The Church's Guide for Reading Paul

The Church's Guide for Reading Paul

THE CANONICAL SHAPING
OF THE PAULINE CORPUS

Brevard S. Childs

WILLIAM B. EERDMANS PUBLISHING COMPANY

GRAND RAPIDS, MICHIGAN / CAMBRIDGE, U.K.

Published 2008 by
Wm. B. Eerdmans Publishing Co.
2140 Oak Industrial Drive N.E., Grand Rapids, Michigan 49505 /
P.O. Box 163, Cambridge CB3 9PU U.K.

Printed in the United States of America

14 13 12 11 10 09 08   7 6 5 4 3 2 1

Library of Congress Cataloging-in-Publication Data

Childs, Brevard S.
    The church's guide for reading Paul: the canonical shaping of the Pauline Corpus /
    Brevard S. Childs.
            p.   cm.
    Includes bibliographical references.
    ISBN 978-0-8028-6278-5 (pbk.: alk. paper)
    1. Bible. N.T. Epistles of Paul — Criticism, interpretation, etc.
    2. Bible. N.T. — Canon.   I. Title.

    BS2650.52.C45   2008
    227′.012 — dc22

                                                            2008011999

www.eerdmans.com

This volume is dedicated to my brothers and sister:

Dick, Wylie, Anne,

for loving care and unswerving support over a lifetime.

Contents

1. The Search for Paul's Theology

I. Recent Historical Attempts

In 1984, when I published a book entitled *The New Testament as Canon*, I had hoped for a reaction similar to the one my earlier *Introduction to the Old Testament as Scripture* (1979) received. In the latter case, the book evoked a heated debate with some sixty reviews in which a few respondents largely agreed with the proposal, others accepted selected features, and others rejected the entire thesis out of hand, often with emotional vehemence.

A similar reaction did not occur within the New Testament guild. There were a few reviews that invariably turned to a defense of the historical critical method that appeared to these reviewers to have been threatened, but the substance of my New Testament proposal was seldom addressed. In general, the book languished in silence, largely unread. Occasionally I heard from colleagues in the New Testament field that they were fully satisfied with their present scholarly methods and saw no need to worry about some allegedly new canonical approach. As a result, when the book went out of print, I turned to other areas of research in the Old Testament, biblical theology, and history of interpretation.

However, recently I had an occasion to return to issues of New Testament interpretation. For some years I had followed at a discreet distance the activities of the Pauline Seminar of the Society of Biblical Literature that extended for more than ten years (1986-1995). Then, stimulated by conversations with friends in the New Testament field, I made the effort to read again carefully the four volumes of collected essays delivered at the seminar entitled *Pauline Theology*.[1] These essays are impressive in many respects. Seldom has a group of scholars showed such sustained interest in a common subject and engaged in serious dialogue for years over central hermeneutical, exegetical, and theological issues of Pauline theology. The seminar was a model of scholars who often disagreed but addressed each other with respect and empathy, devoid of rancor and personal attacks.

From the outset it was agreed that the goal of the seminar would be to investigate Paul's theology by focusing on his "genuine letters," that is, the undisputed letters, each in its discrete historical and literary setting, to see if a larger synthesis of some kind could be discerned lying at the heart of Paul's writings. Initially, J. Christiaan Beker's formulation of the relation in each letter between contingency and coherence offered a starting point, but soon other proposals emerged that also assessed the historical and contextual particularity of each letter. Could one speak of a "core" undergirding Paul's theology, or did the driving force lie in a narrative story forming a symbol system? Was there a logic joining the metaphorical imagery that gave the whole a coherence? Or should one speak only of an activity of the writer in adapting his message to changing cultural and religious issues that evoked fresh formulations from the apostle to meet the new challenges of his churches?

The participants exhibited a growing sense of frustration, especially in volume 4. In spite of the gallant efforts to refine the methodology and to clarify the terminology of such crucial terms as "theology," "conviction," and "process," a broad consensus among the participants had not emerged.

---

1. *Pauline Theology*, vol. 1, ed. Jouette M. Bassler (Minneapolis: Augsburg, 1991); vol. 2, ed. David M. Hay (Philadelphia: Fortress, 1993); vol. 3, ed. D. M. Hay and E. Elizabeth Johnson (Minneapolis: Augsburg, 1995); vol. 4, ed. E. E. Johnson and D. M. Hay (Atlanta: Scholars, 1997). In my opinion, it is correct to focus my interest in the canon of the New Testament initially on the Pauline Seminar of the Society of Biblical Literature (SBL) that extended from 1986 to 1995. The four published volumes of essays reflect a sustained and coherent effort in interpreting Paul's theology by a selected group of well-known scholars. However, I am fully aware that much has happened over the last decade and new SBL seminars have been formed with different agendas and with a younger generation of participants. My decision was recently confirmed when I read Margaret M. Mitchell's highly informative survey of contemporary American research on Paul ("Paulus in America," *Zeitschrift für Neues Testament* 7 [2004]: 10-31). Her emphasis falls on how diverse and widespread the research on Paul has become, which she categorizes under six different rubrics: literary analysis, social-historical, history-of-religions, Pauline theology, ancient and modern social ordering, and history of interpretation. I do not contest the importance of such research, but find much of it peripheral to my focus on Paul and the Pauline corpus.

Some wondered whether focusing on each individual letter, largely in isolation, had fragmented the analysis as the difficulty of moving from the details of exegesis to a larger synthesis became apparent. Paul Meyer, in volume 4, queried whether perhaps the project had been skewed from the beginning and that Paul's theology was an unfolding process continually formulated by the very act of writing each letter.[2] Therefore, the letters could not be summarized within an overarching scheme. In his response, Victor Furnish felt constrained to raise the ontological question of the "truth" in Paul's gospel that, by its prior omission, only enforced the differences in the initial approaches set up to guide the seminar.[3]

From my perspective, what was particularly noticeable was that the subject of canon was never raised. This omission was, of course, intentional. The participants had agreed that their discussion would focus on the writings of the "historical Paul," and that canon was a later, postbiblical development without any exegetical or hermeneutical significance for the subject matter at hand.[4] Nevertheless, certain things in this position struck me as ironical. Although I do not dispute the legitimacy of a search for the "historical Paul" within a certain historical critical context, the hermeneutical questions raised by the seminar concerning a Pauline theology far transcended those of a simple historical reconstruction. Even to speak of a "Pauline corpus" is to enter into the arena of how the historical letters were received, treasured, and shaped, which is of course a canonical question. Can one really search for a Pauline theology when the voices of those are missing who preserved his letters explicitly for an ongoing theological function within the early communities of Christian faith?

The purpose of this monograph is therefore to explore the exegetical and hermeneutical implications of canon for understanding within the context of the church.

II. The Pauline Corpus

The first observation to make is that the earliest manuscript evidence that we have of Paul's letters ($\mathfrak{P}$46, ca. 200) is of a Pauline collection, that is, of

2. Paul W. Meyer, "Pauline Theology: A Proposal for a Pause in Its Pursuit," in *Pauline Theology*, 4:140-60.

3. Victor Furnish, "Where Is 'the Truth' in Paul's Gospel," in *Pauline Theology*, 4:161-77.

an edited corpus. Theoretically, since Paul's letters were originally addressed to individual churches, one would expect that fragments of single letters would first have turned up, but this is not the case. Although Harry Gamble has established the likelihood of an earlier stage when Romans circulated independently,[5] the earliest physical evidence is of a corpus, not of independent letters.

Moreover, it is clear that the corpus offered a selection of his letters, and that by the end of the first century or, at the latest, by the beginning of the second century, an initial Pauline corpus had emerged.[6] At first it was

4. The debate over the definition of canon has been long-standing. Starting with Albert C. Sundberg's Harvard dissertation of 1957, and published as *The Old Testament of the Early Church* (Cambridge: Harvard University Press, 1964), a narrow definition of canon became widespread. The term referred to a list of official authoritative books resulting from the exclusion of those writings deemed noncanonical. This definition is assumed by the essays in *The Canon Debate*, ed. Lee Martin McDonald and James A. Sanders (Peabody, Mass.: Hendrickson, 2002). It is repeated in James VanderKam and Peter Flint, *The Meaning of the Dead Sea Scrolls* (San Francisco: HarperCollins, 2002): "Canon is the closed list of books that was officially accepted retrospectively by a community as supremely authoritative and binding for religious practice and doctrine" (p. 156).

Over against this narrow, history-of-religions definition, I would argue for a far broader definition that does justice to the theological dimension of the term. The early Christian church was never without a canon since it assumed Israel's Scriptures as normative. From its inception the major theological problem was to relate the evangelical traditions of the gospel with its inherited Scriptures. Very shortly one sensed, both in the editing of the fourfold Gospel corpus and in the Pauline corpus, the effects of a "canon consciousness" that I have formulated in terms of "canonical shaping." See the literature cited in my article "The Canon in Recent Biblical Studies," *Pro Ecclesia* 14 (2005): 26-45, and in Christopher H. Seitz, "The Canonical Approach and Theological Interpretation," in *Canon and Biblical Interpretation,* ed. Craig G. Bartholomew et al. (Grand Rapids: Zondervan, 2006), pp. 58-105.

5. Harry Gamble, *The Textual History of the Letter to the Romans* (Grand Rapids: Eerdmans, 1977), p. 12.

6. See on the formation of the Pauline corpus: Andreas Lindemann, "Die Sammlung der Paulusbriefe im 1. und 2. Jahrhundert," in *The Biblical Canons*, ed. Jean-Marie Auwers and Henk Jan DeJonge (Leuven: University Press, 2003), pp. 321-51. Adolf von Harnack, *Die Briefsammlung des Apostel Paulus und die anderen vorkonstantinischen Briefsammlungen* (Leipzig: Hinrichs, 1926), pp. 6-7, suggested an even earlier date of 75-100 for the corpus on the alleged evidence of Polycarp's knowledge of all thirteen of Paul's letters. C. Leslie Mitton reviews the largely discounted debate evoked by Edgar J. Goodspeed and John Knox in the 1930s and 1940s that assumed that Paul's letters had been virtually forgotten by the church for some thirty years until they were formed into a corpus by an intentional editorial activity: *The Formation of the Pauline Corpus of Letters* (London: Epworth, 1955). Finally, the clas-

thought that the earliest form of a corpus was the creation of Marcion, but now it has been generally acknowledged that Marcion was dependent on a still-earlier form.[7] Although there is some variation in the sequence of the letters among the manuscripts, the majority have thirteen letters fixed in the following order: Romans, 1 and 2 Corinthians, Galatians, Ephesians, Philippians, Colossians, 1 and 2 Thessalonians, 1 and 2 Timothy, Titus, and Philemon. Only Hebrews, which was a later addition, varies greatly in its placement, but its presence in the corpus is already attested to by $\mathfrak{P}$46. The order of the sequence appears to have been determined according to length of letter, with the same addressees arranged together in Corinthians, Thessalonians, and Timothy. The letters to particular churches are then followed by letters to individuals.

The formation of a corpus resulted in several effects on the individual letters when joined in a larger canonical context. The letters were provided with similar titles stemming from an editor, not the author himself, which thereby increased the role of an intertextual reading of a unified Pauline collection. While all of Paul's letters share the literary features of first-century Hellenistic conventions (language, structure, addressee),[8] the analogy of the personal letter is only partially true and can be misleading.

Paul's letters were written as an authoritative communication of an apostle, as a vehicle of his presence, and were also received as authoritative by their recipients. Indeed, his letters are the earliest Christian literature to be named "Scripture" (2 Pet 3:15-16), that is, inspired by God (2 Tim 3:16). Nils Dahl was the first to pursue the significance of an early hermeneutical problem related to the formation of a Pauline corpus, namely, the extreme particularity of his letters.[9] How could literature

---

sic essay of Kurt Aland, "Die Entstehung der Corpus Paulinum," in *Neutestamentliche Entwürfe,* ed. K. Aland (Munich: Kaiser, 1979), pp. 302-50. Recently, considerable debate has focused on the illuminating presentation of David Trobisch, *Paul's Letter Collection* (Minneapolis: Fortress, 1994). However, his thesis that Paul himself initiated the collection of his letters has not been widely accepted (see Udo Schnelle, *Einleitung in das Neue Testament* [Göttingen: Vandenhoeck & Ruprecht, 2002], pp. 395-410).

7. See Nils A. Dahl, "Welche Ordnung der Paulusbriefe wird vom Muratorischen Kanon vorausgesetzt?" in *Studies in Ephesians,* ed. David Hellholm et al. (Tübingen: Mohr Siebeck, 2000), pp. 147-63.

8. Ernest Randolph Richards, *Paul and First Century Letter Writing* (Downers Grove, Ill.: InterVarsity, 2004), pp. 210-23.

9. Nils A. Dahl, "The Particularity of the Pauline Epistles as a Problem in the Ancient Church," in *Neotestamentica et Patristica,* Novum Testamentum Supplement 6 (Leiden: Brill,

shaped by such contingent specificity serve as a religious norm for a wider Christian community?

There are many signs that the letters were editorially shaped to enhance a more universal role, but without a loss of the letters' particularity.[10] The textual evidence of manuscripts without a specific addressee (e.g., Ephesians) would indicate a manuscript's possible role as a circular letter. Passages such as 1 Thessalonians 5:27 and Colossians 4:16 ("send to all the brethren") would confirm an intentional inclusion of a wider audience beyond the letter's original recipient. Similarly, the various shorter and longer forms of the ending chapters of Romans would also point to a circulation of the letter with and without the personal greetings of chapter 16.[11] The additional factor that a number of early sources speak of Paul's letters to the "seven churches" would symbolize the universality of his addressing the Christian church at large.[12] Finally, the intensive cross-referencing of the letters within the corpus would indicate their being read together as a coherent collection, which practice was greatly aided by the use of the codex form rather than the traditional Jewish scroll.

Much recent debate has turned on the issue of the sequence of the Pauline letters within the corpus. Bruce Metzger's treatment emphasized the great variety in the order,[13] following the research of Theodor Zahn. Metzger concluded that the sequence was of little significance for the ancient and medieval Christian church, and became an issue only with the rise of later publishing techniques. I would argue that more recent research has not dismissed the significance of sequence so quickly (see Gamble and Trobisch). Gamble reconstructed two early, distinct editions of the collected letters of Paul.[14] The first is that of Marcion (ca. 144), who arranged

---

1962), pp. 261-71. This essay has been reedited in Hellholm et al., *Studies in Ephesians*, with an expansion of the footnotes and bibliography, pp. 165-78.

10. Lindemann is particularly concerned not to see the editorial shaping as a massive redaction that introduced a subsequent theological ideology into the text, but he does perceive early signs of an extension of the letters' initial addressees that led ultimately to canonization ("Die Sammlung," pp. 345-51).

11. Gamble, *The Textual History of the Letter to the Romans*.

12. See Jack Finegan, "The Original Form of the Pauline Corpus," *Harvard Theological Review* 49 (1956): 85-104.

13. Bruce M. Metzger, *The Canon of the New Testament* (Oxford: Clarendon, 1987), pp. 297-99.

14. Harry Gamble, *Books and Readers in the Early Church: A History of Early Christian Texts* (New Haven: Yale University Press, 1995).

ten letters in the order of Galatians, 1 and 2 Corinthians, Romans, 1 and 2 Thessalonians, Laodiceans (= Ephesians), Colossians, Philippians, and Philemon. The other edition that lies behind the large majority of early Greek manuscripts, including the earliest manuscript of 𝔓46, offers a different order: Romans, 1 and 2 Corinthians, Ephesians, Galatians, Philippians, Colossians, and 1 and 2 Thessalonians. What is significant is that Marcion's list reflects the earlier tradition, arranged according to decreasing length, that he then rearranged for his obvious theological reasons to begin with Galatians. Thus, although a common Hellenistic convention of order was followed, it was varied because of content to support his own theological position. One can therefore conjecture that, although the traditional ordering of the corpus beginning with Romans was initially followed according to a literary convention, when the corpus was read together liturgically, the prominent role of Romans, with its unique features, took on a special canonical function. Not only was it the longest letter, but also it exposited Paul's theology with the greatest detail, showed less historical particularity (except chapter 16), and seemed to provide the final and most profound formulation of Paul's theology.[15]

III. The Hermeneutical Problem of Interpreting the Corpus

Up to now my focus on the formulation of the Pauline corpus has been largely formal. However, by the end of the first century or early in the second century, the corpus provided the context in which the church preserved, transmitted, and interpreted Paul's letters. With the growing development of a written New Testament, the Pauline letters took their place as a fixed corpus along with the other literary units: Gospels, Acts, General Epistles, and Revelation.[16]

Nevertheless, it is clear that much of this development is regarded by the New Testament guild as part of later church history and has little relevance for understanding the historical figure who lived in the middle of the first century. It is generally accepted as a critical methodological axiom

15. See Günther Bornkamm, "The Letter to the Romans as Paul's Last Will and Testament," in *The Romans Debate*, ed. Karl P. Donfried, 2nd ed. (Peabody, Mass.: Hendrickson, 1991), pp. 16-28.
16. Trobisch, *Paul's Letter Collection*, pp. 11-12.

that the historical Paul can be recovered only from his seven undisputed letters. Ever since the rise of the historical critical approach to Paul, associated first with Ferdinand Christian Baur (1792-1860),[17] it has been largely assumed that the academic task is to investigate critically the history of the rise of early Christianity, and place Paul within this reconstructed setting. His letters were written to address the many and various contingencies of changing historical, social, and cultural situations. Although F. C. Baur's own critical reconstruction — a conflict between Petrinists and Paulinists — has not been sustained, it has been an assumption of critical reflection ever since that Paul's letters can be understood only by the recovery as closely as possible of his historical environment.

Accordingly, the critical study of Paul's letters over the last 150 years has reached a virtual consensus that Paul's genuine (undisputed) letters consist of Romans, 1 and 2 Corinthians, Galatians, Philippians, 1 Thessalonians, and Philemon. Some scholarly disagreement continues over the so-called deutero-Pauline letters (Colossians, Ephesians, 2 Thessalonians). However, the opinion of the largest majority within the guild has designated the Pastorals (1 and 2 Timothy, Titus) as pseudepigraphical. Hebrews has also not been included within Paul's letters, especially since the letter itself does not claim Pauline authorship. Controversy over its authorship persisted into the early history of the church, especially in the Western Church until the fourth and fifth centuries. As a result, a serious gap has arisen between the historical critical reconstructions of the "historical Paul" and the "canonical Paul" of the traditional corpus.

Within the last half-century the hermeneutical problem of recovering the historical Paul has become even more complex. Even before the rise of postmodernism, Walter Bauer of Göttingen suggested that interpretation of an ancient text should begin, not by inquiring after the author's original intention, but rather by asking how the writer's text was understood by those who first heard or read it.[18] The point being that the various cultural filters through which the text was heard also formed part of its message. Bauer's thesis was of course not formulated to denigrate the importance of an author's intentionality, but to make more precise the hermeneutical is-

17. Ferdinand Christian Baur, *Paul, the Apostle of Jesus Christ* (London: William Norgate, 1873-75; originally published 1845).

18. See J. Louis Martyn, *Theological Issues in the Letters of Paul* (Nashville: Abingdon, 1997), pp. 210-11.

sues involved in the critical exegetical task, and the necessity to expand the range of the cultural conditioning of both author and reader.

Nevertheless, in my opinion, Bauer's thesis opens up a new dimension of the hermeneutical problem involved in assessing the significance of the interpretation of the so-called canonical Paul of the church's tradition. The shape of the canonical Paul emerged from a particular context of the Christian church that developed over hundreds of years. From the beginning Paul's letters had been heard as the source of an authoritative Word from God, borne witness to by the revelation of his divinely appointed apostle. These were collected, preserved, and circulated in time as sacred Scripture on a par with Israel's sacred writings. These writings were received as inspired by God's Spirit to "instruct . . . for salvation through faith in Christ Jesus" (2 Tim 3:15).

The formation of a Pauline corpus also had limited the number of authentic letters of Paul since controversy soon arose within the church regarding writings that came to be rejected as spurious, often after considerable debate (see 2 Thess 3:17). In retrospect, certain criteria were formulated by which to determine the truthfulness of a writing (apostolicity, catholicity, orthodoxy), but the actual determining criterion was the experience of the church in its various forms of usage (liturgical, catechetical, proclamation) in arriving at a writing's conformity to a rule of faith. These canonical decisions were reached over an extended period and only subsequently were given formal ecclesiastical approval.

The theological context in which the Christian canon was formed reflects at the outset a different evaluation of the function of its sacred Scripture. The letters of Paul, although retained in their discrete historical particularity, were always understood as universal in scope and not confined to a particular congregation. Paul's letters were never moored to a historical period in the past, but served as a continuing vehicle by which the church received new and fresh divine instruction, admonition, and a renewed understanding of faith through the presence of the Holy Spirit. The letters became the means through interpretation by which to apply the living Word of Scripture to new conditions in an ever-changing world. Moreover, by understanding each letter within the larger context of the entire Pauline corpus, and indeed, in relation to other parts of Scripture, both Old and New Testaments, fresh constellations of meaning emerged through creative intertextual cross-referencing.

Finally, there is no better way to highlight dramatically the nature of the modern hermeneutical debate over the interpretation of Paul's letters than to contrast the canonical approach outlined above with the recent formulation of Morna Hooker, which for many represents the scholarly consensus. She writes: "[P]iecing together a 'theology' of Paul is thus a kind of detective story. We need to gather those scattered gems and string them together. But also, we shall find some important ones are missing and that the resultant necklace will be imperfect."[19]

In the light of such a jolting disagreement on the basic issues of correct exegetical method, the task before us is to pursue ways of achieving at least a beginning of serious dialogue on just how to proceed.

IV. Historical Criticism and Canonical Context[20]

A crucial hermeneutical problem respecting the interpretation of the Pauline letters arises at this juncture. What is the relation between the church's traditional canonical understanding of its sacred Scriptures and the historical critical approach to ancient writings that was first clearly formulated during the Enlightenment? In the preceding paragraphs I have attempted to outline how the early Christian community of faith heard, received, preserved, and shaped the writings of Paul as authoritative Scripture.

At the outset, a fundamental hermeneutical point must be made that the church's canonical context shares in common all the features of the multifaceted dimensions of human culture: language, history, reason, and the sociological conventions of society. Christians possessed no special grammar. They did not live in a heavenly realm removed from the events of history. They were not immune from all the forces of nature that both sustain human life and bring death and destruction from beyond human

---

19. Morna Hooker, *Paul: A Short Introduction* (Oxford: One World, 2003), p. 29.

20. Some of the best essays on this subject are found in the three-volume set *Verbindliches Zeugnis,* ed. Wolfhart Pannenberg and Thomas Schneider (Freiburg: Herder; Göttingen: Vandenhoeck, 1992-98). For a recent defense of a historicist's position, see Bart D. Ehrman, *The New Testament: A Historical Introduction to the Early Christian Writings,* 3rd ed. (New York: Oxford University Press, 2004), pp. 15-16, 225-29. In spite of a genuine intention to be fair to a confessional approach, which he defines as a "privileged access into the supernatural," Ehrman has not seriously wrestled with the theological dimensions of the biblical text, nor entered into the real hermeneutical questions in any depth.

control. Indeed, in the commonality of all human life lies the basic theological paradox that reveals the core of the hermeneutical debate respecting Scripture.

Fortunately, early in its history the church rejected as heretical the Docetic attempt to isolate the incarnation of Jesus Christ from human history. Rather it affirmed as central to the gospel the mystery that Jesus Christ embraced fully both a human and a divine nature in complete harmony. The creeds did not attempt to explain the mystery, but instead set out largely negative criteria by which to identify errors that distort the mystery of this divine incarnation. Although an analogy between Christ's incarnation and sacred Scripture is far from perfect, as theologians are quick to acknowledge, yet it can be helpful in addressing certain issues at stake in the debate over the interpretation of the church's Scripture, which in its completely human form lays claim to speak truthfully of the divine.

We begin with the problem of history as rendered in Scripture. Beginning in the nineteenth century, it became the object of a new and intense critical scrutiny. Suddenly the profound ambiguities of the term "history" became painfully evident. Did history refer simply to events occurring in time and space, or did history refer to events that could be critically established as having occurred by means of rational evidence? Or again, was biblical history actually a deposit of metaphorical imagery, a form of a symbol system arising from mythical stimuli deeply rooted in ancient community consciousness? In sum, could one even speak of history without some understanding of it as a construct? Our time is too restricted to pursue the various philosophical arguments extending from the late seventeenth century into the twentieth, including the epoch-making contributions of Spinoza, Hume, Kant, Hegel, and Troeltsch, among others.[21] However, within New Testament studies the crucial debate that emerged with great ferocity in the early nineteenth century focused on the critical reconstruction of the life of Jesus. Albert Schweitzer's famous book of 1906 *(The Quest of the Historical Jesus)* is often cited as recounting this largely failed enterprise. However, the search has continued unabated in various new forms into the twenty-first century.

In the 1920s, with the rebirth of confessional theology in Germany, there emerged new interest in a little-noticed book of Martin Kähler writ-

---

21. Louis Dupré, *The Enlightenment and the Intellectual Foundations of Modern Culture* (New Haven: Yale University Press, 2004).

ten in 1892 entitled *The So-called Historical Jesus and the Historic Biblical Christ.*[22] Kähler's major contribution was his effort to distinguish between two different understandings of history. By *Historie* he designated that form of history that emerged in a reconstruction of the past using the critical criteria of "objective," scientific analyses of ancient texts, established by the rational application of cumulative human experience. In contrast, Kähler used the term *Geschichte* to designate another form of history with which he characterized the New Testament's witness to Jesus Christ. Far from being a Docetic isolation of Jesus from history, he insisted that the biblical Christ was indeed historical, but in a sense that arose from the Christian communities' response to the proclamation of the gospel. It was a unique witness that was confessional, kerygmatic, and truthful, evoking faith in the living Christ of apostolic preaching that continues to confront the church and the world in the whole of Scripture.

In my judgment, Kähler succeeded in making an important hermeneutical distinction that has a significant application to the study of the Pauline corpus. Nevertheless, his approach suffered from several inadequacies that his opponents were quick to point out. Kähler failed adequately to explore the hermeneutical relation between these two forms of history, that is, between two very different approaches for reading the New Testament. Frequently his form of *Heilsgeschichte* (e.g., Cullmann) became separated from critically reconstructed history and was vulnerable to becoming an idealistic abstraction. Then again, his distinction was also misused by Rudolf Bultmann, who contrasted *Historie* as a critical reconstruction and *Geschichte,* which was understood existentially.[23] It also became clear that an overall concept of *Heilsgeschichte* could not be maintained for all the New Testament, especially not for Paul.

22. Martin Kähler, *The So-called Historical Jesus and the Historic Biblical Christ* (Philadelphia: Fortress, 1964; originally published 1892). Ernst Käsemann evaluates Kähler's book: "[A]fter sixty years [it] is hardly dated and, in spite of many attacks and many possible reservations, has never really been refuted." Yet Käsemann's understanding of the role of historical criticism remains very different from Kähler's. His claim that historical criticism provides the church with a major check against Docetism fails to grasp the major point of Kähler's book. Another important evaluation of Kähler's hermeneutical contribution is offered by Nils A. Dahl, "The Problem of the Historical Jesus," in *The Crucified Messiah and Other Essays* (Minneapolis: Augsburg, 1974), pp. 59-63. He summarizes his analysis: "Kaehler did not clearly express his opinion about the possibility of genuine historical research into the life of Jesus, but he obviously did not want to exclude this possibility" (p. 167).

23. Rudolf Bultmann, *History and Eschatology* (New York: Harper, 1957).

Equally inadequate was the application by some of Kähler's conservative supporters who assumed that these two forms of history could be simply harmonistically joined. Others had suggested that after the critical foundation of the biblical text had been established by objective, critical analysis, one could then supplement and enrich the "facts" with a homiletical topping provided by Kähler's understanding of *Geschichte*. (This is a criticism often leveled against John Bright's *A History of Israel*.) In the end, Kähler's approach was unable to resolve the growing seriousness of the tension that developed between the reconstruction of a "historical Paul," following the critical lead of F. C. Baur, and the church's traditional understanding of the canonical Paul.

It is my thesis that Kähler was correct to the extent that he brilliantly sensed the church's unique, confessional, kerygmatic understanding of its sacred traditions, testified to in Scripture, but he failed to pursue the relation of sacred and secular history. The two cannot be simply fused, nor can they be permanently separated. I shall shortly attempt to outline how the human and divine dimensions of the New Testament's witness remain inseparably intertwined, but in a profound, dialectical manner. The Bible's testimony to the creative, salvific activity of God in time and space cannot be encompassed within the categories of historical criticism because its method of scientific reconstruction filters out the very kerygmatic dimensions of God's activity that defines the gospel. In hermeneutical terms, the same problems of interpretation addressed by Kähler respecting the Gospels apply equally to the Pauline corpus. It is to this subject that we now turn.

1. Elements of Continuity

We begin by emphasizing the elements of commonality between critical, historical exegesis and confessional, canonical understanding of biblical interpretation, that is, between *Historie* and *Geschichte*, to use initially Kähler's terminology.

a. The two approaches to interpretation share a common Greek text. There is no special holy language, but a form of writing that must be studied critically for its meaning, like any other ancient text. Moreover, critical research, along with fresh archaeological discoveries, has greatly enhanced the philological understanding of the New Testament's Hellenistic environment, while at the same time recognizing the unique features that stemmed from Hebrew and rabbinic traditions. Regardless of how much the content of Paul's letters differs from other contemporary writings, his message does not derive from a unique language functioning apart from the conventional rules of grammar, syntax, and semantics.

b. Text critical analysis of the New Testament is essential for any serious study of Paul's letters, and critical scholarship extending over hundreds of years has discovered the diversity and growth of the biblical texts. It has established rational rules for tracing the textual transmission process, and has been able, in large measure, to interpret the textual linkage between earlier and later stages. No serious biblical interpreter would not acknowledge the inestimable gains achieved in the recovery of the earliest Greek forms of the New Testament, starting with Erasmus, by which to replace the Western Church's dependency on later Latin translations.

c. The historical and sociological contexts of early Christianity have increasingly broadened and deepened the understanding of the multiplicity of forces that shaped Hellenistic Greek and Jewish society. Especially the complexity of gnostic and oriental cults of the Roman Empire has brought new precision in interpreting the rival religious communities at work. Again, the study of the ancient social stratification and the impact of urbanization on the Pauline churches has opened up new dimensions previously unrecognized.[24]

d. Particularly in reference to the Pauline letters, much recent critical comparative literary analysis has greatly clarified the Hellenistic conventions in shaping different genres of letters and described with new precision and fresh insights the structure and literary style of Paul's letters.[25] New archaeological texts such as those of Qumran have added a new understanding of exegetical techniques such as midrash, allegory, and *pesher* readings. Even the recent investigation of the development and employment by Christians of the codex to replace the scroll has provided important information for any serious reader of the New Testament (see 2 Tim 4:13).[26]

e. Recently, renewed interest in the effects of the history of biblical in-

24. Wayne A. Meeks, *The First Urban Christians* (New Haven: Yale University Press, 1983).

25. Abraham J. Malherbe, *Social Aspects of Early Christianity,* 2nd ed. (Philadelphia: Fortress, 1983).

26. See Gamble, *Books and Readers in the Early Church.*

terpretation *(Wirkungsgeschichte)* has also been a welcomed discipline in documenting a full range of interpretation of the Bible. Thus, by illustrating both the levels of continuity and discontinuity of interpretation and the multiple public and private filters through which biblical interpretation has passed, fresh perspectives are gained for future reading.

f. Obviously more controversial as a dimension of commonality between a historical critical and a confessional approach to the Bible is the use of human reason and logical discourse as an indispensable tool for communication and literary analysis. The very nature of Paul's use of syllogism and other logical patterns of argumentation such as a fortiori assumes a common component of human dialogue shared by his readers. However, as we shall see, the move from reason to rationalism as a philosophical disposition is of a different order and requires careful clarification (see 1 Cor 1:18-25).

2. Elements of Discontinuity

When we turn next to approaches of biblical interpretation that reveal elements of divergency and disagreement between the historical critical and the confessional, it is important to stress that the distinction cannot be described in static, black-and-white terms. There is often a fluid relationship in which those elements of commonality begin to shade off into genuine differences. In particular, as the interpretation moves from the formal features to material or content-oriented subjects, the profile of the divergencies grows in sharpness and the heart of the hermeneutical conflict appears in full measure.

a. One of the characteristic marks of the historical critical method in relation to the Bible is its claim not to privilege texts, but to use any and every text as evidence in search of truth. In contrast, the Christian church has designated certain texts as the vehicle of divine truth. This, of course, is the essence of canon. By its use the church confesses to hear the Word of God in the oral and written traditions of the gospel — a rule of faith — which in time was formally designated through a long historical process as canonical. It was not the church's act of canonization that made a writing authoritative, but because it was received and experienced as the authority of the risen Lord, canonization followed. Its authority thus developed from its use and community experience as inspired from God and thus authoritative. Certain texts were thus confessed truthfully to carry the evangelical traditions, while conversely others were not.

b. The essence of canon was not, however, its formal privileging of texts. Rather, the act of canonization derived from its substance, the christological content of Scripture. The canon served as a rule designating the arena within which the truth of the gospel was heard. It functioned also as a negative criterion to mark off those claims of truth that fell outside the circle of faith. Historically, the drawing of these lines was controversial, and it took several generations for the scope of the New Testament to be finalized. First and foremost, Scripture was set apart because of its christological witness to the words of the risen Lord. Just as the incarnation of Jesus Christ was God's unique entering into human time and space, within all the earthly particularity of Israel's history, so the apostolic witness then received its authority as the first testimony to the life, death, and resurrection of Jesus Christ for the salvation of the world through divine rectification on the cross.

c. One of the crucial implications of the formation of a canon as an authoritative christological confession was that the subject matter of its witness was not identical with general human experience. Its *Geschichte* is not the object of critical reconstruction *(Historie)*, but the truth of its witness is measured by its relation to its christological subject matter in its incarnated form. This issue of the referentiality of its witness remains perhaps the most controversial element of the modern hermeneutical debate and is the grounds for denying the identification of a so-called objective historical reconstruction with the church's confession. To insist that the relation is dialectical is simply an effort to maintain the tension between the divine and human interaction essential to Scripture's function in the church.

d. Another feature unique to a confessional reading of Scripture in contrast to the historical critical is what I have sought to describe with the terminology of "canonical shaping." The biblical material has been rendered in special ways by its editors toward the goal of evoking a faith response from its readers. Recently Neil MacDonald has addressed a similar dimension of Scripture in a brilliant new hermeneutical formulation as "the directional eye of the evangelist."[27] He contrasts a reading of the life

27. Neil MacDonald, *Metaphysics and the God of Israel: Systematic Theology of the Old and New Testaments* (Grand Rapids: Baker Academic, 2006), pp. 188-95.

of Jesus offered by various modern film directors that often strives to be faithful to what is "on the pages" of the New Testament but has missed the fundamental objective of the gospel's own vision by failing to view the material through "the directional eye of the evangelist." His major example is a reading that fails to grasp that Jesus of Nazareth is understood in the Synoptics in terms of his soteriological identity with the God of Israel.

e. Finally, a major feature of the difference between the two approaches, the historical critical and the confessional, is that for the latter the person of Jesus Christ is not a figure moored in past history and separated by millennia of temporal distance. Rather the figure testified to in Scripture as having been raised from the dead as a divine vindication of Christ's truthful revelation of God, is confessed as a living presence whose Spirit continues to guide his church until the final rule of God's new age is accomplished apocalyptically at the end of the eschaton. This confession changes dramatically how Scripture is read today by those who "live between the times" (see Rev 22:20).

V. The Role of a Text's Background

The complexity of the hermeneutical problem of interpreting Scripture with its elements of continuity and discontinuity in subject matter becomes immediately apparent in the study of the Pauline letters.

Leander Keck states the problem of interpreting the letters with clarity. For him a crucial issue turns on the role of the background in understanding occasional letters that were evoked by particular historical circumstances of Paul's various churches. He writes: "Because the letters are Paul's responses to what was going on among the readers, it is necessary to understand the situation to which the letters respond."[28] For most biblical scholars Keck's point is so obvious as to border on being a truism. A text is understood only in relation to its historical context. Yet is the issue of background actually so obvious?

In a previous paragraph I discussed the elements of continuity and discontinuity between a historical critical approach and a confessional (canonical) approach. At first glance the supplying of the historical background of Paul's letters seems to be a clear case of the historical environ-

---

28. Leander E. Keck, *Paul and His Letters* (Philadelphia: Fortress, 1979), p. 16.

ment establishing the required context for understanding. Nevertheless, the hermeneutical issue is more complex because of the nature of the biblical literature being interpreted. I offer three illustrations.

1. Shortly after World War II two New Testament scholars of equal preeminence in Göttingen offered two very different understandings of the New Testament text to be interpreted. Joachim Jeremias, after reading the New Testament text in the Greek, started his exegesis by translating the Greek text into Aramaic. For Jeremias the move was legitimate, even mandatory, since all scholars agree that Jesus spoke Aramaic. By recovering an earlier biblical text Jeremias could penetrate behind the Greek to a more accurate, original historical text. In contrast, Ernst Käsemann argued that regardless of the possibility of going behind the Greek, the Greek text of the New Testament remained primary, and was thus the authoritative translation since this was the vehicle through which the gospel was transmitted by the earliest Christians constituting the community. In sum, another hermeneutical criterion was employed in assigning priority to the Greek over a reconstructed earlier stage of the text's original Aramaic deliverance.

2. A second illustration: In the normal circumstances of ordinary life, if one found a page of a modern newspaper, it would greatly assist in understanding the details of the events being reported by acquiring some background information. One assumes a continuity in a historical sequence between human affairs of the past and the present. In contrast, the claim of the Christian gospel is that its content is not identical with the circumstances of ordinary living, but a new divine reality has been announced that often evokes amazement, perplexity, and confusion. When Jesus conversed with the Samaritan woman at the well (John 4), the background of the conversation seemed clear enough. Jesus was thirsty and asked a Samaritan woman to provide him with a drink of water from Jacob's well. Her initial response was completely rational and consistent with the situation. Why would a Jew ask a Samaritan for a drink of water? But then Jesus responded with a word about "living water" that was totally discontinuous with the situation at hand. There is no background that would help her understand. The promise and its fulfillment derived only from the speaker.

3. A final illustration: In ordinary life it is obvious that a person's understanding of a telephone conversation between two people is limited if the person hears only one voice. To some degree this analysis could also be applied to Paul's letters. Keck describes such a one-sided telephone conver-

sation as analogous to the problem of reading Paul's letters, and suggests that most of what we can know of the situations behind the letters must be inferred from the answer of the one voice. He concludes that there is no way out of this dilemma.

However, this reasoning assumes that there is a close continuity always between question and answer. This observation forms the essence of the so-called "mirror image" mode of interpretation.[29] Yet it is precisely at this point that caution is called for. There are many obvious cases of simple continuity between question and answer, but at times there is no continuity. One of the major contributions of J. Louis Martyn's magisterial commentary on Galatians is his insistence on seeing a total discontinuity between gospel and law, and between a continuous *Heilsgeschichte* of Jewish messianism and an apocalyptic invasion by God in the Christ event.[30] If this is true, how much help is offered by a detailed reconstruction of the theology of the "Teachers" (the "troublemakers" of Galatians) in understanding the radically apocalyptical explosion of the gospel proclaimed by Paul? Could an imaginative reconstruction of Paul's opponents as a mirror image to Paul actually serve to blur rather than sharpen Paul's response to the crisis in Galatia? We shall return to this problem in the chapters that follow.

VI. Criteria for Canonicity

When we turn to the important question of the criteria by which the church established its New Testament canon,[31] we must observe several crucial hermeneutical guidelines.

1. Nowhere in the New Testament itself is there an explicit call for a canon. However, the suggestion of some historians that the formation of a canon was a completely accidental occurrence without any warrant from

29. John M. G. Barclay, "Mirror-Reading a Polemical Letter: Galatians as a Test Case," *Journal for the Study of the New Testament* 31 (1967): 73-93.

30. J. Louis Martyn, *Galatians,* Anchor Bible 33A (New York: Doubleday, 1997).

31. Karl-Heinz Ohlig, *Die theologische Begründung des neutestamentlichen Kanons in der Alten Kirche* (Dusseldorf: Patmos Verlag, 1972). See also the essays reprinted in *Das Neue Testament als Kanon* (Göttingen: Vandenhoeck & Ruprecht, 1970), edited by Ernst Käsemann. Finally, Bruce M. Metzger, "Criteria for Determining Canonicity," in *The Canon of the New Testament,* pp. 251-54.

the early traditions of the church cannot be sustained. Even the assumption of an authoritative corpus of Israel's Scriptures would make such a claim highly unlikely. Likewise, to derive the formation of a Christian canon largely from a reaction to the threat posed by Marcion (Harnack's theory) can no longer be historically defended.

2. It is important that the criteria for canon that later theologians presented in a systematic form, especially evident in the early Church Fathers, cannot be separated from the actual history of the canon's development, especially the relation of the evolving canon to the biblical texts themselves. Thus, it is inadequate to ignore the historical growth of a canon consciousness and appeal to the canon solely in terms of a timeless supernatural gift endowed to the church by God and thus authoritative.[32]

3. The fact that the criteria used for establishing a canon were multiple, and often overlapped with each other, would indicate that the process was not a single ecclesiastical decision, or the application of a single principle, but that the criteria for the justification of a canon developed in different ways with varying perspectives that reflect a complex history of confession and controversy. A distinction should be maintained between the later retrospective reflections of the church on its canon and the earlier attestation of a body of authoritative writings that were accepted long before a defense became necessary.

4. It is important that a balance be maintained in recognizing the influence of various local political forces at work, often represented by powerful clerical and secular figures who exercised influence in canonical decisions both in the Eastern and Western Churches, and the explicit theological issues that were constitutive in the struggle to preserve the truth of the tradition from its earliest inception.

5. Finally, the emerging criteria can be analyzed and organized in a variety of ways. In his impressive book *Die theologische Begründung* (see n. 31), Karl-Heinz Ohlig has sought to organize his material under three

---

32. In spite of the brilliance of Jaroslav Pelikan's commentary on the book of Acts in linking the biblical text to its later interpretation by the official creeds of the Eastern and Western Churches, one misses attention to the central theological stance of the Protestant Reformers that all traditions, liturgies, and creeds are continuously to be tested for their conformity to sacred Scripture. Pelikan assumes in his treatment of chapter 11 (Philip and the eunuch) that this chapter provides a warrant for the church's claiming the right of being the sole legitimate interpreter of Scripture, which is far from an obvious inference from this text. *Acts* (Grand Rapids: Brazos, 2005), p. 116.

headings: (a) the qualities for authoritative writings contained in Scripture itself, (b) the theological reasons for canonization, and (c) the effect of the church's use of its Scriptures as canonical. At times his divisions are quite helpful; however, it seems to me that the traditional systematic categories are still to be preferred, especially if the critical hermeneutical issues, previously raised, are respected. These categories are apostolicity, catholicity, and orthodoxy.

1. Apostolicity

Apostolicity was a basic category by which to designate the earliest witnesses of the gospel of Jesus Christ. An apostle was someone authorized to speak on God's behalf. Because the ministry of Jesus was set within a temporal period, his disciples bore a unique confession to his life, death, and resurrection. From the beginning, therefore, there was a historical dimension to the term that set the apostolic testimony apart from timeless myth and legend (see Luke 1:1-4). However, very shortly the term was expanded to a wider circle, and the term was not confined to the Twelve, but included a wider circle of disciples. Clearly, Paul's role as an apostle demonstrated that the term embraced other truthful tradents of the gospel (see chapter 4.I). Paul's own struggle to defend his apostolic office turned on his claim of a direct revelation of Christ appointing him to the ministry of the gospel (Gal 1:11-17).

Harnack defended the thesis that the term "apostle" was only a title that arose as an a priori reflection to cover all the church's institutions without any appeal to a historical confirmation.[33] However, Ohlig has offered a very persuasive refutation concluding that apostolicity was identified with earliest church tradition *(Urkirchlichkeit)*, and far from being just a cipher, became a dynamic term to encompass historical, substantive, functional, and personal qualities of the most basic core of the faith.[34] God used the church to recognize and transmit his revelation.[35]

---

33. Adolf von Harnack, *Lehrbuch der Dogmengeschichte*, vol. 1 (Darmstadt: Wissenschaftliche Buchgesellschaft, 1964), p. 338.

34. Ohlig, *Die theologische Begründung*, pp. 89-94.

35. See the essay of C. Stephen Evans, "Canonicity, Apostolicity, and Biblical Authority," in *Canon and Biblical Interpretation*, ed. Craig G. Bartholomew et al. (Grand Rapids: Zondervan, 2006), pp. 146-66. Evans mounts an impressive argument that the early church,

While initially apostolicity included direct authorship, increasingly it extended to the truthfulness of the gospel when it was also testified to by the deutero-Pauline letters (Colossians, Ephesians, 2 Thessalonians) and especially by the Pastorals. Paul's letters became the model by which all subsequent Christian faith was to be tested. Similarly, the canonical shaping of Acts pointed to the authoritative application of Paul's apostolic ministry for the postapostolic age (Acts 20:17-38).

When the history and function of the church's canon became the object of historical critical scrutiny, it became almost an axiom that the concept arose as an erroneous apologetical device stimulated by political motivation. This misunderstanding, which unfortunately beclouded the issue of pseudonymity, has only recently been subjected to a far more generous interpretation.[36] The great variety within the Pauline corpus in respect to historicity, literary style, and theological perspectives highlights convincingly the complex growth of the letters, but is not determinative in overruling the church's deeming the entire corpus apostolic even when its authorship is only indirectly related to the historical Paul.

2. Catholicity

The criterion of catholicity lay on the universality of the Christian church in its response to the gospel. One of the earliest lists of the Pauline corpus (the Muratorian Canon, late second century) describes Paul's letters to "the seven churches" that sought thereby to symbolize the universality of the church. Then again, very early in the canonical growth of the New Testament the book of Acts was closely linked to the Catholic Epistles, which in some textual traditions preceded the Pauline corpus in sequence. The selection of chosen writings was increasingly set over against other "sectarian" claims, especially in the challenges of Marcion and the gnostics. 2 Peter 1:20-21 expressed the concern for a unified interpretation of the evangelical

---

in making decisions about the New Testament canon, did not identify apostolic authority with direct apostolic authorship. Moreover, the concept of apostolic authority was so central to the formation of the canon as to override even such other criteria as catholicity, orthodoxy, and inspiration.

36. B. S. Childs, *The New Testament as Canon: An Introduction* (Philadelphia: Fortress, 1984), pp. 373-95; see also the recent discussion of pseudonymity by Evans, "Canonicity, Apostolicity," pp. 153-58.

traditions in insisting that no prophecy of Scripture was a matter of private interpretation. Significantly, in the church's continuing struggle to establish a normative, received text of the New Testament, the critically purer text of Alexandria was balanced by the inclusion of the Byzantine text used in the liturgical practices of the widest range of the great churches of Antioch, Rome, and Jerusalem.

In terms of Scripture, catholicity was a confession that the context for its understanding was from within the Christian church. The church was the vehicle for its receiving the continuous life-giving direction of the Holy Spirit that as the "body of Christ" continued to pray for divine illumination. Ohlig[37] rightly insists that the authority of Scripture did not derive from a formal juridical authority bestowed by the church but from the content of the Scripture itself, which was the *norma normans* of its faith. The controversy in the sixteenth century arose when the Roman Church laid claim to the church's priority over Scripture. In contrast, the Reformers sought to assert Scripture's authority apart from the church *(autopistis)*. Fortunately, in the last century there has been a growing reconciliation between the two combatants. Accordingly, the gospel (Word) is acknowledged as the divine source of the church's life, but the church is recognized as the vehicle for its shaping and faithful transmission (tradition). In sum, following the lead of Irenaeus, Word and tradition belong together and are inseparable.

3. Orthodoxy

The criterion of orthodoxy is usually expressed in terms of the "canon of truth/faith" *(regula veritatis/fidei)*, a formulation that appeared for the first time in Irenaeus. This formula became the norm by which the books of the New Testament were measured for their compatibility with the church's tradition of faith. Stephen Evans correctly argues that "orthodoxy," or the degree to which a book embodied that apostolic content summarized in the rule of faith, also served an important function as a negative test.[38]

Yet this criterion was not a later *superadditum* imposed in a political struggle for power, as is sometimes argued, but its roots lay deep within the

37. Ohlig, *Die theologische Begründung,* p. 171.
38. Evans, "Canonicity, Apostolicity," p. 151.

church's oral tradition preceding its stage of a written Scripture. The criterion of orthodoxy (or right doctrine) emerged along with an evolving canon as the church's affirmation of the substantive coherence of Scripture's christological content that was increasingly formulated in trinitarian terminology. Far from its being a late philosophical intrusion from Hellenism (so Harnack), the trinitarian doctrine of orthodoxy formed the grounds by which the Old Testament was embraced along with the New as the divine witness to God's creative and salvific purpose in Jesus Christ for the church and the world. Israel's definitive role in the single purpose of God was established as the anticipation of the inclusion of all nations in God's final victory (see chapters 5.II and 6.VII).

In the New Testament and later Church Fathers, the criterion of orthodoxy was not an abstract norm, or sign of doctrinal ossification. Rather, it was closely joined to that of worship. Scripture's role was continued edification, and was characterized by its clarity, simplicity, and spiritual richness. A rule of faith assured its basic doctrinal coherence that was a mark of the genuine antiquity of its unified faith. In the light of such an appeal to orthodoxy, the full dimensions of the tragic schism between the eastern and western branches of the Christian church emerge.

VII. The Biblical Canon and the Problem of Textual Reception

There is one final but crucial hermeneutical issue to be discussed when treating the relation of the historical critical approach to the traditional confessional (canonical). In fact, within recent decades it has become the main focus of those who include themselves within the overarching rubric of postmodernism. The problem turns on the issue of the reading and reception of a text.

Basic to the hermeneutical theory is the axiom that meaning is not inherent within a text. It cannot be merely identified with authorial intent and thus "excavated." Rather interpretation is an ongoing activity in which sense emerges in the interaction of text, reader, and context. Such an activity is usually not private, but the expression of a community's engagement with the interpretation of a piece of literature. The process of cultural filtering that both the author and reader introduce, whether or not intentionally, becomes part of the meaning itself. Moreover, because of the complexity of the multifaceted sociological influences at work, one frequently speaks of language as a symbol system that is the force that renders a text functional. Because the cultural influences continue to change, no one interpretation can ever claim to be permanent or normative, but remains a transitory instance of a single reading confined within the restraints of time and space.

One particular aspect of this theory of textuality emerges especially in the activity of biblical interpretation. Reception theory often speaks of reading as a "moral discipline" stemming from the ethical responsibility of readership in reinterpreting an ancient historically conditioned symbol system in a fresh manner in order to have it conform to the present demands of moral behavior (see the discussion of Frances Young in chapter 2.III).

For the practitioners of the various forms of postmodernist reception theory, the emphasis on a so-called canonical interpretation is deemed sorely inadequate for several hermeneutical reasons. First, it objects to the claim that any fixing of a text as canonically normative by a reader or community of readers can subsequently remain authoritative because of its fully time-conditioned construal. Second, any claim for restricting a selection of religiously privileged texts is deemed arbitrary. All literature, regardless of ecclesial status, performs a function of truth seeking and cannot be dogmatically circumscribed by boundaries that are inevitably self-serving. No prior claims of biblical unity or coherence can be sustained since meaning is never fixed or determinate. Third, the nature of Scripture as basically metaphorical requires that each generation of readers reinterprets imaginatively its imagery according to new and changing visions of truth and reality. Scripture can therefore never be self-interpreting since meaning requires the active participation in an exegetical dialogue between text and recipient toward an intentional goal (see the discussion of Wayne Meeks in chapter 2.V).

I hope to respond to these serious questions in the following chapters, but a brief anticipation to my reply seems in order. The concept of a New Testament canon derives ultimately from its Christology. The Christian church confessed the uniqueness of the incarnation of Jesus Christ, who entered fully into human time and space and thus rendered that historical activity unique and eternal in its salvific effect. God became human in order to redeem his creation. The incarnation was not a noble idea, a pedagogical example, or a recurring mythical typology, but a divine act of grace that embraced and sanctified this historical entrance forever in all its human frailty and time-conditionality. The four Gospels do not attempt to explain its meaning, but in different and various ways bear witness to its eternal truth. The church, which developed its understanding of canon over many centuries, derived it as a response to the Lordship of Jesus Christ. The apostolic witnesses to the life, death, and resurrection of Christ in human time and space gained their privileged status to perform their function of bearing testimony to the gospel that had been promised in the Scriptures of Israel (Mark 1:1-3).

The function of canon was not only to render a decision on the scope of its Scriptures, but to provide a framework within which the multiple witnesses could be understood. The four Evangelists rendered their witnesses according to the genre of Gospel, not as memoirs of Jesus. The book of Acts followed the Gospels in portraying the Spirit-inspired spread of the gospel that repentance and forgiveness of sins be preached in his name to all the nations, beginning from Jerusalem. Then there followed two corpora of apostolic letters, and a concluding apocalyptic vision of the consummation of the ages. In this sense the church's canonical Scriptures bore testimony to its catholic and evangelical content, a message faithfully rendered commensurate to its faith in a living Lord and Savior.

The Christian canon is not a fixed deposit of traditions from the past, but a dynamic vehicle by which the risen Lord continues through the Holy Spirit to guide, instruct, and nourish his people. The imperative "to search the Scriptures" reveals the need for its continuous interpretation. The activity of hearing, reading, and praying is required, indeed mandated by the Scripture itself. In every successive generation new light has been promised for those seeking divine illumination to provide fresh understanding, new application to changing cultures, and a call for repentance for persistent failure in living out the imperatives of the gospel. In this constant struggle to live a faithful Christian life, the Scriptures of the church afford the abiding context from which to grow into the image of Christ. It is thus a theological gyroscope for maintaining one's direction when buffeted by the ever-shifting winds of change.

To summarize: I have sought to delineate two different approaches from which to interpret the Bible, the historical critical (in all its various forms) and a confessional or canonical. I have argued that the basic hermeneutical problem of interpretation arises because these two approaches can be neither fused nor separated. I have pursued elements of commonality and elements of profound disagreement between them. In the following chapter I shall outline five recent attempts to expand or modify the older forms of historical criticism of the Bible. I shall attempt to analyze both the strengths and weaknesses of the newer proposals. Only then will I return to describe the enduring contribution of the critical approach when its role is seen in proper relationship to the confessional study of the Scriptures of the church, which is the goal of this monograph.

2. Alternative Proposals for the Problem of Interpretation

I. Ulrich Luz: *Wirkungsgeschichte*

Ulrich Luz emerges as one of the most impressive modern New Testament scholars attempting to offer a major reformulation of the historical critical approach to the interpretation of the Bible under the rubric of *Wirkungsgeschichte* (= the effect of biblical interpretation on its subsequent reading, or the history of influence). The term was originally formulated by Gadamer, but it has been refined by Luz, not only in his hermeneutical essays, but above all by his application in his magisterial Matthew commentary.[1] In his writings he distinguishes *Wirkungsgeschichte* from the usual approach of a history of interpretation. The latter is largely interested in tracing how a biblical text was historically interpreted in commentaries and theological tractates, whereas the former focuses on the reception and activation of texts in other media, such as sermons, art, canon law, etc.

Luz is much concerned that the approach of *Wirkungsgeschichte* not be relegated to a secondary appendix following the actual work of exegesis, but rather he argues that it should actually precede the exegesis and inform

1. The following selection is representative of U. Luz's wide-ranging biblical interests: "Wirkungsgeschichtliche Exegese," *Berliner Theologische Zeitschrift* 2 (1985): 18-32; *Das Evangelium nach Matthäus*, Evangelish-katholischer Kommentar zum Neuen Testament I.1-2 (Zürich and Freiburg: Neukirchener Verlag, 1985), ET, *Matthew* (Minneapolis: Augsburg, 1989); "Paulinische Theologie als Biblische Theologie," in *Mitte der Schrift?* ed. Martin Klopfenstein et al. (Bern: Peter Lang, 1987), pp. 119-47; "Kanonische Exegese und Hermeneutik der Wirkungsgeschichte," in *Die Wurzel aller Theologie: Sentire cum Ecclesia. Festschrift Urs von Arx,* ed. H. Gerny et al. (Bern: Stämpfli Verlag, 2003), pp. 40-57.

its self-understanding from the outset. It should work as a critical assumption that shapes the very nature of the exegetical enterprise. I found it ironic that Luz's concept of *Wirkungsgeschichte* provided a major stimulus agreed upon by the participants of the Evangelical-Catholic Commentary series (Evangelisch-katholischer Kommentar), yet in the actual practice of many of the commentaries that have since appeared, *Wirkungsgeschichte* seems to function as an appendix lacking in many of the very components deemed crucial by Luz.

According to Luz, *Wirkungsgeschichte* is an attempt to overcome the distance between the ancient author and its modern interpretation that occurs in the historical critical approach by making more precise the range of inherited assumptions (e.g., Protestant, Catholic) one brings consciously or unconsciously to the text. By reference to the precritical stage of interpretation, one seeks to retain the full richness of the interpretive process, and to understand how the search for a text's substance *(Sache)* can aid in overcoming the gaps perceived by critical exegesis and the present needs of the modern interpreter. The result of recognizing the effect of interpretive traditions serves to free the interpreter from isolating each critical interpretation according to prior confessional assumptions and thus failing to exert the possibility of a variety of rich alternatives that aid in fusing the ancient and the modern. By expanding the interpretive context the interpreter also checks the temptation of trying to move directly from the past to the present without attention to the important in-between periods that often exert an influence on interpretation, even when largely unconscious.

One of the major contributions of Luz, learned in part from Gadamer, was his rejecting the assumption that time is an abyss that must be bridged rather than seeing that understanding is borne by the historical movement with which life itself is lived. Finally, Luz is especially concerned that "confessionalism" be replaced by ecumenicity, an interest that forms the explicit intention of the commentary series (EKK) that assigned books to both Protestant and Catholic scholars.

Luz's program has much in common with my own canonical approach. Both share the concern to overcome the fragmentation of the biblical text often arising from historical critical analysis. Both resist a critical approach that moors the text in the distant past in order for it to be "objectively" dissected, and focuses its interpretation on details largely external to the text itself without attention to the actual content of the biblical witness. Furthermore, Luz accepts a hermeneutical distinction between *erklären* (explanation) and *verstehen* (understanding), a formulation that is dependent in part on Gadamer and Fuchs, but provides a sensitivity to a hermeneutical dimension of interpretation in seeking to penetrate through a biblical text to engage the meaning of its substance. Failure to grasp this dimension of interpretation accounts for, to a large extent, why much of Anglo-American exegesis appears flat and lacking in hermeneutical awareness, despite its impressive learning concerning critical minutiae. Finally, he is also a strong advocate of viewing the New Testament as witness of the church and exegesis as a tool for preaching and proclamation.

However, there are important differences that at first may seem minor but affect the entire enterprise. Luz is also fully aware of these differences, which he outlines in his essay "Canonical Exegesis and the Hermeneutic of *Wirkungsgeschichte.*"[2] Luz shares the view along with the larger biblical guild that interest in the canon can never result in a so-called canonical exegesis of the Bible. Accordingly, the formation of canon is a later, subsequent activity of the church that always must follow the initial historical critical enterprise of exegesis.

However, Luz does concede that one of the functions of historical critical exegesis is to discern "precritical" influences that critical study confirmed were later expanded and developed in the process of canonization. His illustrations include: the replacement of Israel's Torah as the fundamental textual referent with that of the gospel; the function of Mark 1:1 to spring over the temporal distance to the present in a new and living history; the construal of the Gospel of Matthew as a new Genesis, etc. I do not doubt that the New Testament reveals such new canonical shaping. (Of course, I would add a great many more.)

My disagreement is that, in my judgment, such examples that Luz chooses do not belong to a "precanonical" stage. These features by which the message of the New Testament is rendered during various stages of its composition belong to the canonical text itself and have been incorporated within the New Testament's witness as text, not as subsequent commentary. From the very beginning of the process of textualization, "canon consciousness" has been an active force in shaping the authoritative Scriptures. Further, in my opinion the widespread axiom of the New Testament guild that the subject of canon does not belong to critical New Testament study, but is a later activity of church history, reflects a fundamental misunderstanding.

2. Luz, "Kanonische Exegese und Hermeneutik der Wirkungsgeschichte."

This difference might appear to be a minor disagreement, but its consequences for the exegetical task are far-reaching. The apostolic reception of the evangelical traditions ultimately to form a New Testament made use of a concept of canon that influenced its selection, collection, and editorial shaping of the tradition by which to bear testimony to the apostolic witness. Thus the function of the Christian canon established a fundamental difference between the apostolic witness that was received as normative and all subsequent church interpretive traditions that functioned as commentary. The truth of the church's commentary was subordinated to that of the apostolic, and remained in need of constantly being tested for its conformity to the apostolic norm.

This distinction has been sharply formulated by Heiko Oberman as Tradition I (apostolic) and Tradition II (church tradition).[3] Those subsequent traditions that make up Luz's *Wirkungsgeschichte* are not to be fused or identified with the apostolic tradition. Herein lay a crucial hermeneutical debate in the sixteenth century between the Protestant Reformers and Roman Catholics. Church tradition, while indispensable and highly regarded, always stood subordinated as to its truth in reference to the apostolic testimony.

There are several hermeneutical implications to Luz's removal of this canonical distinction. The primary exegesis of a biblical text remains the historical critical approach. *Wirkungsgeschichte* then registers the church's subjective interpretations and performs the task of actualizing the biblical text for the modern reader. Luz has thereby blurred the whole issue of truth, the test of which was offered by the apostolic rule of faith. As a result, Luz, in the spirit of ecumenicity, has understood the Bible as a deposit of rich exegetical stimuli, but he is left with no means of judging its truth, which is still ultimately left to historical exegesis and its *Sachkritik*.[4]

II. Richard B. Hays: Intertextual Reading of Scripture

Richard Hays's book *Echoes of Scripture in the Letters of Paul* emerges as an important contribution to the study of Paul, both in terms of his criticisms

3. Heiko Oberman, "Scripture and Tradition," in *Forerunners of the Reformation* (New York: Holt, Rinehart and Winston, 1966), pp. 51-66.

4. Luz, "Kanonische Exegese," p. 56.

of the reigning approaches of classic historical criticism and in terms of his own highly sophisticated literary proposals.[5] Although working independently from Luz, he expresses several of the same criticisms. Because Paul's letters were interpreted largely by reconstructing his historical and sociological background, the result has been to assign these texts to the past and to distance them from the modern reader. Moreover, the larger narrative structure undergirding the letters has been lost through fragmentation, and the genuine theological content obscured by technical minutiae.

Accordingly, Hays proceeds to outline a different proposal for reading the letters, namely, to assert that Israel's Scriptures provide Paul's context. "[F]or Paul the Word of God is Jesus Christ as experienced in the Spirit-filled Christian community" (p. 4). Thus, by reading Paul as a Christian interpreter of Israel's Scriptures, he opens up a new symbolic world. The key to its hidden illusive meaning is provided by the phenomenon of literary intertextuality, and following the lead of John Hollander, stresses the trope of metalepsis, which is a figurative form arising when a text is linked to an earlier text and the points of resonance are largely unstated. The reader is therefore placed within this field of "whispered correspondences" and allusive echoes to generate new figurations (pp. 14-19).

Next Hays raises the central hermeneutical issue: In whose mind does this intertextual fusion arise? He suggests five possible options (author, reader, autonomous text, etc.), but then he rejects the need to choose only one and argues for the freedom to hold all these possibilities open. This, he argues, is possible because metalepsis does not depend on conscious intention, and the line between Paul's final intent and the later reader is fluid. Indeed, the ensuing conversation between them generates figurations that extend beyond any one historical moment. The effect of such a reading is that all Scripture is seen as a vast metaphorical tapestry (p. 157) in which typology is the central feature of Paul's interpretive strategy. Paul's imaginative act of reading Exodus renders the book as a metaphor for early Christian experiences (p. 95). The echoes are illusive, often hidden, and need to be "teased out" by the reader's creativity. At this point (p. 35), Hays attempts to ward off criticism by insisting that he is not denying the importance of the text's original historical setting, but once affirmed, it plays little significant interpretive role in his proposal.

---

5. Richard B. Hays, *Echoes of Scripture in the Letters of Paul* (New Haven: Yale University Press, 1989).

Of particular importance for Hays is his interpretation of 2 Corinthians 3:1–4:6. Here Paul sets up a dissonance between the Mosaic covenant and the new covenant, with a "heart of flesh" (Jer 31:33; Ezek 36:26) replacing the stony hearts on which God once wrote at Sinai. Just as Christ's words were not inscribed on stone, so Paul's ministry of the new covenant is not of the "script" *(gramma),* but of the spirit. His is a ministry that centers not on written texts but on the spirit-empowered transformation of the human community. Although Hays is aware of Paul's positive use of *graphē* for Scripture (p. 151), the contrast he envisions in 2 Corinthians 3 is between the old covenant as script and the new as spirit. Under the new covenant, direct experience of God is given immediately through the Spirit (p. 143). Consequently "Paul's reading of the sacred text (Exodus 34) reveals that revelation occurs not primarily in the sacred text but in the transformed community of readers" (p. 144).

From my perspective, I think it can be seriously debated whether Hays's interpretation of 2 Corinthians 3 as a direct revelation of God through the Spirit that is no longer in need of *graphē* does justice to this passage (see chapter 4.III). However, I am more concerned with Hays's argument that Paul's interpretation becomes a hermeneutical model "for us," that is to say: "Paul's readings are materially normative . . . for Christian theology and his interpretive methods are paradigmatic for Christian hermeneutics" (p. 183). In sum, those who turn to Christ have the same imaginative freedom as Paul to read the Scriptures according to the spirit. Ironically, Hays even argues that his hermeneutical proposal does not overthrow the canon but upholds it (p. 188)!

My critique of Hays's book *(Echoes)* can be initially summarized in several points:[6]

---

6. *Echoes* has received many reviews. See the collection in Craig A. Evans and James A. Sanders, eds., *Paul and the Scriptures of Israel* (Sheffield: Sheffield Academic, 1993), and Hans Hübner in *Theologische Zeitschrift* 116 (1991): 880-95. I did not find these reviews very helpful. Evans and Sanders wanted Hays to include attention to their program of scribal shaping of the Hebrew Bible before talking of intertextuality. J. C. Beker disagreed with Hays on a few exegetical details, but did not grapple with the larger hermeneutical issues raised by the author. Hans Hübner's extremely learned review criticized Hays for not providing a philosophical analysis of the literary phenomenon of intertextuality, which endeavor Hays had explicitly eliminated as lying beyond the scope of his book. Fortunately, a brilliant dissertation was recently written by Annette Merz, *Die fiktive Selbstauslegung des Paulus. Intertextuelle Studien zur Intention und Rezeption des Pastoralbriefe* (Göttingen: Vandenhoeck &

1. Hays's interpretive proposal rests on the assumption that all of Scripture comprises a metaphorical imagery whose interpretation depends on a literary reading of its potential for generative figuration. Undergirding this metaphorical tapestry is a narrative substructure that provides the Bible with coherence. The initial difficulty here lies with the term "narrative" or "story," which, in my opinion, is an inadequate overarching category to describe the structure and content of Israel's Scriptures. Certainly the Old Testament tells Israel's story, but far more than this. It is a particular kind of history *(Geschichte)* in which God reveals his will as creator and savior of a people in historic time and space. Hays's understanding of narrative shares the weaknesses of the theory of narrativity expressed most eloquently by Hans Frei,[7] who ultimately sought to escape the problem of the Bible's ostensive referentiality by speaking of the narrative's self-referentiality akin to a realistic novel. To read the Hebrew Scriptures only in terms of typology is to denigrate its historical role by rendering it into a timeless narrative figuration.

2. Closely akin to this criticism is Hays's understanding of the role of Scripture in the guidance and shaping of a people to be indirect, illusive, and concealed. The reader is required to exert a capacity for imaginative construal (echoes of postmodernism) to be able to receive its whisperings and hints. In this regard, I would judge that Luz is far more accurate in his essay on Pauline theology when he describes Paul's understanding of the meaning of the Old Testament as "public, open and clear and not with a hidden sense unknown to the prophet himself as is found in Qumran."[8]

3. Perhaps my major reservation is Hays's contention that Paul's figurative interpretation serves as a hermeneutical model for modern interpreters of the New Testament. Hays uses Paul's assertion that Scripture was written "for us" as a warrant for arguing that the modern Christian interpreter has been given the same freedom to render the Old Testament as

---

Ruprecht, 2004). Her work sets a new standard of excellence for the study of intertextuality and the intepretation of the Bible. She offers a serious analysis of Hays's work that is largely positive, pp. 102-4.

7. Hans Frei, *Eclipse of Biblical Narrative* (New Haven: Yale University Press, 1974), is cited both in *Echoes* (p. 224) and in his essay in *Pro Ecclesia* (see n. 10, below).

8. Luz, "Paulinische Theologie als Biblische Theologie," p. 124. See also Frances Young's comment: "The ancient world was far more interested in tradition than novelty. . . . Ancient wisdom was valued rather than creative genius." In Stanley E. Porter and Craig A. Evans, eds., *The Pauline Writings* (Sheffield: Sheffield Academic, 1995), p. 77.

Paul. The present community of faith has also had "the veil removed" and now reads the Scriptures with imaginative freedom "according to the Spirit."[9] A major theological problem with this charismatic understanding of biblical interpretation is that it completely disregards the issue of canon. The assigning by the church of a privileged status to the apostolic witness as the primary testimony to the incarnation of Jesus Christ served to draw a line between Scripture and all subsequent church traditions. The modern Christian is neither a prophet nor an evangelist, but a disciple of Christ whose Christian faith is built upon their witness. Moreover, the basic fact that the church possesses a Scripture that consists of two testaments, both of which bear faithful testimony, is in distinction from Paul, who had but one testament, the Scriptures of Israel. This difference only highlights a basic hermeneutical problem unaddressed by Hays's approach.

It was only after I had completed my critique of Hays's book *Echoes,* published in 1989, that I discovered his new and recent article entitled "Can the Gospels Teach Us How to Read the Old Testament?"[10] It seems apparent that the author is attempting to answer some of his earlier critics by offering a fresh entrance into the same hermeneutical issue of the way that Christians can learn from the New Testament how to read the Old Testament. The focus, however, has shifted from Paul's interpretation of the Old to that of the Gospels. The title of the essay makes it immediately clear that his concern is not in offering an academic exercise in biblical hermeneutics, but, as before, how "we," today's Christian readers of the Old Testament, are to read our Scriptures.

Hays's initial formulation at first sounds like the classic rule expressed by Augustine:[11] the Gospels teach us how to read the Old Testament, and at the same time, the Old Testament teaches us how to understand the Gospels.[12] However, the similarity may be misleading. Hays's proposal is not a simple return to an ancient rubric, but one offering a highly sophisticated and impressive exegetical proposal.

Hays begins his discussion by focusing on the first move of the dialectic: how the New Testament (the Gospels) is interpreted by the Old Testament. He is, of course, aware that for historical critics the claim that Israel's

---

9. Hays, *Echoes,* p. 139.

10. *Pro Ecclesia* 11 (2002): 402-18.

11. Augustine, *Quaestiones in Heptateuchum* 2.73: Corpus Christianorum 33:106, 1279-80.

12. Hays, *Echoes,* p. 405.

Bible influenced the chronologically later New Testament is an uncontested truism. Hays is not concerned to dwell on the historical continuities; rather he pursues the figurative links between the Jewish Bible and the Gospels. He chooses several Gospel passages to describe the mutual relationships discovered by attention to intertextuality. First, in Mark 11:15-19 Jesus' action of cleansing the temple is explicitly set by Mark in the context of Jeremiah's judgment of the Jerusalem temple ("a den of robbers," Jer 7:11) and of Isaiah's oracle, "my house shall be called a house of prayer for all nations" (Isa 56:7). Hays then very skillfully shows how by carefully interpreting and expanding the Old Testament imagery, Mark's use of the Greek Old Testament is far from a conventional proof-texting, but is a way of greatly enriching Jesus' prophetic action by establishing Jesus in a typological relation to Jeremiah. Then Hays turns to Mark 6:45-52 (Jesus walks on the water). He notes that the Septuagintal rendering of Job 9:8 may offer a crucial element for understanding Mark. The Old Testament passage is a reference to God's subduing the watery chaos, and it reads: "[who] walks upon the sea as upon dry ground." Although the Job passage is not explicitly cited, Hays finds that by suggesting an intertextual linkage (whether intentional or not), several features in Mark acquire a far more illuminating interpretation. The Job passage paints a picture prefiguring Mark's sea-walking story as God's sovereignty over all creation.

Next, Hays turns to the second directional move of his dialectic: the Gospels teach us how to read the Old Testament. He focuses his exegesis on John 2:13-22. The story forges a symbolic identification between the temple and Jesus' own body in his enigmatic prophecy: "Destroy this temple and in three days I will raise it up." The meaning of this prophecy becomes intelligible for his disciples only after the resurrection, when they remember what he had said: "They believed the scripture and the word which Jesus had spoken." John 2:17 requires the reference to be from Psalm 69:9: "The zeal for your house will consume me," with Jesus as the speaker. Thus John alleges that the story of Jesus' death and resurrection unlocks the interpretation of Scripture. In a word, Psalm 69 is now to be read figuratively (christologically) as a prefiguration of the resurrection. The second half of the psalm adds more details in portraying Jesus as the righteous sufferer.

Hays's second example of the Gospels teaching us how to read the Old Testament is found in Luke 24:13-35 (Jesus on the road to Emmaus). Jesus scolds his disappointed disciples for not believing the prophets, and "beginning with Moses and all the prophets, he interpreted to them the things about himself in all the scriptures." Hays interprets this chapter to mean that "The whole story of Israel builds its narrative climax in Jesus."[13]

I freely acknowledge that Hays has rendered a brilliant interpretation of the four Gospels' figurative use of the Old Testament. By his appeal to an intertextual interaction, he has convincingly demonstrated how the linkage shows a carefully crafted interpretation of Jesus' ministry by setting these stories figuratively within the context of Israel's Scriptures. However, what Hays has actually done exegetically is to outline variations in the form of christological readings of the Old Testament found in the four Gospels. The fact that the movement between the two testaments can advance in both directions is fully consistent with a christological reading. Although Hays has highlighted his readings by using the modern terminology of intertextuality, the results are that at least four traditional categories of christological reading of the Old Testament have been described, all having countless parallels in the Church Fathers: prophecy and fulfillment (Matthew), type and antitype (Mark), *Heilsgeschichte* as foreshadowing (Luke), and symbolic identification between testaments (John).

I do not wish to be misunderstood. Not for a moment do I dispute that there is a legitimate place for figurative readings of the Bible within the church, and that the exegetical contributions of the Church Fathers remain inestimable. In fact, I have sought to outline in detail the various contexts and resulting approaches to Scripture that try to do justice to a multifaceted hermeneutic of biblical interpretation in today's globalized world.[14] My critique here is rather in the way that Hays addresses this hermeneutical task. Indeed, in my opinion, my earlier criticisms of his earlier book *(Echoes)* have only been further sustained in his latest article.

1. According to Hays, the Gospels' figurative use of the Old Testament provides a model for the modern Christian by which to interpret Scripture. Hays's article on the Gospels now extends Paul's charismatic use of the Old Testament to the typological/christological use by the Gospels as a model for today's interpretation of the Bible. It is one thing to affirm with the Christian canon that the New Testament's use of the Old Testament provides a truthful witness to the gospel ("according to the Scriptures"). It

13. Hays, *Echoes*, p. 416.
14. Brevard S. Childs, *Biblical Theology of the Old and New Testaments* (Minneapolis: Fortress, 1992), pp. 262-87.

is quite another to render the exegetical techniques of the New Testament writers normative for all subsequent Christian exegesis.

2. Once again, the Bible is to be understood metaphorically as a giant tapestry from which to generate figuration. But again, as in *Echoes,* the role of literary figuration and typology does not do justice to the historical (that is, *geschichtliche*) dimension of both testaments. In spite of Hays's repeated denials that he is disregarding the nonmetaphorical content of the Bible, it plays no significant theological role in his exegesis. As a result, the voice of the Old Testament (the Jewish Tanak) is not heard in its own right as an integral part of the Christian canon. Indeed, this issue has not been dealt with either hermeneutically or theologically.

3. Finally, a basic hermeneutical problem raised by historical critics since the Enlightenment, namely, the tension between the literal, historical sense of the Hebrew Bible and the New Testament's interpretation of it, has not been seriously addressed by Hays. In fact, the problem has been exacerbated by Hays's proposal of a repristination of figuration as the church's model for biblical interpretation in the twenty-first century.

III. Frances Young: The Ethics of Reading Paul

The contribution of Frances Young is important and highly relevant to this present project for several reasons. First, she is a leading British scholar in the field of patristics. Second, she has written widely in the area of biblical interpretation, including two methodologically oriented studies on the Pauline epistles.[15] Above all, she has sought to relate both disciplines to the recent insights gained from philosophical hermeneutics and postcritical

15. The following is a selection of Frances Young's most important biblical contributions: *The Art of Performance: Toward a Theology of Holy Scripture* (London: Darton, Longman and Todd, 1990); Frances Young and David Ford, *Meaning and Truth in 2 Corinthians* (London: SPCK, 1987); Young, "The Pastoral Epistles and the Ethics of Reading," *Journal for the Study of the New Testament* 45 (1992): 105-20, reprinted in *The Pauline Writings*, pp. 268-82; "Allegory and the Ethics of Reading," in *The Open Text,* ed. Francis Watson (London: SCM, 1993), pp. 103-20; *The Theology of the Pastoral Letters* (Cambridge: Cambridge University Press, 1994); "Interpretive Genres and the Inevitability of Pluralism," *Journal for the Study of the New Testament* 59 (1995): 93-110; "From Suspicion and Sociology to Spirituality: On Method, Hermeneutics and Appropriation with Response to Patristic Material," *Studia Patristica* 29 (1997): 421-35; *Biblical Exegesis and the Formation of Christian Culture* (Cambridge: Cambridge University Press, 1997).

literary theory. Her synthesis of these two modern disciplines with her formidable classical education has made her a challenging figure.

1. The Development of Young's Understanding

Any attempt to summarize her position must try to do justice to the development of her hermeneutical approach, which extended over several decades. Her early attempt in *The Art of Performance* sought to expand the horizons of biblical interpretation by a focus on artistic, liturgical, and musical interpretation. Then her dissatisfaction with the reigning methods of historical criticism became increasingly sharpened. Her criticism focused on the rendering of a biblical text as an archaeological artifact from the past, separated from the modern reader by an unbridgeable distance, and suffering from the search for scientific objectivity. In her two exegetical studies of Paul she raised the question of "hermeneutics and the ethics of reading," and she presented the notion of a "dialogue" with a text into far greater prominence. Still, in her two studies of Paul she generally defended the traditional critical methods as a needed restraint on those postmodernist scholars who had virtually rejected all claims of referential objectivity. Indeed, at this stage her exegesis of Pauline problems appeared quite conservative and cautious.

However, by 1997, when she published her book *Biblical Exegesis and the Formation of Christian Culture,* her hermeneutical position had become much more aggressive and indeed innovative. The major emphasis now fell on the activity of interpretation as an interaction between reader, text, and context. "Texts 'say' nothing until the reader realizes the black-and-white patterns on the page."[16]

Actually the author herself provides the best guide to her hermeneutical pilgrimage in a highly autobiographical resume of her struggle entitled "From Suspicion and Sociology to Spirituality." She recounts her effort to learn from postmodern biblical studies a way of breaking out of the historicist's impasse that had continued to dominate patristic studies. What she discovered was a new and revolutionary hermeneutical understanding of texts both from philosophical hermeneutics (Gadamer, Ricoeur, Tracy) and from new literary theory (Saussure, Fish, Barthes,

16. Young, *Biblical Exegesis,* p. 10.

Jeanrond). What particularly stimulated her study was the recognition that meaning requires a sophisticated grappling with language that is a symbol system embedded in sociocultural contexts. Texts are not self-interpreting timeless realities, but the social location of language reveals that meaning is bound in discontinuities arising from historical changes. Thus, texts have multiple meanings, and such meanings emerge only in the process of an ongoing dialogue between author and reader.

Young skips over the esoteric debates between the various philosophical giants and focuses on the "practical" issues relating to interpretation. What are the forces at work in constructing a text within a sociolinguistic world? How is meaning grasped by a hermeneutical appropriation? She concludes that there is no meaning apart from interpretation, and an ethical reading is required to enter into the world of the text, not just of the past, and to effect a dialogue between the reader's socially conditioned values and those of the past. In sum, interpretation constantly requires a critical dimension as meaning is transformed into the present and future. The result is that biblical literature is envisioned as metaphorical and yet referential to a God who clothes his divine wisdom by way of tropes, symbols, and imagery. Yet such a suggested reading still leaves an important role for a hermeneutic of suspicion, just so it moves beyond its critical function.

The challenge to a modern reader, whether of biblical or patristic texts, is for a fresh imaginative construal within a learning community centered on Scripture. Authority does not rest in some normative doctrine that is culturally moored in the past, but in a communal effort of interpretation through a transformed behavior that would revitalize a symbol system to reflect the truth and values of the church in common with universal human experience.

Central to Frances Young's fresh formulation of a postmodern hermeneutic is the influence of Werner Jeanrond,[17] who developed the literary and philosophical grounds for an "ethic" of reading. This term is used to designate the conviction that no reading is neutral, but always requires a response to a biblical claim. Every reader is morally responsible for his or her involvement within the enterprise of interpretation. It is this focus on the ethics of reception that Young has developed with great sophistication.

An ethical reading implies a careful balance between empathy and re-

---

17. Werner Jeanrond, *Text and Interpretation as Categories of Theological Thinking* (Dublin: Gill and Macmillan, 1985).

spect for a text's author, whether actual or implied, and a distance needed for critical evaluation. The task of interpretation has thus become a far more sophisticated endeavor that has greatly deepened the initial insight that all interpretation involves an interaction between text and reader. For example, what is the significance that the actual author of a biblical text is often not considered identical with its implied author? Or again, how can interpretation overcome the distance between the reader and the implied audience in which the social world of both can only partially be reconstructed at best? Young also pursues Jeanrond's understanding that there are different "reading genres" that affect interpretation in deciding whether one is reading a text as documentary evidence or liturgically as a religious text.

In sum, the main thrust of this modern hermeneutical exercise in reading is that in an ethical reading one is morally responsible to the "other" and to oneself. Thus, it requires a knowledge and imaginative capacity of the interpreter to enter into this fictional world. Right at this juncture serious theological assumptions are being made that are usually simply taken for granted by all the various postmodernists' proposals.

However, before one turns to a critical assessment of Young's proposal, it should be pointed out that Frances Young, as an avowedly committed Christian scholar, is much aware not only of the potential of postmodern theory for understanding the Bible, but also of the threats that pluralism and relativism hold in undermining every claim of Christian truth.[18]

2. A Critical Assessment of Young's Hermeneutical Proposals

In my judgment Young's mature approach to interpretation has succeeded in appropriating some of the best features of postmodernism. On the one hand, she rightly sets her understanding of Scripture over against a rigid literalistic reading of eternal doctrine. On the other hand, she opposes the historicist rationalism of the older historical critical position that was largely unaware of its own modernist assumptions in a search for objectivity through endless fragmentation. She has also understood the central role of interpretation for meaning and shares a sophisticated theory of

---

18. Young, "Suspicion and Sociology," p. 432.

textuality in the need to enter into the world of the text. Finally, she has made important strides toward moving from suspicion to spirituality with her theory of the ethics of reading, and thus bridging the gap between past, present, and future by locating understanding in the activity of self-participation.

Nevertheless, in my opinion there are serious problems in her understanding of the theological function of Scripture, most of which are related to the role of the Christian canon. First, she shares the widespread misunderstanding that canon was the imposition of an alien dogmatic theory on the Scriptures that sought to preserve one historically conditioned moment in the life of the early church. Rather, the shaping of Scripture into a canon served to provide a way for the authoritative text to be read. It defined for the church the genre within which the text was to be read as witness to Jesus Christ. By establishing the literary structure for a rule of faith, it laid claim for its specific reading function. For the community of early Christians the message of Jesus Christ was thereby communicated as gospel, and all interpretation was anchored fundamentally in this self-understanding.[19]

The theological reason why Scripture has been assigned a privileged status in spite of, indeed because of, its time-conditioned particularity is grounded in the historical specificity of the incarnation of Jesus Christ. The New Testament Scriptures are apostolic and authoritative as the elected vehicle for transmitting the divine purpose in Christ. The church did not create its own canon, but rather responded to what it confessed to have experienced in these texts, namely, the Word of God. Nevertheless, these ecclesial decisions were not infallible since the truth of the apostolic witnesses can be measured only by the subject matter of its testimony, namely, by Christ who entered into human time and space to reveal God's will for the redemption of the world.

The establishing of a canon did not remove the basic activity of the church's understanding through the task of interpretation. The biblical text that constitutes the sacred writings shares all the complexities of philological anomalies, literary obscurities, and multiplicity of conflicting symbol systems, which both Young and Ford have amply outlined.[20] Within the larger structure of canonical shaping, the interpretive task of

19. Jeanrond, *Text and Interpretation*, pp. 120-23.
20. Young and Ford, *Meaning and Truth*, passim.

understanding the biblical texts remains. Young is fully right in rejecting any claims that the fact of a canon removes the text from interpretation, or that it has ossified the interpretation of texts by collapsing the exegetical activity of a dialogue between text, reader, and context into one forever-fixed reading.

Here again I would like to extend the categories of Martin Kähler (*Historie* and *Geschichte*) to the reading of a canonical text. There are the same large areas held in common between a so-called secular, universal interpretation of ancient texts and the church's Scripture. Yet there are also important discontinuities that determine critical features constitutive of the canon's claims respecting issues of authorship, authority, coherence, and truth. The role of canon often calls for a parting of the ways. For example, "apostolicity" is a theological term tied to its evangelical content and cannot be identified with a historical valorization. It will be one of the main functions of the following chapters to try to show in my exegesis of the Pauline corpus those features of historical, literary, and theological continuities and discontinuities.

Another major point of disagreement articulated throughout Paul's letters has shaped early Christian understanding of its Scripture. The addressees of Paul's letters, including the Pastorals, are admonished to listen for the Word of God revealed in the reading of Scripture. The practice rests on the confession that Scripture is not an inert text waiting to be rendered intelligible through the imaginative capacity of its readers. Rather, Scripture has its own voice. Its speaking is often related to the Holy Spirit and the continuing presence of the resurrected Christ with his followers. Because such a confession is either flatly denied or relegated to a harmless metaphor by the academy, it remains a crucial feature of Christian faith that cannot be easily assimilated into postmodern hermeneutical theory.

Another aspect of the church's understanding of the biblical text as having its own voice is the recognition that the text itself exerts a pressure or coercion on its readers. C. Kavin Rowe has further developed this concept in the relation of the Old Testament and the Trinity.[21] The biblical text can be coordinated with the manifestation of the divine will. Rowe rightly

---

21. C. Kavin Rowe, "Biblical Pressure and Trinitarian Hermeneutics," *Pro Ecclesia* 11 (2002): 295-312; see also Christopher R. Seitz, "The Canonical Approach and Theological Interpretation," in *Canon and Biblical Interpretation,* ed. Craig G. Bartholomew and Anthony C. Thiselton (Grand Rapids: Zondervan, 2006), pp. 88-89.

cites from Ernst Käsemann's formulation: "God's power is not silent but bound up with the Word. It speaks . . . so that we experience the pressure of its will."[22] Unfortunately, this quality of the biblical text is foreign to all forms of postmodernism, whether of Jeanrond or Young.

There is one final critique I would make in response to a central feature of Young's approach to biblical interpretation. In her work on 2 Corinthians, she concludes her description of her search for a fresh postmodern way to understand Scripture. She names it a "dynamic hermeneutic," which she set apart from both the older conservative and the liberal interpretive positions. She writes: "We suggest it is possible for scripture to have such a creative bearing on the lives of believers in different ages, cultures and situations, not some kind of search for mechanical correspondences, but by a two-way process of bringing a situation to bear on reading the Bible, and letting the language of the Bible provide a language for expressing and even discerning what is going on in the present . . . and all the needs to be subject to the Spirit of Christ."[23]

There is much in this moving proposal that every Christian can embrace: The Bible remains a living vehicle for divine instruction. The entire Bible is to be used, and we are given the promise of freedom through the work of the Spirit. Yet a crucial distinction remains at the heart of the modern hermeneutical debate: We are not prophets or apostles! Rather our faith is grounded upon their witness to the risen Lord. This means that the postmodern analogy offered is theologically unacceptable. Namely, as Paul once showed remarkable freedom in his use of the Old Testament, so we now possess the same warrant to interpret Scripture apart from the apostolic tradition in order to match the evolving sensibilities of modernity. In spite of its fresh formulation, in this respect Frances Young's portrait of a dynamic hermeneutic within the framework of an ethical reading shares the same error of a misconstrued analogy developed by classic nineteenth-century Protestant liberalism. Both found no place in their theological reflections for the crucial hermeneutical function of the Christian canon, God's gift for an obedient life in a continually changing world.

---

22. Rowe, "Biblical Pressure," p. 309, citing Ernst Käsemann, "The Righteousness of God in Paul," in *New Testament Questions of Today* (Philadelphia: Fortress, 1979), pp. 176-77.

23. Young and Ford, *Meaning and Truth*, pp. 83-84.

IV. Luke T. Johnson: Exegesis and Hermeneutics

Luke Johnson is a leading American New Testament scholar, a Roman Catholic, who has taught both at Yale and at Candler. He has well established himself in the field with at least three commentaries, monographs, and numerous articles. His New Testament introduction *(The Writings of the New Testament)* has been one of the most used in theological education for almost two decades. He has wrestled hard with the theological understanding and application of the New Testament within the historical critical discipline, especially with his book *Scripture and Discernment.* Several years ago he issued a very aggressive attack on the "Jesus Seminar," which he accused of being highly ideologically biased and poor in applying the tools of critical research.[24]

Recently, on the basis of a very impressive critical commentary on 1 and 2 Timothy,[25] Johnson has "confused" the New Testament guild (in the language of Jens Herzer) by challenging the wide consensus that has developed over 150 years concerning the allegedly pseudepigraphical nature of the Pastoral Epistles. What is remarkable is that Johnson has not returned to the older conservative position in defending the Pauline authorship. Rather, by using the tools of critical study with all its new sophistication (philological, literary, historical, and sociological), he has mounted his case for Pauline authorship. In a later chapter we shall return to the details of his exegetical arguments.

Our first concern is to describe how Johnson has offered a new approach to several books within the Pauline corpus that articulates his interest in overcoming the deficiencies of the older historical critical approaches. He thus shares many of the questions raised by Luz, Hays, and Young, while at the same time addressing them from his own distinctive perspective.

---

24. A representative selection of Luke T. Johnson's extensive bibliography includes: *The Acts of the Apostles,* Sacra Pagina 5 (Collegeville, Minn.: Liturgical Press, 1992); *Gospel of Luke,* Sacra Pagina 3 (Collegeville, Minn.: Liturgical Press, 1991); *The Letter of James,* Anchor Bible 37A (New York: Doubleday, 1995); *The Writings of the New Testament: An Interpretation* (Minneapolis: Fortress, 1986; 2nd ed. 1999); *Scripture and Discernment: Decision Making in the Church* (Nashville: Abingdon, 1996); *Real Jesus: The Misguided Quest for the Historical Jesus and the Truth of the Traditional Gospel* (San Francisco: Harper, 1996).

25. Johnson, *The First and Second Letters to Timothy,* Anchor Bible 35A (New York: Doubleday, 2001). Page references to this work have been placed in the text in the following discussion. The commentary is reviewed by Jens Herzer, "Abschied vom Konsens?" *Theologische Literaturzeitung* 129 (2004): 1267-81.

Central to his new approach is his contention, on the one hand, that the historical critical approach to the Bible, seen in its broadest scope, must be even more rigorously employed. Therefore, for example, he rejects the traditional lumping together of the epistles 1 and 2 Timothy and Titus within a unified corpus as "Pastoral Epistles." Rather he feels that each letter must be first treated independently. In a word, he does not embrace the criticism of the historical critical approach as overly prone to fragment the biblical text. On the other hand, and crucial for his new perspective, Johnson proposes that a sharp distinction be made between the exegetical and the hermeneutical tasks (pp. 99, 208-11). By developing his hermeneutical approach after he has completed the exegetical, he feels that he has achieved several important gains, which we shall attempt to describe.

1. Johnson's Interpretive Approach

Johnson's distinction between the exegetical and the hermeneutical tasks in his overall strategy emerges throughout his Timothy commentary. When treating 1 Timothy 1:3-11, he notes in passing: "the present-day struggle of communities with homosexuality is not so much an exegetical as a hermeneutical one" (p. 170). However, the distinction is applied in depth in his chapter entitled "Gender Roles in Worship" (1 Tim 2:8-15). At the outset Johnson notes that Paul's directive concerning public worship is given in gender-specific terminology:

a. First, men are to pray with piety and avoid rancor in discourse. Women are admonished to dress modestly.
b. Second, women are to learn quietly in subjugation to their husbands, to which a general statement of Paul's own opinion is added ("I do not entrust teaching to a woman, nor authority over a man").
c. Third, two warrants are derived from Scripture: the order of creation (2:13) and women's greater susceptibility to moral failure (2:14).

Johnson's exegesis then provides literary parallels from Greek and rabbinic texts to clarify the Hellenistic social contexts of these basic cultural assumptions and to draw some inferences. He further argues that Paul's exegesis of the Genesis passage is deeply flawed since Genesis 3:17 does not blame the woman, but the man, for eating the fruit. In sum, Johnson's exegesis of 1 Timothy 2:8-15 follows in every way the application of historical critical exegesis developed since the nineteenth century in reconstructing the biblical passage according to its putative philological, historical, and cultural contexts.

However, Johnson is not content to leave his interpretation as simply a historical critical exegesis. He adds an important hermeneutical section to address the question: How is a modern Christian reader to deal with such a passage that is obviously highly offensive to modern sensibilities? First, he reviews the commonly used critical options. One option to remove the scandal is to deny genuine Pauline authorship. Another option is to suppress the passage by negating its authority. Johnson then tries to demonstrate why these ploys are both literarily and theologically inadequate and fail to offer a convincing alternative.

At this point Johnson offers his own hermeneutical solution, which he suggests is the only true option: "to engage the words of Paul in a dialectical process of criticism within the public discourse of the church both academic and liturgical" (p. 20). Accordingly, such readings note the peculiar features that render the passage problematic as a normative authority: the passage is gratuitous in going beyond what is required for the situation; it is based on Paul's own private opinion ("I do not allow . . ."), not on a principle intrinsic to the gospel; its injunction is a faulty reading of Torah. Finally, the public dialogue should also acknowledge the harm done to women by a traditional appeal to this biblical passage. It is also interesting to observe that Johnson cites with approval Frances Young's approach to such a critical hermeneutical engagement with this chapter (p. 99).

2. Critical Reflections on Johnson's Proposals

There are several positive features to be gratefully acknowledged. Johnson is critical of many exponents of a "hermeneutic of suspicion" who are unaware of their own assumptions of interpretation that are applied uncritically as if modern sensibilities are always and innately superior to anything of the past (p. 210). Again, the author attempts — if not fully successfully — to take seriously the canonical status of the letters to Timothy that has served the church's tradition in shaping its liturgies and doctrines.

Nevertheless, from my perspective, there are points of major disagreement in Johnson's proposals. First, his sharp separation between exegesis and hermeneutics strikes at the heart of the theological task of biblical interpretation and, in effect, undercuts the very function of the Christian canon. For Johnson, exegesis remains a historical critical enterprise fully in continuity with all the assumptions from the nineteenth century, even in its more sophisticated and expanded form. Accordingly, a biblical scholar seeks to interpret a text as objectively as possible with the tools of philology, history, and literary analysis toward the goal of reconstructing its original setting. Only after its "true meaning" has been determined does the hermeneutical task set in of relating this fully time-conditioned meaning to the modern reader who still holds the biblical text, in some sense, as religiously significant. In contrast, the function of the Christian canon is to provide a very different understanding of the received and shaped apostolic text in its relation both to the past and to future readers.

Second, Johnson accepts uncritically the traditional Catholic interpretation of the Christian canon (indeed, even in its pre–Vatican II form) that canon is a creation of the church, which assigns its authoritative status of canonicity (pp. 210, 422). Over against this view, the whole Reformation debate from the sixteenth century onward turned on whether the gospel (Word) created the church, or the reverse, the church created its Scriptures. Fortunately, most Catholics since Vatican II have acknowledged that indeed the gospel as the preached Word called the church into existence, while at the same time they rightly insist that the church is the indispensable divine vehicle for Scripture's shaping and preservation. The issue is not a minor one since the central theological function of the canon was in distinguishing between the primary apostolic tradition of the Word and the subsequent development of church tradition, the latter standing in continual need of having its truth tested by the former. For Johnson, however, the authority of Scripture does not rest on its "imperatives," that is, on the divine content of its revelation, but on its status of canonicity assigned it by the church.

Third, Johnson has joined an inherited Catholic view of Scripture with a contemporary form of theological liberalism, clearly akin to that of modern liberal Protestantism. Accordingly, the Bible is a completely time-conditioned expression of religious faith that must be constantly adjusted to cultural changes of Christian moral sensibilities affected by the forces of modernity. He writes, for example: "Our growth in understanding of the human person . . . makes it impossible to regard the statements disqualifying women from public speech or roles of leadership as either true or normative" (pp. 208-9). Thus the hermeneutical dialogue of which he speaks turns on negotiating the historically reconstructed biblical texts to our contemporary, culturally shaped sense of morality.

Fourth, Johnson's position reflects little understanding of the theological and hermeneutical implications of the canonical shaping of the New Testament, specifically of the Pauline corpus. The issue of the canonical rendering of the corpus is not a secondary development belonging to subsequent church history, but a force emerging from the inception of the church that registers how the apostolic witnesses were received, shaped, and ordered within a unified corpus. Johnson is correct in seeing that the authority of 1 and 2 Timothy does rest unmediated on the direct authorship of the shaped letters of Paul, but he fails to see the specific new function that these letters have been assigned to Paul's witness as the model for the succeeding Christian church of its true apostolic faith. The corpus has joined the received letters into an authoritative collection while largely retaining the historic particularity of each letter.

The effect is that a canonical context has been provided by which to understand the individual letters in terms of the whole and the whole in terms of the single. There is thus a theological dialectic established within a canonical context that is not simply identified with a reconstructed historical setting. The Pauline corpus was never envisioned as a "noble ideal" of egalitarian values, as often falsely interpreted on the basis of Galatians 3:28, against which all other letters containing hierarchical structures are negatively judged. Nor does the modern cultural criticism of the past provide the means for theologically appropriating the time-conditionality of all the Pauline corpus. Rather, in the plurality within the circle of the canonical collection, a theological dialogue is established among all the witnesses, all of which are ultimately judged in relation to their christological subject matter, namely, by Jesus Christ, the Lord and savior of the church and the world.

In the subsequent exegetical chapters, a canonical approach to the letters within the Pauline corpus, including of course the Pastorals, will be illustrated and defended.

V. Wayne A. Meeks: The Social Context of Pauline Theology

Wayne Meeks is an internationally recognized leader in the field of New Testament and early Christianity. He taught at several American universities before his appointment to Yale, where he worked for some three decades before his retirement. His influence, especially in North America, has been wide, and has continued to spread through his many students.[26] It is frequently acknowledged that this research as a social historian of early Christianity has been a major force in effecting a paradigm shift in the field of New Testament.

Meeks's program did not develop at once. In several of his books he outlined his academic journey. Reviewing his entire corpus, one can discern a deepening, expansion, and even radicalization of his position as increasingly he began to draw out the sociological implications for the study of the Bible within a modern society. Access to his writings is readily obtained. Four of his books have left a major impact and established the range of his remarkable scope.[27] Equally important are his many essays, some of which have been recently republished.[28]

1. Meeks's Approach Outlined

In a real sense, Meeks's basic concerns arose from a simple question: "What was it like to become and be an ordinary Christian in the first century?"[29] Since there were no complete records but only scattered fragments, he concluded that it was the task of a social historian to describe the growth of early Christianity by examining the multifaceted social factors from which Christianity was formed, and which in turn formed its participants. Following the lead of such social scientists as Clifford Geertz, Meeks spoke of a "thick description" of culture consisting of "webs of significance" and of the complex relation between social and symbolic structures.[30] Religion is an integral part of these cultural events providing ac-

---

26. See his Festschrift, *The Social World of the First Christians: Essays in Honor of Wayne A. Meeks,* ed. J. M. White and O. L. Yarbrough (Minneapolis: Augsburg Fortress, 1995).

27. The four books are: *The First Urban Christians* (New Haven: Yale University Press, 1986); *The Moral World of the First Christians* (Philadelphia: Westminster, 1986); *The Origins of Christian Morality* (New Haven: Yale University Press, 1993); *Christ Is the Question* (Louisville: Westminster John Knox, 2006).

28. Meeks, *In Search of the Early Christians* (New Haven: Yale University Press, 2002).

29. Meeks, *The First Urban Christians,* p. 2.

30. Meeks, "A Hermeneutic of Social Embodiment," *Harvard Theological Review* 79 (1986): 179.

cess to Christianity's beginnings, and not obtained by a listing of theological categories. Concern with the primary sources is not so much what people say, but what they do. Social analysis of a community involves its ethos, worldview, and sacred symbols,[31] which can be recalibrated to reveal the way texts worked in the past. Thus, Meeks is equally uninterested in trying to apply a unified sociological pattern on his material, such as that of Max Weber's, which he regards as equally abstract as a traditional theological framework.

At times Meeks describes his method as that of an ethnographer who is concerned with communities. "Individuals do not become moral agents except in the relationships, the transactions, the habits and reinforcements, the special users of language and gesture that together constitute life in community."[32] This is the process named by ethnographers as resocialization that is central to the growth of moral sensibilities. Each people has its own picture of reality from which it derives its own code of behavior. He concludes that the study of early Christianity is not a search for great ethical principles, but an inquiry about the forms of culture within which the moral sensibilities have meaning.

2. Examples of Meeks's Social Interpretation

a. In his famous essay "The Man from Heaven in Johannine Sectarianism" (1972, cited from *In Search of the Early Christians*),[33] Meeks focuses on understanding the function of the Johannine imagery of Christ's "descending/ascending from heaven." He rejects the historical critical solution that the formula was simply an adoption from a prior philosophical scheme, but rather he seeks to let this symbolic language speak in its own way. What is the social function of an image within a community that developed it? He notes that the motifs belong exclusively to discourse, not narrative.

In the dialogue with Nicodemus (John 3), the emphasis falls on Jesus' being incomprehensible to Nicodemus, who is confused by his strangeness. The primary point is the inability of anyone from "this earthly world" to

---

31. Meeks, "Hermeneutic of Social Embodiment," p. 184.

32. Meeks, *Origins of Christian Morality*, p. 8.

33. Meeks, "The Man from Heaven in Johannine Sectarianism," in *In Search of the Early Christians*, pp. 106-14.

understand and accept Jesus who, as an enigma, has descended from heaven. His descent and ascent becomes a cipher for Jesus' unique self-knowledge and foreignness to those of this world. To understand, Nicodemus must be "born from above." Using a Jewish version of the sapiential myth, wisdom sought a home in the world but found no acceptance. Then Jesus signals his own death: he will be "lifted up," and by death he created the community of the Johannine church. These are those who accept his unearthly strangeness and have become an unearthly community.

This mythical symbolism becomes the language by which the Johannine community understands its social identity in isolation from the larger society. The imagery provides an etiology for the Johannine church as a countercultural group. Much like the Sophia myth in Gnosticism, the Fourth Gospel introduces the metaphor of Christ's union with believers, and there remains a dialectical relation in both the using and further developing of the myth into Christology.

b. In his essay "On Trusting an Unpredictable God: A Hermeneutical Meditation on Romans 9–11,"[34] Meeks argues that the heart of the issue in Romans 9–11 lies, not on whether Paul is consistent, but on whether God is consistent in his promises. Chapters 1–8 have focused on God's faithfulness, but now in chapters 9–11 Paul disrupts this confidence. Does not the removal of the distinction between Jew and Gentile also mean the canceling of Israel's election? Accordingly, Paul takes up this basic question of the relation between "Israel after the flesh" and God's new people.

Paul's response is based on his interpretation of the Jewish Scriptures, which is a highly paradoxical reading. In Romans 9:25 Paul cites two verses from Hosea completely out of their context. He takes the prophet's words addressed to Israel to refer to the Gentiles. Christians are the "nonpeople" who have become the people of God. Even more "brazen" is Paul's "misreading" of Scripture (Rom 10:6-8) by interpreting Deuteronomy 30:12-13, which clearly speaks of Torah, to refer instead to Christ and "the word of faith that we proclaim." Paul even extends the tension by inserting Isaiah 8:14 (a stone that trips) into Isaiah 28:16 (the precious, chosen, and honored stone). Meeks interprets the commandeering of Moses' words about the Torah to be spoken by "the righteousness of faith" as a "giant wink" that says "pay attention."

---

34. Meeks, "On Trusting an Unpredictable God: A Hermeneutical Meditation on Romans 9–11," in *In Search of the Early Christians*, pp. 210-19.

According to Meeks, Paul's purpose is not to abolish the plain sense of the Torah's word; he rather requires that the plain sense of the biblical text still functions as a counterweight to his christological reading. The plain sense resides in the mind of the competent reader and serves to establish a provocation pressing toward a resolution of the tension. In sum, where Paul seems to subvert the plain sense of the ancient text, the plain sense continues to exert covert pressure in creating a dialectic with the new reading that brings to light a more complex and inclusive angle of vision. In the end, in spite of the radical change in God's purpose for the nations, the promise spoken to Israel still stands.

Meeks then draws larger hermeneutical inferences from his reading of the "trick played on Israel." The letter of Romans is a social process, and all interpretation takes place within a community sharing a three-way communication among text, interpreter, and reader. Paul's exercise in exegesis lies in establishing a dialectic between the christological interpretation of the Old Testament and the reader's memory of its plain sense. Meeks then draws a modern hermeneutical lesson from Paul's handling of Romans 9–11. Historical critical interpretation can play a role analogous to that of the plain sense vis-à-vis Paul's charismatic misreading. It would thus act as a kind of devil's advocate standing up for the past in a dialogue between the past and the present.

c. Meeks attempts to understand the Johannine language of making Jesus "equal to God,"[35] which evoked the violent hostility of the Jews (John 19:7). His goal is to reconstruct the symbolic bridge between John's language and a mostly Platonic philosophical tradition. What occurs is the development of an exegetical, interpretive process by which a new religious movement of Scripture, of Jesus, and of its own history merged into a complex dialectic.

In the Greek world the formula of being "equal to God" was a means of bestowing honor. The ideal of resembling God by sharing his attributes was commonplace. In the Greek philosophical tradition, to be wise was to strive to be like God. In John 10:31-39 the argument is similar, and the title of being God's equal is innocuous. The issue of Jesus' blasphemy asserted by the Jews in John 10:33 arose because of the novel complex of beliefs clustering around him in Johannine circles that spoke of him as a god. Clearly, the Jews heard this affirmation in a very different way from the Johannine Christians.

---

35. Meeks, "Equal to God," in *In Search of the Early Christians*, pp. 91-105.

How then did the rift develop? Meeks finds the clue in the exegetical process. The idiom of ascending and descending provided a mythical pattern in which Jesus as the Son of Man was rendered equal to God. The glory of Jesus was interpreted by John as his exaltation in death, which was the glorification seen by Abraham (8:56). Thus the Johannine Christians, trying to make intelligible an emerging sense of Jesus' identity, gave the phrase a peculiar twist. Jewish biblical theophanies became christophanies, that is, visions of the divine Son of Man enthroned in heaven, a human form in the image of God.

The force that drove these Christians to make these connections and to separate from the traditional Jewish understanding of man's inability to see God and live, was a classic form of sectarian consciousness. The claims of Jesus established their own identity, and the community exalted in this subordination of the Jewish tradition. As a result, it was the Gospel of John's misreading of the Scriptures that contributed much of what was to form the Christology of the church.

d. Christ is the question. In his most recent book, Meeks focuses on the perennial question of Jesus' identity. He first traces the demise of the traditional dogmatic interpretation of institutionalized Christianity and its replacement by the critical search for the historical Jesus. He then reviews the crises of the old and new quests for the historical Jesus, and why they ended in failure. He concludes that Jesus' identity is not a given profile to be recovered, but a process like all human identity, and is a social issue, an interpretive activity constantly in flux.

Using strategies analogous to Qumran's group struggles to deal with events that challenged traditional beliefs in a God-oriented world, the early Christians searched for appropriate images to express the significance of their charismatic figure's ignominious death. By construing "loaded" texts of Scripture, they sought to explain the group's experience with the claim that God had overruled Pilate's action by raising the crucified Messiah from the dead. The absurdity of such an event was made intelligible by interpreting it as a vicarious death around which the Christian community shaped its own social identity.

In his summary, Meeks concludes that the identity of Jesus is still open since the transactive process by which identity is made is still continuing. "Jesus *is* the persona he becomes in interaction with others."[36] Like the

---

36. Meeks, *Christ Is the Question*, p. 58.

Evangelists who wrote down their different stories, so the modern reader must enter into the same self-involving process by which to discover and invent an appropriate identity.

3. A Critical Evaluation of Meeks's Approach

The basic problem raised by Meeks's approach is a hermeneutical issue that has occupied the field of biblical studies ever since the Enlightenment. How does a modern reader approach the Bible when the traditional ecclesiastical traditions respecting its content and authority have been challenged by a host of new perspectives raised by critics standing outside the prescribed circles of committed religious adherents?

With great clarity in his latest book *(Christ Is the Question)*, Meeks has reviewed the crisis evoked by the rise of historical criticism, and chartered the demise of the nineteenth century's confidence that the various forms of historicism could recover the true meaning of the Christian faith and the identity of its founder. He has also pursued the most recent postmodern attempts to overcome the hermeneutical impasse. He is especially indebted to the analysis of George Lindbeck,[37] whose typology of construing the Bible distinguishes between three modes: the cognitive-propositional (truth claims about objective realities), experimental-expressive (symbols of inner feelings, attributes, or existential orientation), and his own choice of a cultural-linguistic approach (language as communally shaped rules of discourse and action).

Meeks opts for a form of Lindbeck's cultural-linguistic approach in proposing a history-of-religions method that defines the goal of recovering the rise of early Christianity through the discovery of the process by which communities were shaped by a subtle interaction between ethos, worldview, and sacred symbols. The goal according to this model was not belief in objective propositions (doctrine), nor in authentic self-understanding (existentialism), but in a community whose form of life corresponded to the symbolic universe rendered by the text.[38]

In my judgment, the effect of this move is to eliminate from the out-

---

37. George Lindbeck, *The Nature of Doctrine: Religion and Theology in a Postliberal Age* (Philadelphia: Westminster, 1984), pp. 15-45.

38. Meeks, "Hermeneutic of Social Embodiment," pp. 176-86.

set crucial dimensions constitutive to the rise of the Christian faith, including cognitive, experimental, and linguistic factors. (I shall shortly illustrate the problem by returning to the four above-mentioned exegetical examples of Meeks.) What is painfully missing is that the early Christian movement did not inherit a bunch of incoherent Jewish traditions, but a corpus of authoritative writings already formed into a canonical corpus (the law and the prophets) as the context from which the identity of Jesus was revealed, and conversely the meaning of which was transformed by the events of the death and resurrection of the Christ. Israel's story, its life and history, provided a cognitive confessional resource for the rise of Christianity. Similarly, a central feature of the gospel was its bearing witness to a divine reality being revealed in the person of Jesus, the knowledge of whose identity was made known only by the response of faith to the gracious invitation: "Come and see" (John 1:39). Particularly in the Fourth Gospel, the stories recounted stress the qualitatively different knowledge through experience of Christ's true identity from those who knew Jesus only as the carpenter's son (e.g., the Samaritan woman in John 4 and Thomas in chapter 20, etc.).

My initial criticism of Meeks's proposal is that his sociological approach of describing the moral world of early Christianity limits its analysis to the world of human phenomenology expressed in communal patterns of behavior. I do not question that his often brilliant observations are of value in providing a fresh perspective. However, in the end, his approach, while priding itself on its multifaceted quality, is theologically one-dimensional and reminds one of a color-blind art critic attempting to interpret the paintings of a Cézanne or a van Gogh.

I now return briefly to four of Meeks's examples outlined above. First, in "The Man from Heaven," the pattern of Jesus' descent/ascent functions sociologically to shape the identity of the socially alienated Johannine community as separated from the world. Those who accept Jesus' unearthly "strangeness" are drawn into becoming an unearthly community joined to him. For Meeks, much of the imagery of descent/ascent was derived from the Sophia myth in Gnosticism, and in turn helped to develop the elements of the myth that constituted the Johannine Christology.

One only has to compare Meeks's treatment with the classic essay of Nils Dahl to see the one-sidedness of his analysis. Dahl writes: "The whole outlook of the Fourth Gospel is characterized by its consistent christocentricity."[39] Dahl does not doubt that John's language is often akin to Gnosticism, and that John's scriptural exegesis comes close at times to that of the Targum of Isaiah and *merkabah* mysticism, but these comparative, history-of-religions features do not touch the heart of John's Gospel. Dahl then discusses the Christology announced in the prologue. The pre-existence of Christ with the Father is testified to by the Jewish Scriptures, by Abraham, Moses, and the prophets. For John the most important point is that the patriarchs and prophets of Israel are the primary witnesses to Jesus, and only in communion with them can believers outside Israel see what they saw: the glory of Christ incarnate.[40] In Meeks's sociological construal, all the Christology of the Gospel is omitted — by definition a lifeless doctrine — and the theological dimension is flattened into a sociological function of the community.

Second, in his essay "On Trusting an Unpredictable God," Meeks employs Harold Bloom's category of a "misreading" of a text in relation to his interpretation of Deuteronomy 30 in Romans 10. Few would question that Paul has not interpreted Scripture according to its "plain sense." Yet as Leander Keck has convincingly argued, "Paul's reading of Deuteronomy is no more arbitrary than the assertion that the *telos* of the law is Christ, in fact, his interpretives are the logical inference from that assertion."[41] Paul is not attempting to interpret Deuteronomy in the context of Torah apart from its christological goal, but rather to pursue Torah's ultimate role in the light of Christ's cross and resurrection. To claim that Paul is counting on the memory of his audience of the original plain sense of the text in order to form a dialectic is a modern hermeneutical anachronism and a misconstrual of Paul's understanding of Scripture.

Third, in his essay "Equal to God," Meeks attempts to describe an interpretive process in which elements from the Greek philosophical tradition are blended with various beliefs clustered in the Johannine circle by reshaping these elements into metaphors that later constituted much of the church's Christology. Once again, each of the Gospels, along with the letters of Paul, shares a different cultural milieu, and has used a variety of time-conditioned metaphors by which to describe the identity of

---

39. Nils A. Dahl, "The Johannine Church and History," in *Jesus in the Memory of the Early Church* (Minneapolis: Augsburg, 1976), pp. 99-119, here p. 115.

40. Dahl, "Johannine Church and History," p. 114.

41. Leander E. Keck, *Romans* (Nashville: Abingdon, 2005), p. 256.

Christ. Yet Meeks's use of the term "metaphor" functions in such a way that its referentiality constantly blurs into fantasy and mythical speculation. In contrast, when Paul uses a metaphor such as the cross, the referentiality to the historical event of Jesus' crucifixion and death is never lost. When the Gospels speak of bearing witness, the assumption is always that the Evangelists are responding to a divine coercion and not to a linguistic "invention," a word often used by Meeks in tracing the growth of a "symbol system."

Fourth, Meeks's recent book *Christ Is the Question* is filled with a learned and informative history of the move from a precritical period to modernity in the study of the New Testament. Although Meeks does not explicitly align himself with postmodernism, its influence is everywhere felt. The major concern of the book is to demonstrate that Jesus' identity, like every other human being, is developed through a complex interpretive process. The result is that the various filters that now separate the ancient texts and the modern reader have become virtually impenetrable. He speaks repeatedly of obscurity, and characterizes the traditional Reformation doctrine of Scripture's perspicuity as absurd.[42] He agrees with Maurice Wiles in renouncing altogether the concept of the Bible as "binding authority."

The identity of Christ is shrouded in uncertainty and obscurity. The gap separating the past from the present is clouded by innumerable, unrecoverable cultural forces. Moreover, the modern reader is also rendered unable to recover the past because of countless cultural, psychological, and ethnic patterns both consciously and unconsciously at work, with the result that even the questions raised about Jesus' identity must be radically recast. Because Jesus' identity is not a fixed entity but an interactive practice, his identity is still developing and each new generation reconstructs it according to their time-conditioned sensibilities. (In the last decade, Jesus' egalitarianism seems to have replaced his idealism as his highest virtue.) Although Meeks tries valiantly to conclude his book on a positive note, the question remains whether his prescribed journey can provide a way for a joyful entry into the divine mystery of life that generations of Christians confessed to have found in Jesus Christ.

---

42. Meeks, *Christ Is the Question*, p. 118.

4. The Role of the Canon and Jesus' Identity

In this final section I would like to offer my own hermeneutical proposal as an alternative to Meeks's program, and to pinpoint the nature of our fundamental disagreement over exegetical method in interpreting the Bible. I shall again try to delineate a christological, confessional approach under the rubric of canon over against Meeks's sociological history-of-religions approach as an exercise in social history.

Meeks builds his description of the rise of modernity largely on Hans Frei's account in *The Eclipse of Biblical Narrative*.[43] Frei traced the move toward modernity from an initial assumption by the Reformers of the unity of meaning and its referent. The separation began in the seventeenth century when rational evidences were thought necessary by which to establish this unity (Spinoza, Locke), and then came apart dramatically when the Enlightenment critics used evidences to contest and deny the unity of the biblical text with its putative referents.

Recently Neil MacDonald offered an important corrective to Frei's explanation of the hermeneutical transition from the precritical to the critical era.[44] The problem did not involve merely a shift from history-like meaning to ostensive reference, but the hermeneutical alteration occurred in the domain of belief, at the level of epistemic stance regarding "truth telling." The change took place when belief in the biblical narrative was no longer held according to a traditional hermeneutical assumption of truth, but now required critical evidential justification. To use my canonical terminology, the change occurred when the truth-telling role implicit in the concept of an authoritative canon was replaced by the need for a critical context supported by external proof of its veracity.

Meeks, along with a majority of New Testament scholars, regards the subject of canon as largely irrelevant to the growth and development of early Christianity. He assigns it to a late-second-century introduction by Irenaeus as part of Christianity's increasing institutionalism. I judge this interpretation of the role of the New Testament canon to be a serious misunderstanding of a crucial element in the development of early Christian-

43. Hans W. Frei, *The Eclipse of Biblical Narrative* (New Haven: Yale University Press, 1974).

44. Neil B. MacDonald, "Illocutionary Stance in Hans Frei's *The Eclipse of Biblical Narrative*," in *After Pentecost: Language and Biblical Interpretation*, ed. Craig Bartholomew et al. (Grand Rapids: Zondervan, 2001), pp. 312-28.

ity. The Christian church was never without a canon. When the New Testament writers spoke of Scripture *(graphē),* the reference was to the Scriptures of Israel, later called the Old Testament by Christians, which was assumed to be authoritative. As Hans von Campenhausen has forcefully stated, the problem of the early church was not what to do with the Old Testament in the light of the gospel, but rather the reverse.[45] In the light of the Old Testament, which was acknowledged to be the true oracles of God, how was one to understand the good news of Jesus Christ?

The struggle to understand the identity of Jesus involved a dialectical process from the church's inception. The gospel was interpreted in the light of the Old Testament, while conversely the Old Testament — now largely read in Greek — was understood from the witness of the gospel. The lengthy formation of the Christian canon underwent a process in which the church in all its diverse forms confessed to hear the truthful witness to Christ in certain books. The Church Fathers never described the selective process as their own creation, but rather the selection was seen as a response to the pressure of the four Gospels experienced in liturgical and catechetical contexts as truthful.

The early determination of the scope of the gospel and later of the Pauline corpus served to set the boundaries of the New Testament Scriptures. Inside the circle of received authoritative writings, there was the recognition of a unity within a wide range of witnesses. There was only one gospel but four Evangelists testifying to it in different ways. Outside the circle were listed the nonauthoritative books, at times still judged edifying, but at other times flatly rejected as heretical. The formation of a New Testament canon involved a long, often controversial process. Cultural and regional factors were always at work, but the intent of the establishment of a written Scripture was to bear truthful testimony to Jesus Christ. All three of the modes designated by George Lindbeck were at work in the process: a cognitive truth confessed, experiential modes of response sounded, and a shaping of cultural, linguistic patterns of the faith rendered.[46]

Meeks assigns the formation of a New Testament canon to the late second century as part of the church's political ploy to institutionalize a form of Catholic orthodoxy, a position already projected by Harnack. One of

45. Hans von Campenhausen, *The Formation of the Christian Bible* (Philadelphia: Fortress, 1972), pp. 64-65.
46. Lindbeck, *The Nature of Doctrine.*

the major purposes of this monograph is to argue that the formation of a New Testament canon was, above all, a hermeneutical exercise in which its anonymous apostles and postapostolic editors collected, preserved, and theologically shaped the material in order for the evangelical traditions to serve successive generations of Christians. The canonical shaping was indeed an interpretation of the traditions, but its rendering of the gospel into its written form echoed the earlier, oral christological rule of faith, and established a norm by which all subsequent traditions were to be tested.

The concept of an authoritative canon is built on two crucial factors that play no role whatsoever in Meeks's understanding of early Christianity. First, the formation of a canon, in a variety of ways, was a confession of the historical reality of the church. The followers of Jesus assembled together at first in small house communities spread over Asia Minor and Greece, but the term *ecclesia* (church) also included the concept of the larger universal people of God. Jaroslav Pelikan writes: "it does not do violence to the text of Acts to make 'the church' a major doctrinal theme running through the entire book."[47] It was thus not arbitrary that the later Niceno-Constantinopolitan Creed of 381 identified the marks of the Christian church as "one, holy, catholic, and apostolic." It is constitutive of Meeks's sociological description of the early church to disregard this claim as an alien dogmatic formulation, and to include in his reconstruction of the history of early Christianity every conceivable religious grouping as playing an equal role in its development. But does not such a historical account need to recognize the sharply differing perspectives of those inside (the "emic") and those outside (the "etic") communities? In his commentary on Galatians, J. Louis Martyn makes a penetrating observation that by reading Paul through the lenses of second- and third-century sources (Aristides and Pliny the Younger), Meeks runs the risk of flattening the uniquely apocalyptic stance of the early church in his reconstruction of an alleged process of resocialization.[48]

Second, the writers of the New Testament, especially John, Paul, and his successors, assigned a crucial theological action within the life of the church to the role of the Holy Spirit, the living spirit of Christ, who "quickened" the Scriptures in a continuous activity of interpretation, in-

---

47. Jaroslav Pelikan, *Acts* (Grand Rapids: Brazos, 2005), p. 56.
48. J. Louis Martyn, *Galatians*, Anchor Bible 33A (New York: Doubleday, 1997), p. 533.

struction, and application (John 16:13; Rom 15:6; 2 Tim 3:16). It is therefore quite impossible to describe the rise of the Christian movement without recognizing the church's understanding that in the wrestling with its Scriptures, it was being constantly instructed by a living Lord. Whatever metaphors the church developed in this endeavor, they were always understood in relation to a perceived divine reality.

To conclude: I consider the debate with Wayne Meeks to be of greatest importance because the contrast in approaches serves to illustrate two dramatically opposed understandings of the task of biblical studies, and to demonstrate how high are the theological issues at stake.

3. The Shaping of the Pauline Corpus

Up to now we have discussed the significance of interpreting the Pauline letters within the context of the Pauline corpus. How exactly does one proceed? I suggest that the initial and crucial problem turns on determining the form and function of Romans within the corpus.

I. The Letter to the Romans

Much of the lengthy debate over Romans during the last century turns on the question of the purpose of Paul's writing of Romans. Karl Donfried suggested that two major theses have emerged.[1] One stressed external factors (historical and sociological) respecting the Roman church; the other emphasized internal problems tied to Paul's understanding of his mission. Of course, alongside these two methodological assessments of Paul's purpose was the attention paid to the literary form of his letter that has been carefully analyzed in relation to the multifaceted conventions of letter writing especially in the Greco-Hellenistic traditions.

After presenting a wide variety of different formulations of these two options, Donfried concluded by offering his own methodological principle that he thought formed a fundamental axiom on which all further research should proceed, namely, the letter of Romans was written to deal with a concrete situation in Rome,[2] the exact form of which could be fur-

---

1. Karl P. Donfried, ed., *The Romans Debate,* rev. ed. (Peabody, Mass.: Henrickson, 1991).
2. Donfried, *The Romans Debate,* p. 109.

ther debated. However, this so-called axiom on an understanding of Romans over the last half-century has not produced anything like a consensus. In fact, just the opposite has resulted, with no clear sense on how to resolve the problem. The move toward focusing rather on Paul's own situation for writing the letter has probably gained strength.

If one therefore begins with Paul's own declaration in Romans 15:19, he had ended his missionary enterprise in the eastern part of the Roman Empire. He was now at last able to accomplish his plan to visit Rome, and hoped from there to advance to Spain (15:24-28). Also imperative to Paul was his task to deliver the collection to Jerusalem that he had assembled from some of his Gentile congregations. The apostle is not personally acquainted with the Roman congregation and appears somewhat uncertain of his reception (15:31). Yet of equal importance is Paul's desire for fellowship with the Christians of Rome: "to impart some spiritual gifts," "to be refreshed in your company," and "to be sped on my journey by you." In sum, he writes his letter as a form of self-introduction, offering in a letter a provisory substitute for his actual presence in their midst.

Yet it is in the prescript of his letter (1:1-7) that one sees most clearly the intensity and full scope of Paul's purpose in writing to the Romans.[3] One is struck immediately by the length of the prescript and the solemnity of his salutation. By an expansion of the Hellenistic Greek epistolary prescript, he has foreshadowed most of the major themes of his letter: his apostolic authority; his commitment to Christ as servant like the Old Testament saints; the content of the gospel he proclaims, promised by the prophets; the continuity of his faith with the early kerygmatic preaching (1:3-4); the inauguration of a new age effected by Jesus Christ; Jesus Christ's rule in power through his resurrection; and Paul's apostleship for the sake of the nations.

What is crucial to the entire letter and adumbrated in this prescript is that Paul covers a range of topics that he has previously addressed throughout his earlier letters that he had targeted to a particular historical situation. In an impressive essay Günther Bornkamm lists some sixteen

---

3. See Robert W. Wall, "Romans 1.1-15: An Introduction to the Pauline Corpus of the New Testament," in *The New Testament as Canon*, ed. Robert W. Wall and E. E. Lemcio, Journal for the Study of the New Testament, Supplement 76 (Sheffield: Sheffield Academic, 1992), pp. 142-60.

topics recurring in Romans that have parallels in the earlier letters, including the debate over Paul's claims of apostolicity (Gal 1; Phil 3); justification by faith (Gal 3; Phil 3); Abraham's rectification apart from works (Gal 3); the antithetical typology of Christ and Adam (1 Cor 15); baptism and the new life (Gal 3); the role of the law, gifts of the Spirit, and the ethics of the weak and the strong (1 Cor 8–10).[4]

Moreover, Bornkamm goes to great lengths to explain the unique shape of Paul's letter in setting forth these previously discussed topics in a far more detailed, and profound, theological manner, as if to offer a summation of his life's mission. Bornkamm is aware that Paul is not writing a systematic theology. The epistolary style continues and is confirmed especially by chapter 16. (The various theories to interpret the recipients of Paul's greeting lie outside the scope of this chapter.) Yet the attempts at postulating some external force (e.g., the edict of Claudius) driving Paul's theological reflections have failed to do justice to the uniqueness of the letter in which a holistic perspective dominates that deepens, corrects, and develops his letter to the Romans. In my judgment, Bornkamm's own suggestion of a "last will and testament" is not fully satisfactory and goes beyond the expressed purpose of the letter.

In his conclusion, Bornkamm makes the interesting observation in an almost offhanded remark that he does not pursue: "Nevertheless this letter, even if unintended, has in fact become the historical testament of the Apostle." Not only do I concur with this evaluation, but I feel that Bornkamm has touched on a crucial point. Regardless of Paul's intention, the letter to the Romans has been heard in a particular way in the subsequent development of the Pauline corpus. Moreover, this move was not an accidental construal, but one that found its warrant in the perspective of the prescript with its universal scope, the appeal to "all," the promise to the nations, and the new eschatological era of Christ's Lordship.

To suggest that the prescript of the book of Romans has been received by its structure, content, and position to serve as an introduction to the entire Pauline corpus does not in itself entail that it thereby provides a self-evident interpretation of the rest of the book. Far from it! The complex literary and theological problems of the book's coherence continue to chal-

---

4. Günther Bornkamm, "The Letter to the Romans as Paul's Last Will and Testament," in *The Romans Debate*, pp. 16-28.

lenge each new generation of readers. A canonical approach to the book does not presume to escape the exegetical problems of interpretation that rightly have engaged generations of scholars. What is the nature of the letter's coherence? How do the various parts relate: chapters 1–4, 5–8, 9–11, 12–13, 14–15, and 16, and how are the multiple tensions to be interpreted? Can one work with a dialectic between coherence and contingency, as once suggested by J. Christiaan Beker?

In sum, the range of interpretive problems addressed in the Pauline Seminar of the Society of Biblical Literature in volumes 3 and 4 remains an existential challenge for anyone seeking a new approach for breaking out of the scholarly impasse. I thus agree with Frances Young that an appeal to a canonical shaping of the Pauline corpus does not imply that textual meaning can be gained apart from the activity of interpretation.

That being said, I would nevertheless argue at the outset that the canonical shaping of the corpus in assigning a critical role to Romans does serve to guide the range of possible interpretations. It offers, at the very least, negative criteria by which to eliminate certain alternatives. First, from a canonical perspective that receives the biblical text as authoritative Scripture, and treasures it as a divine word from God to a community of faith and practice, any interpretation that derives the major content of the book of Romans from external, nontheological forces is judged to be a misreading of the literary genre of this religious text. It is to read against the grain of the author's intent and thus to highlight features that are peripheral to the literature's purpose.

Second, the canonical shape of the corpus serves to bear testimony to how the letters were received within a living tradition that culminated in the Pastoral Epistles. The very fact that Paul's teaching became identified with "sound doctrine" as a measuring rod for its faithfulness to the gospel would act as a restraint against an interpretive move that would set in opposition to Paul's dynamic kerygma an allegedly static deposit of the Pastorals. Or again, to characterize Paul's preaching of justification by faith apart from the law as "a secondary crater" (Albert Schweitzer) is to disregard its programmatic role in Romans 1:16-17 and 3:21-26 and the resonance it received in the Pastorals, namely, in Titus 3:5 ("he saved us, not by deeds done by us in righteousness . . . that we might be justified by his grace") or in 2 Timothy 1:9 ("who saved us and called us with a holy calling, not in virtue of our works according to his own purpose"). In a word, a disregard of the *Wirkungsgeschichte* (aftereffect) of Romans that overlooks its ecclesial (canonical) perception in order to reconstruct an alleged ideology of the "historical Paul" is deeply flawed.[5]

Third, any interpretation that so moors Paul's message in exclusively time-conditioned contingencies of the past as to make succeeding theological actualization impossible, or so to render his message in such contradictions as to deny any rational consistency, conflicts with a serious engagement with Paul's thought.

To summarize, Romans was shortly received as the introduction of the Pauline corpus, from its content, position, and majestic formulation of the Pauline gospel. However, before returning to the relation of Romans and the particularity of his earlier letters, it is necessary first to describe another crucial canonical structure of the Pauline corpus, namely, the Pastoral Epistles.

II. The Pastoral Epistles

We began our discussion on how to proceed with a canonical interpretation of the Pauline corpus by attempting to demonstrate how the book of Romans was shortly understood and shaped as the introduction to the Pauline corpus. Now we turn to the end of the canonical process respecting the formation of the corpus, namely, to the function of the Pastoral Letters.[6]

---

5. Sadly, this is the effect of Bart D. Ehrman's chapter in his recent book *The New Testament: A Historical Introduction to the Early Christian Writings,* 3rd ed. (New York: Oxford University Press, 2004), pp. 285-301.

6. S. E. Porter offers a thorough assessment of modern theories of when the Pauline corpus was compiled: "When and How Was the Pauline Corpus Compiled? An Assessment of Theories," in *The Pauline Canon,* ed. S. E. Porter (Leiden: Brill, 2004), pp. 95-127. Recently several scholars have challenged treating the Pastorals as a literary unity, and sought to analyze each letter individually by itself. An extreme example of this approach is found in William A. Richards's book *Differences and Distance in Post-Pauline Christianity: An Epistolary Analysis of the Pastorals* (New York: Lang, 2002). Using a method of "epistolary analysis," Richards seeks to reconstruct the historical development of early Christianity by means of this sophisticated literary analysis. He discovers three different genres of letters, three different fictive authors, and three different addressees. Although I do not reject his method out of hand, I feel that the level of speculation in moving from literary genre to historical evidences is unpersuasive. Especially what is missing are the controls of how the Pastorals were received and heard in the late first and early second centuries by Polycarp and Ignatius. Annette Merz provides just this needed information, and even concludes in her study that

Several reasons motivate this move. The Pastorals are generally recognized as the last addition in the growth of the corpus. (The role of Hebrews is a separate issue without a claim of Pauline authorship.) They are judged to be more distant from the core of Paul's "genuine" (undisputed) letters than even the so-called deutero-Pauline letters (Colossians, Ephesians). Nevertheless, by jumping to the final stage of the canonical shaping of the corpus — some would speak of a "trito-Pauline" collection — one can best establish the widest parameters of the corpus and thus determine the literary structure within which the earlier letters have been set. Whereas the letter to the Romans introduces the corpus with Paul's most comprehensive formulation of his theology by reviewing the topics central to his entire missionary activity, the Pastorals reflect a portrait of the apostle offering his final testimony as he awaits his imminent death (2 Tim 4:6-8). Once the parameters of the corpus have been analyzed, the hermeneutical implications will be addressed by which to interpret the main body of the remaining letters within the canonical circle.

Ever since the early nineteenth century, the heated debates over the Pastoral Epistles largely concentrated on the issue of authorship (e.g., Schleiermacher, F. C. Baur). As a result, by the middle of the twentieth century all but a small minority of critical scholars denied the authorship of Paul and classified the letters as "nongenuine." It is unnecessary once again to review this history or to rehearse the reasons for this conclusion (see B. S. Childs, *Introduction to the New Testament as Canon*, pp. 373-95). However, often as a consequence the importance of these letters has been disregarded and they continue to be designated by many as inferior in quality.[7]

Fortunately, there has been a decided shift in direction within the last several decades, largely led by German Roman Catholic scholars (Brox, Trilling, Lohfink, Trummer, Löning, etc.). The change in perspective has led to a variety of significant insights. There is a renewed recognition that the nature of the Pastoral Epistles is unique and cannot be identified with later pseudepigraphical writings of the New Testament (e.g., *Acta Pauli*).

---

the Pastorals were already received by these apostolic fathers, not as individual letters only, but as a corpus (*Die fiktive Selbstauslegung des Paulus* [Göttingen: Vandenhoeck & Ruprecht, 2004], pp. 114-26, 141-94).

7. Typical is the evaluation of Anthony T. Hanson, "The Domestication of Paul: A Study in the Development of Early Christian Theology," *Bulletin of the Johns Rylands Library* 63 (1981): 402-18.

The Pastoral Letters are not about Paul, but rather lay claim to the direct voice of Paul himself, even though this Pauline legacy has been extended and often transformed to address issues of the post-Pauline era. The motivation behind this fusion of genuine Pauline tradition and non-Pauline extension reflects a fresh development that is inadequately expressed in the terminology of pseudepigraphy.

Running somewhat parallel to the German research on the theological dimensions of the Pastorals was a fresh sociological enterprise carried on largely by North Americans and British.[8] Although the two movements did not often intersect, with hindsight we can see no good reason why these two different approaches could not enrich each other, if related with hermeneutical sophistication.

This search for a deeper understanding of the relation between the undisputed Pauline letters and the Pastorals agrees that the earlier statistical studies of scholars such as Percy N. Harrison and Albert E. Barnett have been instructive,[9] but that these analyses were far too narrow and their scope failed to discover the continuing, living oral tradition at work. The shaping of the Pastorals occurred within an active *Wirkungsgeschichte* and stood within a developing Pauline interpretation that joined together earlier and later stages of growth. A holistic approach is therefore required that would further the study of the ecclesiastical milieu out of which the post-Pauline letters developed.[10]

Although the literary dependency of 2 Timothy 1:3-12 on Romans 1:8-17 has long been recognized, the theological claims of continuity as well as the transformation of the content has not been fully exploited. In 2 Timothy 1:8 Paul is concerned above all with the gospel for the sake of which he is suffering. Elsewhere in the Pastorals the *euangelion* is mentioned with the promise of eternal life, and a call for its proclamation (1 Tim 1:11; 2 Tim

---

8. See David C. Verner, *The Household of God: The Social World of the Pastoral Epistles,* Society of Biblical Literature Dissertation Series 71 (Chico, Calif.: Scholars, 1983); Margaret Y. MacDonald, *The Pauline Churches: A Socio-Historical Study of Institutionalisation in the Pauline and Deutero-Pauline Writings* (Cambridge: Cambridge University Press, 1988).

9. Percy N. Harrison, *The Problem of the Pastoral Epistles* (London: Oxford University Press, 1921); Albert E. Barnett, *Paul Becomes a Literary Influence* (Chicago: University of Chicago Press, 1941).

10. Peter Trummer, *Die Paulustradition der Pastoralbriefe* (Frankfurt: Lang, 1978); Gerhard Lohfink, "Die Vermittlung des Paulinismus zu den Pastoralbriefen," *Biblische Zeitschrift,* n.s., 32 (1988): 169-88.

2:8). Paul is an apostle of Jesus Christ, a servant of God (Titus 1:1//Rom 1:1) who has been empowered by God's pure grace (1 Tim 1:13; 2 Tim 1:9) as apostle and teacher of the gospel (2 Tim 1:11). In the Pastorals the content of the gospel has been designated as *parathēkē*, the sacred tradition that has been entrusted both to Paul and to his coworkers (1 Tim 6:20). Or again, the gospel has been interpreted as "sound doctrine," a doctrinal content that stands opposed to false teachings (1 Tim 1:10; 6:3; 2 Tim 1:13; 4:3; Titus 1:9, 13).

It is precisely at this point that the Pastorals have been accused of changing the genuine Pauline understanding of the gospel as the power of God for salvation (Rom 1:16) to a static, formalized concept of right doctrine.[11] Unquestionably there has been a shift in vocabulary, but I would agree with the arguments of Gerhard Lohfink,[12] among others, that the gospel has not been interpreted by a concept of sound doctrine, but the reverse, that sound doctrine has been defined by the gospel (cf. the parallel in Rom 6:17, in spite of Bultmann). What has changed in the approach of the Pastorals is not the concept of the gospel, but the manner in which the content is appropriated and treasured.

One of the most important changes introduced by the Pastoral Letters was the shift in the portrayal of Paul. There is a marked distance between the Paul of the earlier epistles and that of the Pastorals. Heinz Schürmann describes it as the distinction between the apostolic and postapostolic age reflected in the Pastorals and in Acts 20.[13] In contrast to the rest of the letters, the Paul of the Pastorals does not apply his understanding of the gospel to a new and particular historical situation. He does not develop the implications of his theology on a new front as, for example, in Galatians or Corinthians. There is a shift from an active to a passive Paul. This characterization is not meant in a psychological sense, but rather that Paul does not break fresh ground in direct confrontation with a specific historical

11. This position is articulated in detail by Rudolf Bultmann, "Right Teaching and New Testament Canon," in *Theology of the New Testament,* part 3 (New York: Scribner, 1955), pp. 119-42.

12. Gerhard Lohfink, "Paulinische Theologie in der Reception der Pastoralbriefe," in *Paulus in den neutestamentlichen Spätschriften,* ed. Karl Kertelge, Quaestiones Disputatae 89 (Freiburg: Herder, 1981), pp. 96-105.

13. Heinz Schürmann, "Das Testament des Paulus für die Kirche," in *Traditionsgeschichtliche Untersuchung zu den synoptischen Evangelien* (Düsseldorf: Patmos, 1968), pp. 310-40.

crisis within a distinct congregation. Instead, his teachings have become the medium by which others are to confront falsehood and heresy. Paul as teacher has become the model by which sound doctrine is measured. The decisive point to make is that the Pastorals do not attempt to update Paul for a later age. His theology was not extended in this way, nor did its actualization function according to this pattern. Rather, the canonical move sought to collect Paul's letters into a normative corpus of Scripture.[14] The process of canonization, which was adumbrated long before the Pastorals, was now to encompass Paul's theology within the category of "sound doctrine." His teachings were assigned the function of establishing the normative context from which the later generations of leaders were to combat the threats of heresy.

A further transformation reflected in the Pastoral Epistles was in terms of the addressees of these letters. No longer are the recipients particular congregations, but rather individual coworkers, Timothy and Titus, who earlier were minor leaders and were sent on specific tasks by Paul. Now they are major leaders of the church, delegates entrusted with the responsibilities of caring for all the communities of faith. They receive rules and directives to discharge in establishing continuity with the past, and instructions for the future. Especially central has been their role in resisting heresy that clearly had moved the central challenge no longer in relation to Judaism, but to various forces within and without the church who "swerve from the truth" (2 Tim 2:16-19; 4:3; Titus 3:9-11). The ordering of leadership within the church has also been developed beyond that of the earlier letters (1 Tim 3:1-13). New directives are offered to regulate the care of younger and older widows (1 Tim 5:1-16) and how wages are to be distributed fairly, particularly in regard to communal support for those who "labor in preaching and teaching."

The point has been made that the Pastorals reflect the growing force that culminated in the formation of a Pauline corpus. In his essay, Alexander Sand focused on how Paul's "occasional" letters could have developed into a corpus.[15] Nils Dahl had earlier addressed the problem of appropriating such highly particularized letters into a normative role within a

---

14. James W. Aageson in his recent essay, "The Pastoral Epistles, Apostolic Authority, and the Development of the Pauline Scripture," pursues this issue with fresh insight. In *The Pauline Canon*, pp. 5-26.

15. Alexander Sand, "Überlieferung und Sammlung der Paulusbriefe," in *Paulus in den neutestamentlichen Spätschriften*, pp. 11-24.

larger circle of churches.[16] Sand notes signs of an evolving corpus in the role of the public reading of Scripture (1 Tim 4:13) and the admonition to remain in the faith of his childhood acquired through the sacred writings (2 Tim 3:15). Such references to the exchange of his letters (1 Thess 5:27) and the reference to Paul's other letters (2 Pet 3:15-16) would also point to the growing sense of a unified collection, rather than just single letters. Moreover, the extension effected by the deutero-Pauline writings (Colossians and Ephesians) would also have served as preparation for a further growth toward a fixed corpus represented by the Pastorals. Then again, the development of the portrait of Paul who became the model of the faithful teacher showed signs of a living Pauline legacy that had been culled from his other letters in an organic growth.

Finally, the effect of an evolving Pauline corpus becomes evident in the development of a doctrine of sacred Scripture most clearly expressed in 2 Timothy 3:16-17. The force behind this move turns on the issue of how Paul's teaching legacy was to be actualized by the Christian church for the future generations. We have already suggested that this appropriation was not achieved by simply updating Paul, or by extending to Paul's coworkers his apostolic office. Rather, Paul's writings became the measure of right doctrine, not as a lifeless deposit of fixed doctrinal creeds. The formulation in 2 Timothy 3:16 derived from a highly practical goal of how Paul's written legacy, now formed into a corpus, was the means of continuing guidance for the life of the church. These writings were given to instruct "for salvation through faith in Christ Jesus" (3:15). Then the Pauline corpus is identified with Scripture, much according to the manner of 2 Peter 3:16. Because it is inspired by God (God-breathed), it is useful for teaching, for admonition, for training in righteousness toward the goal of generating in the believer the good works commensurate with Christian faith.[17]

---

16. Nils A. Dahl, "The Particularity of the Pauline Epistles as a Problem in the Ancient Church," in *Neutestamentica et Patristica*, Novum Testamentum, Supplement 6 (Leiden: Brill, 1962), pp. 261-71.

17. See Robert W. Wall's essay, "The Function of the Pastoral Epistles within the Pauline Corpus of the New Testament: A Canonical Approach," in *The Pauline Canon*, pp. 22-44. Despite an informative review of the history of the canonization of the Pauline corpus, I do not think his major thesis concerning the canonical role of the Pastorals is persuasive. He argues that the Pastorals function to offer "a necessary theological balance to Pauline theology," "a rounding off" of the theology of the genuine letters by focusing on anthropological features: "the believer's life style," "moral habits," and the "need for good works." I would argue that

To summarize, by first focusing on the beginning of the Pauline corpus, especially on the programmatic function of the Romans prescript, and then by turning to the final stages in the growth of the corpus reflected in the Pastorals, we have been able to describe the shaping and scope of the collection. However, only when we turn to spelling out the hermeneutical function of how to encompass the remaining letters, indeed the bulk of the Pauline legacy, can we determine how the entire corpus functions exegetically for the present generation of modern Christian readers.

III. The Hermeneutical Significance of the Canonical Structure

The letter to the Romans with its prominent position as the introduction to the Pauline corpus sets forth the most comprehensive formulation of Paul's missionary message. The presentation is the most universal, the least shaped by external contingency influences, and with the widest scope of any of Paul's letters. Moreover, Paul reviews in Romans the great majority of topics already addressed in his earlier letters but written to address highly particularized, historical situations within certain of his local congregations.

At the other end of the Pauline corpus are the three Pastoral Epistles. They were included in the corpus at a later date, at the conclusion of a lengthy historical process of canonization extending most probably into the early second century. However, the Pastorals function as Paul's final witness as he anticipates his imminent death (2 Tim 4:6-8). By their structure and content the Pastorals stress the continuity of the apostolic faith both preached and preserved. Yet there is a shift from the active Paul of the earlier letters to the passive Paul who has completed his assigned call to serve the gospel, and now looks to passing the torch to his trusted coworkers. Paul's legacy remains active and living. Indeed, Paul's witness has become the model of apostolic teaching, the measure of "sound doctrine." In the process of canonical shaping Paul's message has been extended and given a new form from its initial reception as it was assigned a new function within the Pauline corpus. Paul's letters serve no longer as simply oc-

---

these features are peripheral to the letters and derive from the later Hellenistic milieu rather than reflecting actual canonical shaping. I feel strongly that the analyses of Sand and Lohfink (see above) are far closer to the central theological concerns of these letters.

casional writings, but now have been received as sacred Scripture to become the written vehicle by which his gospel is continually actualized by the Holy Spirit for every succeeding generation.

The structure of these books at the beginning and end of the corpus sets the canonical context for its interpretation. They address the crucial hermeneutical issue of the interpretation of Paul, namely, how are his letters in their highly particularized, time-conditioned, historical settings to be used by future generations of Christians?

The initial hermeneutical key is offered by the letter to the Romans, which covers the same topics dealt with in the earlier letters in a lengthy and profound reformulation. Romans and the Pastorals represent two very different literary genres from the highly particularized letters that form the bulk of Paul's missionary message. How are they to be related? The solution is not one of harmonization. Nor is the proper hermeneutical approach one that blunts the particularity of the letters within the corpus by various appeals to creedal abstraction. Rather, the canonical structure sets up a dialectical interaction within the context of the corpus between the general and the specific, between the universal content of the gospel and the unique needs of each congregation, between the sound doctrine of Paul and the particularity of its application by the apostle who labored to target the continuing theological crises with the gospel of Jesus Christ.

The critical exegetical task is performed within the canonical context formed by the Pauline corpus. (Of course, ultimately the Pauline corpus will have to be related to the rest of the New Testament, especially to Acts, and to the Old Testament.) Accordingly, for example, the interpreter seeks to reflect on the particularized application in Galatians 3 of Abraham's justification by faith with Paul's often quite different emphasis in Romans 4 of a similar theme, but within a much wider theological context. Obviously this is an exegetical issue that has long exercised critical biblical scholars. What, then, is different in the canonical approach being outlined? The decisive difference lies in the goal of the exegetical activity. According to the approach of traditional historical criticism, the goal of such comparisons is largely to reconstruct the theology of the historical Paul. A comparison between Romans and Galatians could result in the tension between the two providing evidence that Paul's theology had changed and developed. Or, one could conclude that the conflict between the two reports only showed the rational inconsistency of his argumentation. Or again, the critical interpreter might infer that the application of Paul's theology to the contingencies of Galatians was skewed and expressed little in common with the theology of Romans.

In contrast, the goal of the canonical hermeneutic that is being suggested is to reflect on the theology expressed in various forms within the Pauline corpus. It would allow that a distinction at times between the theology of the "historical Paul" and that of the Pauline corpus can be made, but it would resist any permanent separating of a reconstructed "historical Paul" from the witness of the "canonical Paul." Indeed, at the heart of the failure of the SBL's Pauline Seminar in recovering Paul's theology was the assumption that one could recover Paul's theology apart from its ecclesial reception.

There is one further point of difference between these two approaches. It concerns a hermeneutical move actually formulated more recently by postmodernists. Namely, the exegetical task involves not just recovering a historical intention of an ancient author, but embraces as well the activity of the modern reader in the activity of interpretation. The dialectical endeavor of establishing a dialogue between the particularity of the original Pauline letters and the canonical shaping of the Pauline tradition involves an additional element in the enterprise, namely, the goals and intentions of the modern Christian reader. The major motivation for comparing the contingency and the coherence within the Pauline corpus is to gain insight on how the apostolic witness to the gospel from the past can be actualized through the work of the Spirit to instruct the church of the present. The promise of such an actualization is most clearly formulated in 2 Timothy 3:16.

At this juncture of how the actualization of the past witness of the Bible is understood, a major difference with the recent postmodern proposals emerges. As discussed above in chapter 2, Frances Young is much concerned that the interpretation of the Bible not result in anchoring the text to the distant past. She appeals for an "ethical reading," by which she means that the ancient biblical text be interpreted from the context of the new and changing values of modernity in order to render its message accessible and compatible with the present. Closely akin to Young's program is the approach of Luke Johnson, who would separate sharply the critical exegetical task, which reconstructs the text's allegedly original historical meaning, from the hermeneutical task, which brings its own modern moral sensibilities to bear for today's culturally shaped contemporary recipients.

The canonical approach is also concerned with establishing a bridge between the apostolic witness of the biblical canon and the context of the modern reader. However, the search for the actualization of the past is achieved through the interpretation of Scripture. By setting reflection on the particularity of Paul's witness in relation to the coherence of the gospel according to its canonical shaping, the modern reader is led to seek theological analogies from within the diversity available in Scripture in providing direction to address the changing challenges of a faithful application of the gospel today. In the chapters that follow, an attempt will be made to demonstrate with specific examples how such an exegetical activity is applied within the parameters established by the Pauline corpus.

However, one final hermeneutical issue must be discussed before turning to an application of a proposed canonical approach. It concerns the perennial, highly existential question of how this proposed canonical approach relates to the historical critical approach to exegesis, which is actually the issue that evoked, in large measure, this monograph.

For my response, I shall turn again to the formulation I employed in chapter 1, first proposed by Martin Kähler with his contrast between *Historie* and *Geschichte*. I maintain that this contrast can be extended to apply to the historical critical approach to Paul and to that of the canonical. Again I would argue that the two approaches to the biblical text cannot be simply fused, neither can they be separated into two sealed vacuums. The same dialectic applies to the life of Jesus research and to the Pauline corpus. Clearly a canonical approach to Paul's letters depends on the use of all the critical tools of exegesis (philological, historical, literary, sociological). The use of these tools has resulted in a far sharper reading of the letters and has been greatly aided by the recovery of the Hellenistic literary conventions employed by Paul. Or again, the discovery of the gnostic texts has provided an access to the actual voice of the ancient gnostics who up to now had been largely filtered through the polemical descriptions offered by the Church Fathers.

Nevertheless, in the end the confession by the church to the privileged status of its Scripture because of its unique witness to Jesus Christ establishes a context for interpretation that strives to respond to the coercion exercised by the subject matter of its testimony. No claim is being made that would assign the quality of infallibility to the church's hearing and shaping of its Scripture, but in spite of its continual frailty and painful failures from its inception, it lives from the promise that Scripture continues to transmit truthfully to the church through the divine Spirit the gospel of Jesus Christ, quickening and guiding its life.

4. Exegetical Probes:
Introduction and Guidelines

The approach that I have chosen is to illustrate the method being proposed by focusing on selective critical exegetical problems from within the Pauline corpus. The intention is not to attempt an exhaustive commentary on specific books within the corpus, but to traverse a whole range of classic exegetical problems that then will be addressed from a different perspective. Only in the concluding chapter will the attempt be made to draw some larger implications from these selective probes. At the outset, it may aid in clarifying the approach by offering a few guidelines to the exegetical method employed.

1. The literary context for the study will be the traditional Pauline corpus consisting of Romans, 1 and 2 Corinthians, Galatians, Ephesians, Philippians, Colossians, 1 and 2 Thessalonians, 1 and 2 Timothy, Titus, Philemon, and Hebrews.

2. To speak of these books as composing the Pauline corpus is not to assume direct Pauline authorship of all these letters, but rather to acknowledge their status within a traditional apostolic collection.[1] The church's designating a canonical status to these books as received was reached, after considerable debate, by the fourth century, but does not rule out the significance of secondary literary growth, signs of historical

---

1. For the implications of this statement on the doctrine of the inspiration of Scripture, see the fresh reflections of Stephen B. Chapman, "Reclaiming Inspiration for the Bible," in *Canon and Biblical Interpretation,* ed. Craig Bartholomew et al. (Grand Rapids: Zondervan, 2006), pp. 167-206. Chapman addresses in great detail Carl F. H. Henry's theological criticism, and concludes that a canonical approach is an ally of orthodox Christian theology, not its foe.

tension, and conflicting theological perspectives. However, such evidence will be handled in relation to the final literary context, ultimately recognized by the Christian church as canonical, that is, theologically normative.

3. The canonical context of the Pauline corpus is not to be understood as a unified theological collection devoid of tensions, or as a whole requiring a rationalistic harmonization. Rather, the corpus is understood as forming a circle of apostolic writings within which the church's apostolic faith is located. Its canonical status sets the scope of its witness and is drawn to exclude works that were judged either nonauthoritative for the life of faith or heretical in their teaching.

4. The interpretive task within such a canonical context is part of the church's role of hearing the various witnesses each in its singular historical and literary context, and in its larger theological role within the Pauline corpus. The goal of the exegesis is to understand the singular witness in terms of the whole corpus, and conversely, the whole in the light of the diversity of the singular.

5. The reflective task of interpretation is to take seriously the effect of the corpus's shaped traditions but not to limit interpretation to recovering only past authorial intent. The effect of the reader's context, the nature of the new questions raised by each new generation, implies that fresh meanings will emerge in new combinations between the reader's changing situations, which are held in a continuing dialectic with the received corpus of the Pauline legacy.

6. A canonical interpretation as envisioned does not consist in simply a synchronic analysis of the letters within a literary context. Rather, the dialectical relation between *Historie* and *Geschichte,* regarding both its kerygmatic distinctiveness and its cultural commonality that was outlined in chapter 1, will be constantly applied. The evidence for historical growth beyond Paul's own lifetime (e.g., the Pastorals) will be evaluated in providing its unique canonical roles. Likewise, the philological characteristics, literary conventions, and historical particularity will be exploited.

7. The interpretation of the letters within the larger literary context provided by canonical shaping will attempt to do justice to the interpretive task cogently raised by Frances Young (see chapter 2). This means that the interpretive process of studying the Pauline corpus involves the search by its modern readers for its moral instruction fully within its contemporary historical and cultural setting. The letters are not a deposit from the past,

but a divine vehicle for continuing engagement with God. This search for "discerning the Word of God" in the Pauline corpus lies in finding the proper analogy from the past for the future. The goal is fully "practical" in its aim of being instructed toward a life of righteousness according to the gospel. The crucial dialectic between canonical shaping of the apostolic tradition and the exegetical task of understanding the interaction between text, reader, and contemporary situation will be pursued. Attention will also be given to the crucial role played in Paul's letters by his appeal to the Scriptures of Israel, which Richard Hays has brought to the forefront (see chapter 2).

8. The emphasis of the exegesis will fall on the effect of the larger canonical context provided by the corpus, and its theological, that is, apostolic, claims to address a congregation of faith with a Word of God. The appeal to the role of the Holy Spirit in addressing a divine message for continuing instruction for the ever-changing conditions of the world is not a hermeneutical method, but a confession of the Christian reader toward a participation in the life of the Spirit in accordance with Scripture.

In sum, the exegesis will be deemed worthwhile by this writer if it succeeds in raising new perspectives for breaking out of some of the impasse that has increasingly paralyzed the understanding of Scripture.

I. Paul's Apostolate and the Gospel

The place to begin in describing the canonical shape of the Pauline corpus lies with Paul's description of himself as an apostle. Not only does the title come in the superscriptions of the great majority of his letters (Romans, 1 and 2 Corinthians, Galatians, Ephesians, Colossians, 1 and 2 Timothy, Titus; the exceptions being Philippians, 1 and 2 Thessalonians, and Philemon), but also the defense of his apostolate occupies a central role, usually in a highly controversial setting, especially in Galatians, 1 and 2 Corinthians, and the Pastorals. The complexity and difficulty of the subject are also evident because many aspects of the growth of the early Christian church are concealed in a fragmentary state. Finally, the subject inevitably merges into the even more perplexing topic of the order and offices of the church that will be treated in the succeeding chapters.

There is little need to present a detailed history of the debate over the origin, meaning, and function of the term "apostle" because this history has

81

been reviewed many times.[2] Still, to draw a few of the main lines from the controversy may be helpful in establishing a context for the important exegetical issues to be addressed. It is generally agreed that the modern nineteenth-century debate over apostleship began in 1865 with Joseph B. Lightfoot's excursus "The Name and Office of Apostle,"[3] when he separated the title of apostle from that of the Twelve and directed the focus to Paul. Later, Lightfoot's insights were greatly developed by Hans von Campenhausen, who then insisted on the necessity of focusing the debate on Paul's apostolicity apart from the various Gospel constructs.[4] The next major turn in the debate was evoked by the classic article of Karl H. Rengstorf on "apostle" in Kittel's *Wörterbuch*,[5] in which he sought to show the origin of the apostolate in a pre-Christian Jewish, rabbinic office of the *šaliah* as a commissioned agent sent to act in the name of another. However, in spite of its wide impact, there were a number of serious problems with this identification. Not only were the rabbinic functions very different from those of the New Testament apostle, but the sources for the institution could be literarily documented only in the period following the destruction of Jerusalem. Next, a very powerful opposition to Rengstorf's theory arose from monographs by Günther Klein and Walter Schmithals,[6] scholars associated

2. Olaf Linton, *Das Problem der Urkirche in der neueren Forschung* (Uppsala: Almqvist & Wiksell, 1932); Jürgen Roloff, *Apostolat–Verkündigung–Kirche. Ursprung, Inhalt und Funktion des kirchlichen Apostelamtes nach Paulus, Lukas und den Pastoralbriefen* (Gütersloh: Gerd Mohn, 1965); Rudolf Schnackenburg, "Apostolität, Stand der Erforschung," in *Katholizität und Apostolizität,* ed. R. Groscurth, Kerygma und Dogma, supplementary issue 2 (Göttingen: Vandenhoeck & Ruprecht, 1971), pp. 51-73; Francis H. Agnew, "The Origin of the New Testament Apostle-Concept: A Review of Research," *Journal of Biblical Literature* 105 (1986): 75-96; Anthony C. Thiselton, "Some Misleading Factors in the History of the Interpretation of 'Apostle,'" in *The First Epistle to the Corinthians* (Grand Rapids: Eerdmans, 2000), pp. 669-78.

3. Joseph B. Lightfoot, *Saint Paul's Epistle to the Galatians* (London: Macmillan, 1865), pp. 89-97.

4. Hans von Campenhausen, "Der urchristliche Apostelbegriff," *Studia Theologica* 1 (1947/48): 96-130.

5. Karl H. Rengstorf, "Apostolos," in *Theologische Wörterbuch zum Neuen Testament,* ed. G. Kittel and G. Friedrich, vol. 1 (Stuttgart, 1933), pp. 397-448 = *Theological Dictionary of the New Testament,* ed. G. Kittel and G. Friedrich, vol. 1 (Grand Rapids: Eerdmans, 1964), pp. 407-47.

6. Günter Klein, *Die Zwölf Apostel. Ursprung und Gestalt einer Idee* (Göttingen: Vandenhoeck & Ruprecht, 1961); Walter Schmithals, *The Office of Apostle in the Early Church* (Nashville: Abingdon, 1961).

with Rudolf Bultmann, who focused in differing ways on a form of Hellenistic Gnosticism as the source of the concept. Then, picking up on earlier insights from Harnack, other scholars attempted to trace the growth of the concept as a reaction to a variety of cultural forces within the early Christian church. In spite of the enormous stimulus evoked by these scholars, including the learned monograph of Dieter Georgi,[7] little consensus emerged. In the end, perhaps one of the most substantial contributions to the debate has been that of Ferdinand Hahn.[8] He summarized the objections to the *šaliaḥ* hypothesis by emphasizing the contrast of the New Testament's understanding of apostleship as basically religious rather than legal. Moreover, he called attention to the Old Testament in providing closer analyses to the New Testament without limiting the analogies to an exact philological transference. He suggested that there are frequent Old Testament references to prophetic sending (e.g., Isa 61:1) that are closely compatible to Paul's eschatological understanding of his own prophetic vocation.

1. Characteristic Features of Paul's Apostleship

The basic elements in Paul's understanding of his apostleship appear right from the start in the Pauline corpus, in the introduction to the letter to the Romans. Paul is "called" to be an apostle, "set apart" for the gospel, to "preach" the good news to the nations, through the power of the resurrected Christ. There is a basic connection between apostle and gospel. The apostle has been commissioned by God to proclaim as an eschatological herald a new age dawning from the death and resurrection of Christ. A new state of affairs has entered, and its good news unleashes the power of God for salvation. Therein the righteousness of God (objective genitive) is manifest. Moreover, Paul has received with his apostolic commission the charisma toward the end of bringing about an obedient response among all the nations. However, it is only when one turns to the rest of the Pauline letters that the full dimension of the term "apostle" emerges.

---

7. Dieter Georgi, *The Opponents of Paul in Second Corinthians* (Edinburgh: T. & T. Clark, 1987).

8. Ferdinand Hahn, "Der Apostolat im Urchristentum," *Kerygma und Dogma* 20 (1974): 54-77; Hahn, "Apostel," in *Religion in Geschichte und Gegenwart*, 4th ed., vol. 1 (1998), pp. 636-38. See also Otto Kuss, *Paulus. Die Rolle des Apostolat in der theologischen Entwicklung der Urkirche* (Regensburg: Pustet, 1971).

a. Galatians 1–2   The full impact of Paul's apostolic authority and divine legitimation emerges in the conflict with the churches of Galatia.[9] Paul confronts churches he had earlier founded with an accusation that they had turned to a different gospel from the message he had preached, and thus their action was threatening to pervert the faith they had once received. Moreover, it is clear to Paul that this betrayal instigated by "troublemakers" (1:7) involves also an attack on his apostleship. Thus, he launches into a vigorous defense of his authority. First, he rules out two false options as the source of his message. It was not derived from a human source, nor was it mediated by a teacher. Rather, it came by a revelation *(apokalypsis)* of Jesus Christ. When he then recounts his early life of opposition to the gospel, he does so to stress the absolute reversal caused by divine intervention. He did not confer with anyone, but followed his commission to preach among the Gentiles away from Jerusalem.

Both in the exercise of his apostolic authority through his letter to them and in the account of his confrontation with Peter in chapter 2, Paul does not base his accusation of a betrayal of the gospel on his own spiritual or ecstatic experience. Nor does he challenge Peter's apostolic office. Rather, he makes his claim on the grounds of the "truth of the gospel" (2:14). His disagreement with Peter does not derive from a differing political ploy but from what he names an act of hypocrisy motivated by fear of the Judaizers. Peter's response is not recorded in Galatians, but rather Paul spells out in his letter the theological implications of the gospel: no one is justified by the works of the law, but through faith in Jesus Christ (2:16). It is significant that nowhere in these chapters does Paul explicitly elaborate the content of his gospel. Rather, there is the assumption that it is known. Paul spells out only the theological implications of the content of the gospel that he has preached and that is now being challenged.

In his interpretation of Galatians 1 and 2, John Schütz argues that Paul understands his apostolic authority as an interpretation of power that he correctly links to the proclamation of the gospel.[10] Yet Schütz tries to make the case that the content of the gospel remains for Paul very nebulous. It is certainly not a static doctrine, but it is an event, an effective force, an area

---

9. See J. Louis Martyn, "The Nature of Paul's Apostolate," in *Galatians,* Anchor Bible 33A (New York: Doubleday, 1997), pp. 92-95.

10. John H. Schütz, *Paul and the Anatomy of Apostolic Authority* (Cambridge: Cambridge University Press, 1975), pp. 35-78, 114-58.

in which "to stand." In the end he characterizes Paul's understanding as "pregnant" or "dynamic."[11] Then Schütz contends that the only ground on which he can establish his apostolic certainty against the *Ersatzevangelium* of his opponents is his autobiographical experience. Because his whole being is an embodiment of his gospel, his biography of radical reversal provides the evidence for his authority. Yet this conclusion is certainly to blur the controversy in Galatians.

In my judgment Heinrich Schlier is far closer to the truth in stating that for Paul the gospel was the concrete content of what he had preached.[12] Of course, the gospel is not a flat, static proposition, but Schütz has stretched the wide, dynamic qualities of the gospel — its power, effective force, event character — to such a limit as to undermine its substantive content. It is not to be overlooked that Paul could also speak of the gospel as the "standard of teaching" (Rom 6:17) and the "doctrine you have been taught" (Rom 16:17). As a result of Schütz's reading, the Pauline understanding of gospel and authority is defined in such a way as to make any continuity with the deutero-Pauline letters difficult, and with the Pastorals impossible.

b. 1 Corinthians   When one turns to 1 Corinthians, one observes a wide variety of issues directly relating to Paul's understanding of his apostleship. The immediate problem Paul addresses is strife and dissension within the community that had been reported to him (1:11). Much of the initial problem concerns the application of spiritual gifts (1:7), but before he seeks to address specific issues of their abuse (chapters 12–14), he moves to strike to the heart of the problem. The gospel he preached to them was not of human words of wisdom or eloquent speech. Rather, he came to preach Christ crucified, foolishness to the world, but to those called in faith, Christ the power and wisdom of God (1:24). The strife among different parts of the community only demonstrated that they were still immature Christians not understanding the life in the Spirit that he had preached (2:14–3:4).

However, the dissension within the Corinthian community emanates

---

11. Schütz, *Paul and the Anatomy*, p. 53.

12. Heinrich Schlier, *Der Brief an die Galater*, 12th ed. (Göttingen: Vandenhoeck & Ruprecht, 1962), p. 38. See also Jost Eckert, "Die Verteidigung der apostolischen Autorität im Galaterbrief und im zweiten Korintherbrief," *Theologie und Glaube* 58 (1975): 1-39.

not just from split loyalties between members, but involves those who directly dispute Paul's apostolic authority (9:1). One of the accusations brought against Paul by his opponents — this is an issue to which we shall return — was that he did not "act" like an apostle when he refused to accept financial support from the congregation. Paul, of course, defends his freedom to refrain from accepting as his apostolic right (9:3-27). Paul's initial defense in 9:1 makes use of the traditional criteria of being an apostle: he should be a witness to the resurrection of Jesus (Acts 1:22) and should preach the gospel of Christ crucified (Acts 9:15). However, Paul's reference to these "qualifications" almost appears at this point rhetorical. His major warrant for his apostleship is his congregation: "You are the seal of my apostleship in the Lord" (1 Cor 9:2).

What is crucial to Paul's defense is the manner in which he exercises his authority. He is a servant of Christ and steward of God's mysteries (4:1). He is a fellow workman for God (3:8), and it is immaterial to him who first plants the seed or who later waters it, because only God gives the growth (3:5-10). In contrast to those Christians who exalt in their spiritual gifts before others (4:6-8), Paul describes his apostleship as being sentenced to death, as a fool for Christ's sake (4:9-13). His whole being as an apostle is being an imitation of Christ, which imitation he mediates to his congregation (4:16). Paul does not laud his authority over his church. Rather, he speaks of his being to them a father in Christ (4:15) and of Timothy as a beloved child (4:17). Yet, whatever his title, Paul does exercise his authority even when he is not present (5:3). He hopes he will not have to "wield a rod," but wishes his commands could be delivered "with love and a gentle spirit" (4:21).

Of course, the issue arises whether Paul understood his apostolic role as an *Amt* (an official ecclesial office with special gifts and status). Much of the answer depends on what one understands by *Amt*. It has long been noted that the Greek language is rich with titles that denote positions of rulership or of special honor (see the philological details by Eduard Schweizer).[13] What is noteworthy is how seldom such vocabulary occurs in the New Testament. Rather, the New Testament uses the word *diakonia*, which designates a service or ministry that carries with it no special honor

---

13. Eduard Schweizer, "Das Amt. Zum Amtsbegriff im Neuen Testament," in *Gemeinde und Gemeindeordnung im Neuen Testament* (Zürich: Zwingli, 1959), pp. 154-64 = *Church Order in the New Testament* (London: SCM, 1961), pp. 171-80.

or status. When Paul speaks of his apostolic authority, it is in terms of his ministry that is measured by the standards of the cross through the power of the Spirit (2 Cor 12:12; Rom 15:18-19). Although Paul often speaks of "grace *(charis)* and apostleship," or "grace given to him" (Rom 12:3; 15:15), he seems to avoid naming his apostleship as a charismatic gift. However, this problem becomes even more complex in 1 Corinthians 12:28. Here, when mentioning the various charismatic gift-bearers, he speaks of God's appointing in the church "first apostles, second prophets, and third teachers, then healers, workers of miracles, and administrators." Hahn seeks to resolve the problem by noting that in the two lists of the various charismata (1 Cor 12:7-11; Rom 12:6-8), the apostolate is not included.[14] Therefore, he concludes that Paul lists the apostolate among the three important charismatic functions of the church, but he does not include the apostolate as a charismatic office. This issue will return for further discussion when we examine the apostolic office of Paul in the Pastoral Letters.

Finally, there is another crucial text in which Paul's understanding of his apostolate involves a different set of problems, namely, 1 Corinthians 15:1-58. The issue at stake turns on the central factuality of the resurrection of Christ. Paul is confronting a teaching regarding the resurrection in the Corinthian church that he feels is not only erroneous but also strikes at the heart of the central belief of the faith. To be sure, it has become a major problem of commentators to discern the exact reasons for this denial of the resurrection. The traditional view was that the denial arose from a rationalistic stance that rejected any form of a postmortal existence. Such a position would allegedly have been represented by the Epicureans in the Greco-Roman world or by the Sadducees within Judaism. However, this explanation did not serve to illuminate the logic of Paul's defense of the resurrection in chapter 15. A more convincing reconstruction urged that there was no future resurrection because the resurrection had already occurred, and that Christian believers had already been exalted into the new life of the Spirit (see 2 Tim 2:18). Since this theory was first defended, especially by Julius Schniewind,[15] further modifications of it have related to the issue of the soul's immortality. However, in general, it seems convincing that the denial of the resurrection arose within Greek Hellenistic Christian

---

14. Hahn, "Der Apostolat," pp. 59-60.

15. Julius Schniewind, "Die Leugnung der Auferstehung in Korinth," in *Nachgelassene Reden und Aufsätze,* ed. E. Kähler (Berlin: Töpelmann, 1952), pp. 110-39.

beliefs regarding the life of the spirit that was thought freed from the human body. How and why Paul refutes this denial is of the greatest importance, and in fact may cause chapter 15 to be the crucial chapter from which to understand the entire letter.[16] Still, our present concern is more narrowly conceived in terms of Paul's apostleship and will not address many of the remaining perennial problems of the chapter.

Modern New Testament scholars generally agree that Paul is citing a pre-Pauline summary of the Christian faith that he has "received." In the opening verses of the chapter, the apostle first reminds his readers of the gospel that he preached to the Corinthian congregation, and that was received by them. Then he links his preaching with a summarizing of the Christian tradition he had inherited. The tightly shaped and paralleled structure of the tradition may well point to a catechetical form of the creedal affirmation: "Christ died for our sins in accordance with the scriptures and was buried, that he was raised on the third day in accordance with the scriptures, and that he appeared to Cephas, then to the twelve." Then an additional witness is included. Last of all, Paul adds, Christ appeared to him, "the least of the apostles." Moreover, Paul sees no tension between his message and that which he shared with the earlier apostles. Just so the gospel is preached, he is indifferent to the means of its proclamation.

One of the main problems that arises from these verses in relation to an understanding of Paul's apostleship is how to relate this position of continuity with his vehement denial in Galatians of his dependence on human tradition, especially as mediated by those apostles before him (Gal 1:16-17). Over the years, various hypotheses have been developed to harmonize the two positions. However, they appear often as abstract constructs without concrete textual support. Whatever one in the end decides, one can conclude only that the tension was not expressed as a problem by Paul himself. He could affirm both the independence of his revelation of the gospel from human mediation and the continuity of his gospel with the traditions of a larger circle of apostles.

This problem also has ramifications for the larger problem of how the gospel Paul received from Christ relates to the *paradosis* (tradition) he received according to 1 Corinthians 15, which became the vehicle by which the gospel was transmitted. During the hegemony of Bultmann and his students in the mid–twentieth century, much emphasis was laid on distin-

16. Karl Barth, *The Resurrection of the Dead* (London: Hodder and Stoughton, 1933).

guishing the existential preaching of the gospel as kerygma from an increasing attempt at its institutional objectification into church doctrine. This important issue will again surface when the role of the deutero-Pauline letters is discussed, but then, above all, with the role of the Pastorals and the identification of the gospel as a "deposit to be guarded" (see below).

c. 2 Corinthians The issue of Paul's apostleship assumes major proportions in 2 Corinthians.[17] In 2:14–4:6 Paul offers a lengthy description of his apostolic ministry entrusted to him by God. He begins with an outpouring of praise to God for the sheer privilege of having this service. He is not a huckster of the Word of God, but has pure motives as commanded by God to preach in the name of Christ. He is bold in his confidence that he is equipped and qualified for the challenges he faces. Then addressing a theme, of the Corinthian opposition lurking in the background, he rejects the need for any letters of commendation. Rather, the fact that a Christian community of faith exists in Corinth is his best defense. The transformed lives of the Corinthians themselves — a letter written on the heart — is proof enough of his true ministry.

Then Paul turns to what some have termed a digression to compare his ministry as a new order of the Spirit with that of the old economy represented by Moses according to the code of law. This important passage (3:7–4:6) will occupy us in detail in a later chapter. However, it is important to note that before he enumerates the nature of his apostolic ministry as one of suffering and trial (4:7–6:13), Paul again shifts his glance away from himself. His ministry is completely dependent on the mercy of God (4:1). Thus he does not preach himself, but Jesus Christ as Lord and himself as a servant.

We next turn to chapters 10–13, where it has long been recognized that the Pauline apostolate provides the real theme of the debate reflected in these chapters. Several major problems call for resolution: (1) Who are Paul's opponents? (2) What are the charges brought against him? (3) How and why does Paul defend himself in this manner?

Right from the beginning of chapter 10, it is clear that Paul is defending himself against opponents who challenge his apostolic authority. 10:2

---

17. See the excellent selection of essays edited by Eduard Lohse, *Verteidigung und Begründung des apostolischen Amtes (2 Kor 10–13)* (Rome: Abtei St. Paul vor den Mauern, 1992).

speaks of some persons who "suspect us of acting according to worldly standards." In 11:13 he identifies some as "false apostles, deceitful workmen, disguising themselves as apostles of Christ." His rivals commend themselves as servants of Christ (11:23). Finally, in 12:11 he contrasts "the signs of a true apostle" with "these super-apostles." During the 1960s and 1970s there was an explosion of monographs and articles that sought to identify these opponents. One thinks especially of the learned contributions of Käsemann, Bultmann, Barrett, Schmithals, and Georgi,[18] among a host of others. The opponents are identified with Hellenistic-Jewish Christians, gnostic Christians, itinerant charismatics, or Judaizers boasting of their special relationship with Christ. Although this heated debate raged for decades without reaching a consensus, it did succeed in eliminating certain options.

Käsemann's provocative interpretation of 11:4-5 argued that Paul distinguished between the "false prophets" and the "super-apostles."[19] The latter, that is, the intruders in verse 4, are now understood as the leaders of the Jerusalem church, and the dispute about apostolic jurisdiction (10:12-18) relates to the earlier agreement of Paul with the Jerusalem leaders about the division of missionary responsibilities. Accordingly, a parallel was sought with Galatians 2:9. By and large, this hypothesis has not generally commended itself. In the end, the debate over the identity of Paul's opponents illustrates well both the strengths and the weaknesses of a method of mirror reading, and is certainly not to be categorically disparaged. However, a defense of the method can still be mounted even when the identity of Paul's opponents continues to remain considerably blurred.

Second, what are the charges being brought against Paul? Some of them overlap with those leveled in 1 Corinthians. He is regarded as unskilled in speech (2 Cor 10:10); he has acted in a way "according to the flesh," that is, for things personally expedient; his weak appearance is contrasted with his letters (10:1, 10); and he lacks the signs of a true apostle. Finally, Paul does not behave as a true apostle by his refusal to accept financial support (1 Cor 9:3-18; 2 Cor 11:7). These parallels support in part the hypothesis that Paul's opponents also in 2 Corinthians have a different pneumatic un-

---

18. Ernst Käsemann, "Die Legitimität des Apostels. Eine Untersuchung zu II Korinther 10–13," *Zeitschrift für die neutestamentliche Wissenschaft* 41 (1942): 33-71; Rudolf Bultmann, *Exegetische Probleme des zweiten Korintherbriefes*, Symbolae Biblicae Upsalienses 9 (Uppsala: Wretmans boktr., 1947); Charles K. Barrett, "Paul's Opponents in II Corinthians," *New Testament Studies* 17 (1971): 233-54; Georgi, *The Opponents of Paul in Second Corinthians*.

19. Käsemann, "Die Legitimität des Apostels," pp. 41-42.

derstanding of spiritual gifts, especially in the exercise of an apostleship. Yet the accusations brought against Paul appear even more complex in 2 Corinthians. Using the method of mirror reading, it would appear that some of his opponents are claiming the privileges of their Hebrew ancestry (11:22). They also claim as apostles of Christ a message that is superior to that of Paul (11:5), which Paul can only reject as a work of Satan (11:14).

Third, in the light of such charges, why does Paul defend himself in the manner he does in chapters 10–13? Several commentators are quite perplexed why Paul, who is noted for his straightforward talk especially when the truth of the gospel is at stake, should content himself with a convoluted and tangled defense that remains on the grounds set by his opponents. Käsemann recognizes the problem, and seeks to resolve it by claiming that Paul's dual enemies (false apostles and super-apostles) forced him into a dialectical response.[20] Paul walks a tightrope trying to defend his apostolic authority against a rival perversion from pneumatics and yet at the same time is careful not to offend the Jerusalem apostles whose influence has been detected in 11:4. Despite Käsemann's many penetrating observations, his solution remains speculative in relation to the apostles from Jerusalem.

Quite a different hypothesis is mounted by John Schütz.[21] He argues that the central disagreement lies in the ego of those who claim to be apostles. Paul decides to meet his attackers on their own grounds. Because there are no objective marks of the apostolate by which to prove one's claim, his opponents use the habit of self-commendation (10:12). But Paul's ego is that of a "controlled self," restrained by the love of Christ, a power that lies outside himself (5:14). Paul will not boast beyond limits, but will keep to those boundaries apportioned to him by God (10:13). They claim to speak through Christ (13:3), but Paul identifies their claim with "another spirit" (11:4). His opponents find their identity from the past with an appeal to Moses, but Paul's life has been shaped by the event of the death and resurrection of Christ. This marks the profound difference between the two perceptions of the apostolic ego. Paul can defend his authority only by describing his role as servant. Paul's apostolic ego is subordinated to the gospel. Therefore, he turns to a "catalog of hardships" (2 Cor 11:23-33; 1 Cor 4:8-13). He contrasts thereby his humiliation with the Corinthians' own exaltation. According to Schütz, Paul is not interested in his apostolic legitimacy, but

---

20. Käsemann, "Die Legitimität des Apostels," pp. 36-40.
21. Schütz, *Paul and the Anatomy,* pp. 114-58.

only in the question of authority. The attackers are not true apostles because they have made themselves authors of the standards they proclaim.

Schütz has offered an impressive interpretation of Paul's defense. My major question is whether Schütz has overemphasized the contrast between authority and legitimacy. Schütz is certainly correct in asserting that Paul's main defense of his apostleship was in terms of his authority. Yet to make the case that Paul's lack of any sense of legitimacy forced him into a vulnerable position with his opponents, whose attack he could overcome only with great difficulty, seems overdrawn. I would rather argue that the dialectical form of argument that dominates chapters 10–13 arises largely from the substance of Paul's theology. Of course, much of his rhetorical force and probing irony is dictated by the radical contingencies of the crisis in Corinth. Paul is fully aware of the irony of his boasting. Yet in a contest with proud adversaries, it served increasingly to highlight the contrast between the true identity of an apostle whose strength is revealed only in weakness and those who parade their prideful strength. He does resist the temptation to boast of his heavenly vision (12:1-5). Rather, it is in his hardships that the power of Christ is revealed. For the sake of Christ he is content with "weaknesses, insults, hardships, persecutions, and calamities, for when I am weak, then I am strong."

It is interesting to observe that in spite of the hesitancy of his responses against the charges brought against him that seem constantly to push him into a defensive position, when Paul comes to actualize his authority over the Corinthians, he exercises it without any sign of misgivings. "I warned those who sinned before and I warn them now while absent" (13:2). "I write this . . . in order that when I come, I may not have to be severe in my use of the authority which the Lord has given me, indeed for building and not for tearing down" (13:10).

d. Colossians and Ephesians Our major concern in this section is to trace the reception of Paul, the apostle, in Colossians and Ephesians,[22] the so-called deutero-Pauline letters. This canonical way of posing the question assumes the results of generations of critical research on the complex

---

22. Helmut Merklein, "Paulinische Theologie in der Rezeption des Kolosser- und Epheserbriefes," in *Paulus in den neutestestmentlichen Spätschriften. Zur Paulusrezeption im Neuen Testament,* ed. K. Kertelge, Quaestiones Disputatae 89 (Freiburg: Herder, 1981), pp. 25-69.

issues of authorship and literary and historical setting,[23] but it attempts to shift the focus toward seeing how these letters understood and reconfigured the shape of his apostolate within the Pauline corpus.

In the previous sections, which analyzed the major features of Paul's apostolate on the basis of his undisputed letters, the initial emphasis fell on the close coupling of the gospel with that of Paul's apostolic office. Within Colossians and Ephesians, this same close interlinkage continues. The object of Paul's proclamation is the gospel, the "word of the truth, the gospel" (Col 1:5; Eph 1:13; 3:6; 6:16). Yet at the same time, there is a marked shift of focus. The object of Paul's proclamation is the "mystery," hidden for ages but now made manifest (Col 1:26-27; 2:2; 4:3; Eph 1:9; 3:3, 4, 9; 5:32). This mystery is no longer identical with Paul's gospel, but is the worldwide extension of Paul's earlier "secret" (1 Cor 2:7-13). This mystery is God's plan to reconcile to himself all of creation by overcoming the wall of separation between Jew and Gentile to create a unified household of God (Eph 2:14-22). "He is the head over all things for the church, which is his body, the fullness *(plērōma)* of him now fills all in all" (Eph 1:22-23; see Col 1:18-20).

Paul, the apostle, is now himself part of the content of this proclamation and belongs to the mystery of God's plan. He is named a "minister of the gospel" (Col 1:23) afflicted with Christ's suffering for the sake of the church (1:25). But more, the church is now described as "built on the foundation of the apostles and prophets, Christ Jesus himself being the chief cornerstone" (Eph 2:20). There is now a structure joined together and growing into a holy temple (2:21). Using the metaphor of a building, of members of Christ's body (4:12), "of one new man" (2:15), the writer establishes the role of the apostle as a model or norm in which Christology and ecclesiology have been reconfigured.

From this new reflection on the relation of Paul the apostle to the mystery of the church, Merklein draws an important hermeneutical implication,[24] and thereby offers a theological interpretation to explain the "pseudonymous" form of these two letters. Because the church is anchored

---

23. Besides the older critical introductions such as Werner G. Kümmel, *Introduction to the New Testament* (London: SCM, 1975), and Ernst Käsemann, "Epheserbrief," in *Religion in Geschichte und Gegenwart*, 3rd ed., 2:517-20, see the introduction by Rudolf Schnackenburg, *Ephesians* (Edinburgh: T. & T. Clark, 1991), pp. 21-37, and Nils A. Dahl, "Einleitungsfragen zum Epheserbrief," in *Studies in Ephesians*, ed. David Hellholm et al. (Tübingen: Mohr Siebeck, 2000), pp. 3-105.

24. Merklein, "Paulinische Theologie," p. 35.

in the apostolic gospel and the mystery of its divine plan is grounded on the foundation of the apostles and prophets, its proclamation can be understood only in the continuing speaking of the apostle Paul to the church and world in the present time. Merklein concludes that this perspective affords the theological warrant for the literary form of both letters that has been used to describe hermeneutically — I would say "canonically" — the ongoing function of Paul's apostleship.

e. The Pastoral Epistles We turn finally to offering a description of Paul's apostolate from an analysis of the Pastoral Epistles. Jürgen Roloff begins his very thorough chapter on the subject by conceding that the topic has been overshadowed by the continuing controversy over the authorship of these letters.[25] For those who argued for their pseudonymity (e.g., von Campenhausen), the sharpest contrast is made between the charismatic understanding of Paul's apostleship in the "genuine letters" and the institutional rendering of the Pastorals. Conversely, for those defending their direct Pauline authorship, the differences were played down and various historical hypotheses were mounted to explain Paul's adaptation to the changing cultural circumstances. Roloff is therefore intent to break out of this impasse. He concludes that the Pastorals cannot be understood as standing in a simple historical continuity with the earlier Pauline letters. Nevertheless, in terms of the subject of ecclesiastical offices *(Ämter)*, the Pastorals present a picture equally distant from the Church Fathers of the early second century, such as Clement. Therefore, Roloff chooses to focus on the subject of apostle by first restricting his investigation to the language of the letters themselves to uncover the particularity of the Pastorals lying between these two time lines.

The Pastorals designate Paul as apostle in only five places: 1 Timothy 1:1, 2 Timothy 1:1, Titus 1:1, 1 Timothy 2:7, and 2 Timothy 1:11. Roloff argues that the first three occurrences are simply stereotypical prescripts and the last two are hermeneutically insignificant. He thus concludes that the term is never given an emphasized role and that the author shows no interest in developing the title.[26] It is against this position that Gerhard Lohfink voices his strongest objection.[27] First, he observes the literary dependence

---

25. Roloff, *Apostolat–Verkündigung–Kirche,* pp. 236-71.

26. Roloff, *Apostolat–Verkündigung–Kirche,* p. 241.

27. G. Lohfink, "Paulinische Theologie in der Rezeption der Pastoralbriefe," in *Paulus*

of 2 Timothy 1:3-12 on Romans 1:8-17. Not only is there a remarkable parallel in the larger structural pattern of the two proems, but there is a close similarity of shared vocabulary in six instances. Moreover, the proem of Romans has one phrase that occurs in none of Paul's other letters but recurs in 2 Timothy 2:3. He concludes that there is the highest probability that the author of the Pastoral Letters had knowledge of Romans and was intentionally developing his introduction in relation to that of Romans.

Second, to score the importance of the apostolate of Paul in the Pastorals, Lohfink notes that of the superscriptions in the thirteen letters within the Pauline corpus, only Romans has a more lengthy scope (seventy-two words) than Titus (forty-seven words), which exceeds all the other letters by a great measure and reveals the most complete description of Paul's apostolate within the Pastorals.[28] Lohfink then turns his attention to two questions: What did the Pastorals *not* take over from the earlier epistles, and how was what was received, shaped?

In the earlier epistles Paul's entrusted commission as an apostle was closely connected with the revelation of the risen Christ (1 Cor 9:1; 15:8-9; Gal 1:15-17). With the Pastorals the decisive moment in the life of Paul was formulated in terms of the appointment to his office (Titus 1:3; 2 Tim 1:11-12). Rather than being an apostle to the nations (Rom 11:13), he is the teacher of the nations (1 Tim 2:7), indeed the unique and true teacher. In the earlier epistles Paul was seen as one among many apostles (Gal 1:17, 19; 2:7-8), while in the Pastorals Paul is seen as the one apostle, the unique and true teacher of the nations (1 Tim 2:7).

However, of greater significance is the adaptation by the Pastorals of features of his apostolate from the undisputed letters. Paul is designated "apostle of Jesus Christ" (1 Tim 1:1; 2 Tim 1:1; Titus 1:1). His office is described as a *diakonia* (service, ministry) (1 Tim 1:12; 2 Cor 5:18). He is an apostle "through the will of God" (2 Tim 1:1; 1 Cor 1:1; 2 Cor 1:1), and "by command of God . . . and Jesus Christ" (1 Tim 1:1; Gal 1:1). His apostolate is inseparably joined with the service of the gospel (1 Tim 1:11; 2:6-7; Titus 1:3; Rom 1:1; 1 Cor 1:17). The apostolate office is a pure gift of God's grace (1 Tim 1:12-17; Rom 1:5; 12:3; 1 Cor 3:10). Its goal is to engender belief (Titus 1:1; Rom 1:5). His office is worldwide and directed to the nations

---

in den neutestamentlichen Spätschriften, pp. 70-121, and "Die Vermittlung des Paulinismus zu den Pastoralbriefen," *Biblische Zeitschrift,* n.s., 32 (1988): 169-88.

28. Lohfink, "Paulinische Theologie," p. 72.

(1 Tim 2:7; 2 Tim 4:17; Rom 1:5; 11:13; Gal 1:16). Paul as the first of sinners (1 Tim 1:15-16) is the model of true faith. He is not an example in a moralistic sense, but is to be imitated as the model of God's gracious action toward all humanity. The suffering of Paul occurs for the sake of the gospel (2 Tim 1:8, 10-12; 4:5, 17), and his suffering encompasses his entire existence that is a witness to the gospel in his trials, imprisonment, and ultimately death.

Above all, Paul the apostle is the guardian of the faith against all heresy. He is the source of sound doctrine that is identified with the gospel. He instructs his coworkers, Timothy and Titus, and every generation of Christian leaders (*episkopoi, diakonoi;* 1 Tim 3:1-13) to guard sound doctrine as a sacred trust *(parathēkē)* and to oppose those who reject "the healthy words" of our Lord Jesus Christ (1 Tim 6:3; 2 Tim 4:3). Finally, Paul speaks of his apostolic presence that is carried first by his coworkers and then by his letters (1 Tim 3:14-15). Paul's apostolate is unique to him and not shared by the next generation, but his teachings continue to be the standard by which Christian doctrine is to be measured for the next generations, indeed until the parousia (2 Tim 1:12).

2. The Theological Implications of Canon

What are the implications to be drawn from the Pastoral Epistles' understanding of the apostolate of Paul? In the first place, there are multiple indications of the strongest continuity between the earlier, undisputed letters of Paul and the Pastorals. Paul's apostolic office has not changed, but remains unique and the ground on which his proclamation of the gospel is based. Second, there have been equally important accent changes in the function of his office. Paul has become the model of Christian faith with a new predominance, and the guardian of sound doctrine against the increasing threat from heresy. In a following chapter the problem of the development of institutional offices within the early church will be discussed in depth and the relation of charismatic functions to ecclesiastical offices pursued. Here our purpose is to focus initially on Paul's apostolic office.

To suggest with some commentators that the Pastoral Epistles reflect a retreat, indeed, a serious misunderstanding of the Pauline gospel, is to fail in grasping the significance of the history of Paul's reception in the church that has been carefully analyzed by Gerhard Lohfink and his colleagues.[29] In a word, the failure to understand the true significance of the role of canon results when one disregards the canonical shaping of the Pastorals as a guide toward rendering the entire Pauline corpus. The content of the message of Paul has not been altered, but the function of the apostle has been reformulated. The active Paul, the missionary and founder of churches, has been reshaped to form a new and canonical role for the apostle. His "occasional" letters have been collected and acknowledged as a part of the church's sacred Scriptures. His presence has, in a genuine sense, been textualized to become a written vehicle by which the church, guided by the work of the Holy Spirit, is continually instructed by his letters. Thus the canonical function of the Pastorals within the corpus is to offer the means by which the active Paul, the missionary, the apostle, has been rendered continually accessible to later generations of Christians by transforming his role into an analogical norm along with the rest of Scripture by which to discern the will of God in the changing historical crises facing the church in the future.

II. Abraham's Faith in Galatians 3 and Romans 4

1. J. C. Beker's Categories of Contingency and Coherence

J. Christiaan Beker sets up the problem of the contingency and coherence of Paul's letters by focusing on the differing interpretations of Abraham's faith in Galatians 3 and Romans 4.[30] He argues that Paul's interpretation of Abraham's faith is set firmly within the polemical setting of a crisis evoked in the churches of Galatia by troublemakers (Gal 1:7) who have preached another gospel from that delivered by Paul, and have convinced some within the Galatian churches of their position. By calling into question Paul's apostolic authority, these troublemakers have argued that Paul's message of a law-free gospel is a distortion of the teaching of the mother church. Rather, Gentile Christians are still under obligation to observe the Jewish law, particularly that of circumcision, the essential sign of gaining entrance into the line of salvation history that started with Abraham and finished its fulfillment in Christ.

---

29. In *Paulus in den neutestamentlichen Spätschriften.*
30. J. Christiaan Beker, *Paul the Apostle* (Philadelphia: Fortress, 1980), pp. 23-131.

Paul's response is both polemical and substantive. He sets forth the sharpest possible antithesis between the promise of blessings for the Gentiles by faith alone and the works of the law (Gal 2:1-6). Then he seeks to establish his argument by several different appeals to Abraham. Citing Genesis 15:6, he argues that Abraham was reckoned righteous on the basis of his trust in God alone, and Israel's Scriptures further confirm that those who share Abraham's faith are blessed by God, apart from the works of the law (Gen 12:3; 18:18). Then again, by citing Habakkuk 2:4 Paul demonstrates that no one is justified by God through the law because Christ has redeemed us from the curse. In fact, Beker maintains that Torah in Galatians almost takes on a demonic role. Next, in Galatians 4:22 Paul offers an allegory of two covenants on the basis of Abraham's two sons: Hagar's offspring is of slavery, that of Isaac of freedom. Paul concludes that we are children of the free woman, not of slavery. Finally, he interprets Abraham's seed in Genesis 12:7 as referring only to Christ. The promise made to Abraham was given 430 years before the Sinai covenant with Moses and cannot be added to.

Over against this focus on stark discontinuity in Galatians, Beker interprets Paul's portrait of Abraham in Romans as focusing on continuity. Paul is not opposing an apostasy of Judaizers, but is engaged in a dialogue with Jewish Christians. His emphasis on Torah is one of persuasion. Indeed, he offers an apology for the law (Rom 7:7-12). He places the law within the context of God's faithfulness and his plan of salvation history. Abraham is here an example of faith. His justification rests on his faith, and he becomes the father of all who believe without circumcision. The law is necessary because it functions as the negative counterpart (Rom 4:13; 5:13, 20) to the righteousness of God in Christ. By citing Psalm 32, Paul identifies the blessings of forgiveness expressed by David with God's reckoning Abraham righteous. Moreover, in contrast to Galatians where the promise is restricted to Christ alone as the seed, in Romans the promise to Abraham is also to his descendants. Beker also tries to show that Paul's argument in Romans was addressed to particular circumstances of the Roman church, which he plans shortly to visit.

When Beker turns from describing the sharp contrasts between the portrayal of Abraham in Galatians and in Romans, he appeals to a dialectical hermeneutic that reveals the wide diversity of interpretation. He is adamant that this biblical tension cannot be resolved by any moves of harmonization, but Paul's theology can be understood only by retaining the tensions arising from the particularity of the historical situations being addressed by Paul. However, it is interesting to observe that Beker's dialectic always seems to move from contingency to coherence. One wonders how it would change this hermeneutic if the movement were reversed.

2. J. Louis Martyn's Analysis of the Role of the "Teachers"

An even more impressive example of relating Paul's interpretation of Abraham's faith has been mounted by J. Louis Martyn, both in his monumental commentary on Galatians[31] and in a series of essays on the relation between Galatians and Romans.[32]

For several important reasons, Martyn's commentary on Galatians has been widely recognized as introducing a new critical phase in the study of Galatians. First, he has sought to reconstruct the historical critical context of the letter by focusing on the crises provoked by the "troublemakers" (1:6-9; 3:1-2, 5; 4:17; 5:7-12; 6:12-14), which he names "the Teachers," who have set the agenda for Paul's polemical defense of his apostolic message. By using both inner-biblical and extrabiblical historical texts of Hellenistic Judaism, Martyn has sought to reconstruct in the greatest detail the exact nature of their teachings. Then he uses his reconstruction in the form of a mirror image to interpret Paul's response to this challenge.

Second, Martyn has argued at length that the key to Paul's theology in Galatians is found in his application of an apocalyptic form of discourse that shapes every aspect of his response to the Teachers. The center of Paul's apocalyptic lies in the certainty that God has invaded the present evil age by sending Christ and his Spirit into it. This disjunctive apocalypse evoked the birth of his gospel mission. "[H]is gospel came into being when God apocalypsed [*sic*] Christ to him."[33] As a result of God's invasion, two pairs of opposites are at war with one another, which evokes diametrically opposed antinomies between spirit and flesh, gospel and law, evil age and new creation, freedom and slavery. The Christian, grasped by Christ's invasion, now understands the whole world as trapped in the power of this present evil age. He sees the world bifocally, both the old and new simulta-

---

31. Martyn, *Galatians*.
32. J. Louis Martyn, *Theological Issues in the Letters of Paul* (Nashville: Abingdon, 1997).
33. Martyn, *Galatians*, p. 99.

neously, but is confident of God's final victory. Paul calls this apocalyptic good news the gospel.

Both of these perspectives — Martyn's reconstruction of the opposition of the Teachers and his focus on Paul's apocalyptic theology — are so central to Martyn's understanding of Galatians that they must be briefly addressed before turning to interpret the tensions between Galatians and Romans.

First, it should be noted that Martyn's concern for a reconstruction in such detail of the Teachers' message is closely connected with his larger hermeneutical goals borrowed from Walter Bauer's suggestion.[34] Accordingly, Martyn seeks to reconstruct how the first Galatian recipients of Paul's letter would likely have understood the text of Galatians that we now read. In this sense he is going beyond a search for Paul's authorial intent, but he rather seeks to sit in the congregation at Galatia and to experience imaginatively how the letter was first received and understood.

Immediately several hermeneutical problems, raised earlier when we spoke of a mirror image reading, come to mind. The danger of over-interpreting, psychologizing, and speculating is always present. But more serious from a canonical perspective is how such a surplus of meaning relates to the received written letter of Paul that was soon read by other churches unable and unaware of the Teachers' role beyond the written canonical text. Is there not a hermeneutical parallel with Käsemann's objection to Joachim Jeremias's giving exegetical priority to his reconstructed Aramaic original over the Greek New Testament text?

Several examples arise that raise the question whether Martyn's sharpened reconstructions have at times actually served to skew the message of Paul's written text by filling in the silences and supplying motivations not explicitly stated. For instance, Martyn conjectures that "the false brothers" may have cleverly approached James by scaling down their appeal, by omitting the issue of circumcision, and by focusing on observance of the food laws.[35] They may well have left aside the controversial demand of circumcision only for the moment in order to provoke a confrontation with Paul, who was the leader of the Gentile mission sponsored by the church of Antioch. However, is this not speculation going beyond the actual text?

---

34. Martyn, "John and Paul on the Subject of Gospel and Scripture," in *Theological Issues in the Letters of Paul*, pp. 209-10.

35. Martyn, *Galatians*, p. 461.

Or again, he writes: "[T]he important point is that Paul must also have come away from this political defeat with heightened distrust of the Jerusalem church itself."[36] Whether this inference is true or not, it is important to note that Galatians 2 draws none of these conclusions, but turns to expound the theological signification of this past confrontation for instructing the Galatians on justification by faith and not by works of the law (2:16).

Finally, Paul writes in Galatians 5:2: "If you undergo circumcision, Christ will be of no help to you." Martyn comments: "The instruction of v. 3 is thus a polemic tightly focused on the message the Teachers are preaching to Gentiles, not a polemic against Judaism."[37] The effect of Martyn's reconstruction is to limit Paul's understanding of the law to a particular, time-conditioned, inner-Christian debate and thus to separate Galatians from the theological confrontation with Judaism found in Romans (Rom 2:1–3:4).

In addition, Martyn's apocalyptic reading of Galatians has been widely regarded as unusually perceptive and has evoked remarkable agreement by its sheer persuasiveness. An issue that still causes debate is the terminology of apocalyptic. How does such an interpretation of its use by Paul in Galatians relate to other apocalyptic images, say, in 1 and 2 Thessalonians, not even to speak of the usage in the Old Testament and in the Pseudepigrapha? In a subsequent chapter (4.VIII), I return to this issue in more detail. Its immediate relevance will also become apparent when we discuss how Martyn relates Galatians to Romans.

We are now in a position to return to our central question, first raised by Beker, but greatly expanded by Martyn. How is one to resolve the tensions between the two Pauline letters (Galatians 3 and Romans 4) regarding the faith of Abraham? In a special essay, Martyn has set forth his hypothesis.[38] Building on his earlier understanding that the Teachers were still active in the Galatian churches and were continuing to offer their hostile interpretation of Paul's letter, Martyn suggests that three matters in his letter would emerge as unusually provocative to these law-observant Teachers: (1) Paul's critical reference to the Jerusalem church (Gal 4:25-27);

---

36. Martyn, *Galatians*, p. 461.

37. Martyn, *Galatians*, pp. 470-71.

38. Martyn, "Romans as One of the Earliest Interpretations of Galatians," in *Theological Issues in the Letters of Paul*, pp. 37-45.

(2) his "outrageous" comment about the law (3:19-20); and (3) his controversial reference to the noncircumcised Jewish Christians as the "Israel of God" (6:16). Martyn then argues that Paul took steps to correct or modify these three matters that were so offensive to the Teachers. Initially, he apparently wrote a second letter (subsequently lost) referred to in 1 Corinthians 16:1-2 expressing his concern for the unity of the Christian churches and proposing a plan to collect funds from the Greek churches to aid the Jerusalem church.

More importantly, Martyn suggests that Paul's subsequent letter to the Romans was his attempt to modify his earlier positions of the Galatian letter. Thus, while not repudiating his stance of a connection between Sinai and tyranny, Paul now insists on the law itself as holy and even spiritual (Rom 7:12). Then again, he shifts the christological focus from Christ as the single seed of Abraham (Gal 3:16) to speak explicitly of the whole line of patriarchs. Abraham, Isaac, and Jacob are the first embodiment of God's gracious election (Rom 4:16). Moreover, in chapters 9–11 of Romans Paul explicitly corrects any slighting of historical Israel by speaking of God's mysterious intent of faithfulness to all Israel (11:26). Paul has revised his earlier view by affirming Israel's ultimate salvation along with all human beings.

In sum, Martyn suggests that the relation of the two letters is to be interpreted in terms primarily of a historical sequence. Romans is to be understood as a corrective of Galatians offered by Paul at a later date. This solution thus affords him an interpretive access to both letters without the need for Beker's hermeneutical dialectic between contingency and coherence.

Nevertheless, I would question Martyn's solution from two directions, both of which relate to the role of canon. First, Martyn continues to interpret Romans according to a reconstruction of Paul's putative intention for writing Romans because of what he had earlier written in Galatians, especially his concern to remove any offense he might have caused. Accordingly, Martyn has introduced psychological and political speculations regarding his intentions in order to explain the shape of Romans. Second, Martyn does not adequately take into consideration, in my judgment, the canonical function of Romans within the Pauline corpus, not only its specific theological shape, but also its predominant role in outlining the coherence of Paul's theology in a fresh, comprehensive manner. This function is not in terms of chronological priority, but rather as an example of Paul's application of the gospel in a holistic manner by reviewing the contingencies of the past in a deepened sense of the theological coherence of his entire ministry.

3. A Canonical Reading of Abraham's Faith according to Paul

In a previous chapter I tried to set forth the canonical shape of the Pauline corpus. I stressed the canonical function of the letter to the Romans as providing an interpretive key to the corpus as an introduction to the most extensive and comprehensive review of his theology dealing with the very topics he had treated in his earlier letters. How does this canonical shaping of Romans affect the way Galatians is now to be read?

a. The first observation to make is that the conflict of Paul with the Teachers who are challenging his law-free presentation of the gospel by insisting that the Jewish law remains still obligatory for the Christians of Galatia, receives a different focus when read in the light of the letter to the Romans. In Romans 1–3 Paul sets forth the plight of all humanity alienated from God. In his thematic formulation of 1:16-17, he defines the gospel as the power of God for salvation, first to the Jew and then to the Gentile. However, in his unfolding of this theme Paul reverses the sequence by addressing initially the Gentile world that evokes God's righteous wrath against his creation. Then, using the form of a debate, God turns to the Jew, who is found equally guilty. Romans 2:12 offers a summary: all who have sinned without the law will perish without the law, but all who have sinned under the law will be judged by the law. Thus, the universal character of the indictment is clear. All of humanity is without excuse and judged guilty (3:23).

Paul next addresses the obvious question: What advantage, then, has the Jew? To answer this question Paul turns to the theme of the righteousness of God manifested apart from the law and uses the figure of Abraham (Gen 15:6) to provide his scriptural warrant for justification by faith without circumcision. It is at this point that the discussion regarding Abraham's justification by faith overlaps with Paul's debate with the Jewish Christians in Galatia. In his reconstruction of this debate within the Galatian churches, Martyn goes to great lengths to argue that Paul's attack on the role of the law in God's rectification is not related to Judaism,[39] but

---

39. Martyn, "Galatians, an Anti-Judaic Document?" in *Theological Issues in the Letters of Paul*, pp. 77-84.

rather is an inner-Christian debate between Jewish Christians. As a result, in my judgment, Martyn's reconstructed critical context respecting the central role of the Teachers has replaced the larger canonical context provided by Romans. That a canonical issue is involved is made explicit by Martyn when he suggests that Romans should be read through the lens of Galatians, which is the reverse of its canonical shaping.[40] Rather, when Romans is used as the lens for understanding Galatians, the debate over justification by faith apart from the law is indeed a controversy with Judaism and not just an inner-Christian debate.

When Paul in Galatians 3:7 defines the sons of Abraham as "those of faith," the implication is certainly directed against the traditional Jewish understanding that the sons of Abraham were the adherents of the Torah. Likewise, the term "Israel of God" (6:16) implies a new definition of Israel that is incompatible with the Jewish understanding of its divine election.

b. Second, the tensions outlined by both Beker and Martyn respecting the law take on a different face when attention is paid to the canonical shape of the larger Pauline corpus. Both scholars, in treating Galatians 3, place great emphasis upon the radical discontinuity in Paul's presentation of the law. Accordingly, in his effort to destroy completely the Teachers' position that Christian faith in Christ still mandates observance of the Jewish law, Paul expends great energy to establish in the boldest possible antithesis justification before God by the law and justification by the faith (faithfulness) of Jesus (3:11-14). Martyn sees the radical discontinuity threatening to identify the law with a demonic tyranny. Even Paul's subsequent "apology" for the law to serve as an "addition" because of transgression (3:19) does not fully remove its denigrating function that is further made by mention of the law's being mediated by angels (3:19) to become a vehicle of God's curse. Martyn continues to refer to the Sinai law as given "in the absence of God," which interpretation presses the theme of discontinuity to an unwarranted extreme (see Acts 7:53).

The critical issue at stake is not to deny the element of radical discontinuity respecting the gospel and the law in Galatians, but to see the effect of reading Galatians in the light of Paul's mature and comprehensive treatment of the law and the faith of Abraham in Romans. The key passage is Romans 7:7–8:8. Paul does not for a moment weaken his earlier sharp contrast between law and gospel, but in Romans Paul provides a far broader

40. Martyn, "Romans as One," pp. 37-45.

context for his interpretation of the relation between the two. The law it-self is not sinful. God forbid! Such a thought is a horror for Paul. It is not the source of tyranny, but rather it is holy and the commandments are just and good (7:12).

Ernst Käsemann, in his commentary on Romans 7, follows the traditional Lutheran emphasis in ascribing the law completely to the old aeon.[41] The law is the counterpart to the gospel, and radical criticism of the Torah is the inalienable mark of Paul's theology. Käsemann continues to emphasize the radical discontinuity of God's action: "Incorporation into the rule of Christ and total separation from the law coincide."[42] The crisis being described in Romans 7 is "mankind under the law," including specifically the pious Jew.[43]

It is at this point that Paul Meyer's essay on Romans 7 breaks fresh ground.[44] In fact, Meyer uses chapter 7 as an example of how Paul's understanding of the law has developed since Galatians. Meyer insists that Paul is not concerned in chapter 7 with the malevolent power of the law, but rather with that of sin. Nor is he describing a divided self with one part under the power of sin and the other not. Rather, chapter 7 concerns the demonic force of sin in perverting the law that was intended by God to procure life, but has actually brought forth the exactly opposite result. Indeed, the demonic nature of sin lies in its power to distort the highest and best of all human piety. By isolating works from law, Paul is able to contrast God's righteousness, not with righteousness from the law, but with Israel's own righteousness. The just requirements of the law have been fulfilled by Christ, and are now made available to all who walk in the Spirit (8:4).

As a result of this new formulation of the righteousness of God based on faith, Paul can now summon two witnesses, Moses and the personified "righteousness from faith," to offer complementary testimonies. In contrast to Galatians, where law is identified with doing, Paul redefines "doing" as believing in what God has done in Christ. Citing the words of the law itself (Lev 18:5), Paul argues that the law points to Christ as its goal

---

41. Ernst Käsemann, *Commentary on Romans* (Grand Rapids: Eerdmans, 1980), p. 186.

42. Käsemann, *Commentary on Romans*, p. 189.

43. Käsemann, *Commentary on Romans*, p. 335.

44. Paul W. Meyer, "The Worm at the Core of the Apple: Exegetical Reflections on Romans 7" (1990), in *The Word in This World* (Louisville: Westminster John Knox, 2004), pp. 57-77.

(telos) and that the righteousness from the law finds its fulfillment in the righteousness from faith.[45]

c. Third, another important implication is to be drawn from Paul's use of Israel's Scripture to serve as warrant for this presentation of the righteousness of God. In the past, there have been several attempts to isolate the positive role of Jewish Scriptures from its negative role. One approach, first developed by Hartmut Gese,[46] was to distinguish between "Zion-Torah" and "Sinai-Torah," but such a distinction has not been generally accepted. Another impressive attempt by Martyn has been of Paul's hearing two voices in the law, one referring to the voice of the Sinai law with its curses (Gal 3:10, 13, 19; 4:3-5, 21), and another referring to the voice of pre-Sinai law, God's own mind (3:8; 4:21).[47] Although Martyn correctly recognizes the different senses of Paul's handling of the law, in the end the positive voice of law continues to be only the pre-Sinai voice, the law's original voice, the voice of God's promise to Abraham. The Sinai voice remains from the old aeon, the bearer of the curse, the source of death and tyranny.

However, Paul's reflections in Romans 9:30–10:13 would indicate a very different dialectical understanding of law. Rather than emphasizing the radical discontinuity of Galatians — Christ is the termination of the law — Romans speaks of the law pointing to its goal in Christ (10:4). Thus, when properly understood (9:30–10:13), the law of Moses is also a witness to the righteousness of God's law.

d. Fourth, there is still another aspect of Paul's use of Romans that effects a canonical understanding of Galatians. The issue turns on the promise of justification by faith made to Abraham in Galatians 3. Both Beker and Martyn have stressed the radical quality of Paul's restricting the promise to Abraham alone as the sole seed (Gal 3:16). This element of radical discontinuity has been further expanded by Martyn,[48] who hears Moses' voice in Romans 10:5 as a falsification of the gospel and which calls for critical discernment between the spirits. Martyn's reading of the singularity of the promise to Abraham is consistent with his emphasis on Paul's apoca-

---

45. J. Ross Wagner, *Heralds of the Good News: Isaiah and Paul in Concert in the Letter to the Romans* (Leiden: Brill, 2003), p. 160.

46. Hartmut Gese, "Erwägungen zur Einheit der biblischen Theologie," *Zeitschrift für Theologie und Kirche* 67 (1970): 417-36; Gese, *Essays in Biblical Theology* (Minneapolis: Augsburg, 1977), p. 82.

47. Martyn, *Galatians*, pp. 506-14.

48. Martyn, *Galatians*, p. 333.

lyptical stance in establishing the sharpest possible contrast between the old age of the law and the new age of the Spirit. Nevertheless, it is quite clear that in Romans 4 the promise to Abraham is not restricted to the patriarch himself, but also applies to his descendants (v. 13). Moreover, attention to Israel's history, to Sarah and Rebekah, to Jacob and Esau, is included in God's salvific intent.

In the climax of Romans 7, Paul contrasts God's law and sin's law: "There is no condemnation for those in Christ Jesus, because God's law, the law of the Spirit of life in Christ, has set me free from sin's law" (Rom 8:1-2). God has done what the Mosaic law could not do, namely, set us free from the law of sin and death. God's purpose in sending the Son was "in order that the just requirements of the law might be fulfilled in us, who walk according to the Spirit" (8:4).

e. Finally, there is an important change in Paul's manner of expounding the problem of the law. In Romans 9:30–10:21,[49] Paul addresses in new detail why Israel failed to obtain righteousness. He alters the earlier metaphor of contrasting righteousness by faith and of the law, to that of a race. Why did Israel fail to obtain righteousness? In 9:31 Paul claims that Israel failed "to catch up," not with righteousness, but with the law *(nomos)* itself. Israel had not obtained the goal of righteousness; it had not even caught up with the law that would lead it to the goal. Moreover, Paul does not criticize Israel for pursuing the law. Rather, it failed because it did not seek the law in the right manner. It pursued the goal not from faith, but by works. Israel's zeal was not "according to knowledge"; rather it sought to establish its own righteousness. It pursued the law as if it were "from works" *(ex ergōn)*. In contrast, God's righteousness, the righteousness of faith revealed in Jesus Christ, was the goal *(telos)* all the time. The effect is that the law has also a positive role for Paul. He terms it "the law that leads to righteousness" because its goal is Christ (10:1-4).

The larger theological question to which we shall return in a subsequent chapter is the relation of Paul's apocalyptical theology to the use of *heilsgeschichtliche* categories. Even from Paul's understanding of the positive witness of the law of Moses, one cannot avoid seeing that his theological framework includes the entire history of Israel in which the promised salvation in Christ was already adumbrated.

---

49. Wagner, *Heralds*, pp. 119-217.

4. Justification in Philippians

Before attempting to draw some larger hermeneutical implications respecting the canonical effect of Romans on the interpretation of Galatians, it is necessary to throw the interpretive net even wider by including a brief reflection on other biblical parallels to our topic within the Pauline corpus. The parallel closest to the subject matter of Galatians 3 and Romans 4 is from Philippians 3:2-11.[50] Paul is writing to one of his Gentile Greek churches, above all to express his thanks for the support he received from them. However, in chapter 3 the tone of the letter shifts quite suddenly and dramatically (the reasons for the change in style and content continue to be debated by academics), and he quite unexpectedly warns his congregation against evil workers who appear to be demanding the Jewish rite of circumcision. Whatever the exact nature of the conflict, Paul offers a rare autobiographical account to illustrate how trust in Christ replaces any claims of confidence through religious piety "according to the flesh." All human activity is deemed worthless when measured by knowledge of Christ. Then Paul describes his life in Christ in terms familiar from Romans and Galatians. He has "gained Christ," not by having a righteousness of his own, based on the law, but that which is through the faithfulness of Christ, the righteousness from God that depends on faith. Furthermore, he seeks to share in the power of Christ's resurrection, identifying with his suffering and death, that he may attain in death a life reflecting Christ's glory.

In Philippians 3:9 Paul contrasts two kinds of righteousness: "a righteousness of my own based on the law" and the righteousness from Christ "through the faith of Christ" *(dia pisteōs Christou)*. The highly controversial issue of the phrase *pistis Christou* found in Galatians 2:16 has now been extended into the letter of Philippians. Is Paul using an objective genitive (faith in Christ) or a subjective (or authorial) genitive (faith of Christ)? I have been persuaded by the arguments of Richard Hays[51] and J. Louis Martyn[52] that the latter option is to be preferred. Martyn paraphrases Galatians 2:16 in support of his understanding also of Philippians: "We

---

50. See particularly the illuminating commentary of Markus Bockmuehl, *The Epistle to the Philippians* (London: A. C. Black, 1998).

51. Richard B. Hays, *The Faith of Jesus Christ*, 2nd ed. (Grand Rapids: Eerdmans, 2002).

52. Martyn, *Galatians*, pp. 246-60.

have placed our trust in Christ Jesus, in order that the source of our rectification might be the faith of Christ and not observance of the law." This contrast is not between two human alternatives, to observe the law or to have faith in Christ, but rather, to emphasize justification is God's initiative carried out in Christ's faithful death in obedience.

Yet I think it important that *pistis* (faith) be understood much like the Hebrew *'emunah* as the faithfulness of Jesus. Paul is not interested in the personal piety of Jesus. Nor does Paul or the Gospels seek to *share* the story of Jesus' religious experiences.[53] For this reason, I am uneasy when Hays extends his important grammatical analysis to a larger theory of a narrative story undergirding the New Testament. According to his hypothesis, Paul marks a historical development toward the formation of the Gospels by his implicit literary reference to the Jesus story.[54] My difficulty with Hays's larger interpretation of the theological significance of the "faith of Jesus" is that it moves in the direction of Albrecht Ritschl,[55] who shifted the center of gravity from religion about Jesus to a religion of Jesus himself, indeed making Christ's own relation to God the basis for justification by faith. In my judgment, this is not the function of faith in the Pauline letters, nor even the canonical role of Acts (see chapter 5.I), both of which move in a very different direction from supporting this alleged narrative substructure.

One of the significant points to observe in this passage from Philippians is that it contradicts the proposal once defended that Paul's teaching of justification by faith, not by the law, was a peripheral topic for the apostle and was restricted to a peculiar situation in which Paul was defending the inclusion of the Gentiles into the promises of Israel (Stendahl). This passage from Philippians shows that Paul uses the doctrine within a much wider context than in a debate over the inclusion of Gentiles. Moreover, the theme of justification by faith is also joined with Paul's other theme of participation in the death of Christ through sharing his sufferings as he awaits a transformed life in the presence of his Savior. The familiar polemical notes associated with Paul's defense of a doctrine of justification by faith in

---

53. I suspect that this liberal theological misunderstanding may account in part for Gordon D. Fee's continued defense of an objective genitive reading in his commentary, *Paul's Letter to the Philippians* (Grand Rapids: Eerdmans, 1995), p. 325.

54. Hays, *Faith of Jesus Christ*, p. 219.

55. See Horst Stephan, "Die Theologie Albrecht Ritschl," in *Geschichte der evangelischen Theologie* (Berlin: Töpelmann, 1938), pp. 193-203.

Galatians are lacking largely in his exposition of the church at Philippi, but a closely akin doctrinal formulation provides the grounds for his continued striving after faithful obedience, as he awaits his union with Christ.

5. Justification in the Pastorals

Finally, it is highly significant that an appeal to salvation as justification through God's grace without human deeds of merit appears in the Pastoral Epistles, namely, in Titus 3:5-7. The context for the Pastoral Letters is far different from the earlier Pauline epistles. There is no one crisis to which the letter of Titus is addressed, but rather pastoral advice is offered to Paul's younger coworker in the ministry of the gospel for the next generation of Christians.

The appeal to justification by faith is completely without polemics, indeed it has become a conventional, even formalized recounting of God's goodness that has been poured out so richly by the Savior. The main point of the letter is to urge Titus to be faithful in preserving Paul's teachings befitting "sound doctrine." He offers advice on various subjects of fitting behavior so that good deeds correspond to a life reflecting God's gracious will, as those of a common faith await the blessed hope of the appearing of "our great God and Savior" (2:13).

The canonical significance of the Pastorals respecting the doctrine of justification does not lie in any fresh or innovative interpretation of Paul's teaching. Indeed, the profound theological depths of Paul's theological expositions, both in Galatians and in Romans, have been somewhat diluted and rendered quite pale in comparison. Rather, the significance of the Pastorals is in showing how Paul's letters have been preserved for use by the succeeding generation and that his letters, now received as sacred Scripture, are the measure of sound doctrine for the church. The practices and teachings of the Pastoral Letters do not serve canonically as a substitute or replacement for Paul's earlier letters; rather, they provide the hermeneutic by which Paul's ministry is to be continually employed as instruction for the future crises that will undoubtedly threaten his churches. It is crucial to recognize that the Pastorals do not attempt to describe in detail the contents of Paul's theology. Rather, they indicate Paul's enduring role as the model of sound doctrine and designate where his teachings can be found, namely, in Scripture (see 2 Pet 3:15-16).

The next generation of the church's teachers (Timothy, Titus, etc.) is to instruct their communities in Paul's teachings through the vehicle of sacred Scripture (1 Tim 4:13; 2 Tim 3:14-17). They are to study these writings with the guidance of the Holy Spirit to find in his letters analogies by which they are to respond to the coming crises in a manner commensurate with sound Christian tradition. In this respect the Pastorals are crucial in providing an additional hermeneutical guide for exploring Paul's legacy. He is not a figure of the past, but a living vehicle ministering to every future generation of Christians. These are the sacred writings that are able to instruct them for salvation through faith in Christ Jesus (2 Tim 3:15).

6. Hermeneutical Implications

In conclusion, what are the hermeneutical implications to be derived from a canonical reading of the Pauline corpus in respect to the subject first broached in Galatians 3 and Romans 4, namely, justification by faith?

a. First, there are clear differences of emphasis and tensions between Galatians and Romans on a variety of issues related to the promises to Abraham. These are not to be merely harmonized, but rather reflected upon in a dialectical fashion within the canonical framework by which the corpus has been shaped. A careful balance must be maintained throughout between elements of contingency and coherence, especially led by the canonical role of Romans within the corpus.

b. The reader can see that Galatians has been constructed in a particular fashion due to the contingent events of the crisis evoked by the Teachers. When Galatians is compared with Romans, one can note that the former is not only highly polemical, but that only one side of the issue has been addressed. To meet the challenge of the Teachers, Paul has focused his attention completely on the discontinuity between law and gospel, between works and faith. An initial implication of this characteristic for those seeking from Galatians an analogy in confronting future heresies is that Paul chose to formulate his defense of the gospel in different ways. He allowed the urgency of the contingent crises to shape his message in a particular fashion, in fact, in a form that, without the framework of Romans, would have skewed the full richness of his understanding of the law. The fact that in Galatians the language focused exclusively on the radical discontinuity of the apocalyptic meant that the formulation of Galatians would remain in some tension with the *heilsgeschichtliche* approach of Romans. The hermeneutical implication is that both the dimension of apocalyptic and of *Heilsgeschichte* must be retained and their particular functions determined from their discrete context within the entire Pauline corpus. In addition, the function of Romans when reading Galatians assures that the context for Christian theological reflection will include the Old Testament and Israel's struggle for God's justification of his chosen people.

c. The goal of the Pauline corpus was not to lie in a reconstruction of a purified "theology of Paul," but rather to understand how his letters, in both their contingency and their coherence, could serve to guide the church through the new crises of history within the larger context of the Christian Bible. To search for a "historical Paul" can be helpful, even essential in certain situations, but only as it serves better to understand the full range of the message of the Pauline corpus whose witness continues to instruct, admonish, and sustain the apostolic faith of the church.

III. Life in the Spirit

The subject of the Spirit[56] and spiritual gifts is of central importance for understanding Paul's theology. Unquestionably the two subjects belong close together (1 Cor 12:1-3; 2:10-14; Rom 12:1-13). Exactly how the two subjects relate must be addressed at some point in the analysis. Nevertheless,

---

56. The following is a selective bibliography on the subject of Spirit: Beker, *Paul the Apostle*, pp. 272-94; Hans von Campenhausen, "Spirit and Authority in the Pauline Congregation," in *Ecclesiastical Authority and Spiritual Power* (London: Adam and Charles Black, 1964), pp. 55-76; Gordon D. Fee, *God's Empowering Presence: The Holy Spirit in the Letters of Paul* (Peabody, Mass.: Henrickson, 1994); Gerhard Friedrich, "Geist und Amt," *Wort und Dienst. Jahrbuch der theologischen Schule Bethel*, n.s., 3 (1952): 61-85; Ernst Käsemann, "Geist und Geistesgaben im Neuen Testament," in *Religion in Geschichte und Gegenwart*, 3rd ed., 2:1272-79; Leander E. Keck, "The 'Law of Sin and Death': (Romans 8:9-14): Reflections on the Spirit and Ethics in Paul," in *The Divine Helmsman: Festschrift Lou H. Silberman*, ed. James L. Crenshaw and Samuel Sandmel (New York: Ktav, 1980), pp. 41-57; Barnabas Lindars and S. Smalley, eds., *Christ and Spirit in the New Testament: Studies in Honour of Charles F. D. Moule* (Cambridge: Cambridge University Press, 1973); Paul W. Meyer, "The Holy Spirit in the Pauline Letters: A Contextual Exploration," in *The Word in This World*, pp. 117-32; Eduard Schweizer, "Pneuma," in *Theological Dictionary of the New Testament*, ed. G. Kittel and G. Friedrich, vol. 6 (Grand Rapids: Eerdmans, 1968), pp. 415-39.

the exegetical problem is that these two aspects of the same subject often appear apart from each other and have developed in somewhat different directions within the Pauline corpus. Thus, it is crucial to see how the Spirit is first understood in Romans 8, where the noun *pneuma* (spirit) appears more frequently than in any other letter. Similarly, the parallel in Galatians 5 must be seen in relation to Paul's particular battle with the "troublemakers," while the parallel in 2 Corinthians 3 also has its own special context.

It is therefore my concern to focus in this chapter on the subject of the Spirit, following the previously developed method of comparing and contrasting the different functions of the Spirit within Paul's corpus. Ultimately the task will be to reflect theologically on how a canonical reading affects the interpretation. Then in the following chapter we will turn to the subject of the gifts of the Spirit. We begin with Paul's most comprehensive treatment of the Spirit in Romans 8 before turning to Paul's earlier references in Galatians and 2 Corinthians.

1. *Romans 8:1-27*

It has long been recognized by commentators that the content of Romans 1–4 differs from that of Romans 5–8,[57] and what exactly accounts for the shift remains a chief exegetical problem. Some initial insights are gained by observing the change in vocabulary. In chapters 5–8 the theme of the righteousness of God appears infrequently, as does that of faith and trust. The juxtaposition of Jews and Greeks is largely replaced with a focus on the Christian community along with infrequent citations from the Old Testament. Instead the topics of reconciliation, slavery versus freedom, adoption and peace prevail. Above all, God's love and the Spirit move to center stage. Yet it would be a serious misreading to suppose that the goals and concerns of chapters 1–4 have been abandoned. Rather, the chapters that follow draw out the theological implications for the Christian community from the foundations established in chapters 1–4.

An initial structural problem emerges in determining the function of the initial paragraph, Romans 5:1-5. Do these verses serve as a conclusion of chapters 1–4 or as the introduction to chapters 5–8? Strong arguments

---

57. Paul W. Meyer, "Romans: A Commentary," in *The Word in This World*, p. 174.

have been mounted for both options, but a definitive decision does not seem necessary at this juncture. The initial verses clearly summarize what has previously been argued, yet at the same time the topics of the paragraph of rejoicing in suffering and of God's love poured out through the Holy Spirit introduce major themes that follow in chapters 5–8.

The implications of what God has done in Jesus Christ in justifying the ungodly and removing the grounds for divine enmity are spelled out now in terms of the gifts of God in Christ and of establishing a reordered life of hope and joy in sharing the benefits of God's grace through the power of his Holy Spirit. In the chapters that follow, justification is interpreted as an acquittal for life, which has now replaced the reign of sin in a new life of freedom. In chapters 6 and 7 Paul returns to the subject of law to demonstrate that the new order means we are united with Christ, and that the old order with its power of sin and death has been overcome. We are discharged from the law, "dead to that which held us captive," to serve in the new life of the Spirit.

Then in chapter 8 Paul reaches the climax of his description of the new life in Christ by turning to his most powerful exposition of the role of the Spirit. The key word is *pneuma,* which occurs twenty-one times in the chapter and offers the apostle's most profound explication of the indwelling of God's Spirit as the divine fulfillment of his promise of freedom in Christ. Chapter 8 begins with the bold affirmation that summarizes the major themes of the preceding chapters. "Therefore, there is no condemnation for those in Christ Jesus" (v. 1). The power of sin to condemn has been broken for those who have been baptized into Christ's death, and whose old life has been ended. Then verse 2 interprets this newfound freedom in terms of the role of the Spirit. The law of the Spirit of life, God's Spirit in Christ Jesus, has set humanity free from the law of sin and death. It is highly significant that the polarity between law and grace has been reformulated in terms of a law of life, Christ's law, and the law of sin and death.

In verse 3 Paul continues to contend that God's action in sending his Son does what the law is unable to accomplish. He overcame the power of sin in order that the "just requirement of the law might be fulfilled in us" who walk according to the Spirit that is life and peace. In verse 9 Paul amplifies the significance of life in the Spirit. The spirit of God, namely, his very presence, dwells in the Christian. Without the Spirit, one does not belong to Christ. But if Christ is in you, then God who raised Christ from the dead will give life to every Christian through his Spirit. The gift of the

Spirit is here joined with the death and resurrection of Christ, whose life is shared with the believer. The contrast is between living by the flesh, which is death, and living by the Spirit, which is life. The choice between life and death recalls Deuteronomy 30:15.

Next the corporate nature of those sharing in Christ's life by the Spirit is emphasized. All who are led by the Spirit are children of God. The Spirit produces a truly filial union with God, enabling us as heirs (Paul moves to the plural) to address God as Father. The appeal to the Aramaic *abba* supports the view that corporate worship by the community of faith is intended, one not limited to personal prayer.

When Paul further characterizes the nature of the obedient life, it is in terms of Christian suffering with Christ. The suffering of the saints is not an unexpected accident, but the quintessential opposition of evil against those who have been freed from slavery. Then Paul sounds the eschatological hope of those led by the Spirit. He develops the theme to encompass the entire creation that actually groans to be delivered from its bondage and awaits the freedom already experienced by those led by the Spirit. Paul comforts the suffering saints by reminding them to wait for God's plan with patience because the divine Spirit continues to intercede for them. He concludes with the confident confession that nothing can separate us from God's love — he includes himself — in the life of suffering, but that all things are under the control of God's love whose purpose is only that of good.

Up to this point the exegetical task has been to establish the literary context of Romans 8 within the Pauline letter, and then very briefly to outline the major themes of the chapter concerning the subject of the Spirit. Our next task is to focus on another major parallel passage respecting the Spirit in Galatians 5. Only after this has been completed can we explore the canonical relation between Romans 8 and Galatians 5.

2. Galatians 5:13-26

Traditionally it has often been argued that Galatians has been loosely structured into three different parts: chapters 1–2 autobiographical; chapters 3–4 doctrinal; chapters 5–6 homiletical. However, recent scholarship has largely been dissatisfied with this formalistic division that failed to grasp the nature of the book's internal coherence. Upon reflection, Paul's fundamental rejection of his opponents' appeal for a continued observance of the requirements of the law left the question open whether the law has any continuing role whatsoever for the Christian. Or again, how does the freedom of the Spirit-filled life gained by the victory of Christ on the cross relate to the everyday life of the Christian still living in the world with all its temptations?

Galatians 5:1 begins with a bold affirmation of the freedom that Christ has gained and a warning against returning to slavery. Although this verse serves very well as a summary of chapters 3 and 4, it also sets the context for what follows in the rest of the chapter. It also reminds the reader that Paul's "homiletical" exposition is not a general, timeless admonition, but still is directed specifically to the crisis of the Galatian churches. Thus, do not "again" return to a slavery from which you have been freed before the arrival of the "troublemakers" (2:4).

Verses 2-12 continue to spell out Paul's warning. Although the issue of circumcision does not play a role in his arguments against justification by works of the law in the main body of the letter, it clearly is the crucial symbol for Torah observance and lies everywhere in the background of Paul's conflict with the troublemakers (cf. 2:3; 5:10). Therefore, it is not strange that it is introduced to signify the sharpest either/or contrast between law and grace.

In 5:13 the apostle returns to the subject of freedom. It is not to be misused as "an opportunity for the flesh." For Paul, the flesh (sarx) is the willing instrument of sin, and the vehicle of all forms of sin in which no good thing can live.[58] In contrast, Paul sounds the central note of his new ethic: through love become slaves to one another. The grounds for his appeal are then given in verse 14: "The whole law is summed up in a single command. You shall love your neighbor as yourself."

In verse 16 Paul returns to the subject of the Spirit (see 5:5), but this time he offers a detailed exposition of the role of the Spirit who is the divine agent for the new life in Christ. The Christian is to live by the Spirit in conscious opposition to gratifying the impulses of the flesh. The two ways of life are set in the sharpest possible opposition. Then the contrast is further emphasized. The two forces are locked in mortal battle (see Eph 6:10-20). Next Paul contrasts the life in the Spirit with those living under the

---

58. See F. W. Danker, W. Bauer, W. F. Arndt, and F. W. Gingrich, *Greek-English Lexicon of the New Testament and Other Early Christian Literature,* 3rd ed. (Chicago, 1999), p. 915.

law. Thus he shifts the earlier imagery of justification of chapter 2 (faith in Christ and not works of the law), but the change has already been adumbrated in 2:19: "I died to the law that I might live in God."

Next, Paul describes the works of the flesh that run the gamut of human sinfulness: idolatry, impurity, anger, envy, drunkenness, and the like. He ends his list with an eschatological warning. By contrast are the fruits of the Spirit. These are not classified as good works, but spring forth from the divine Spirit. The list begins with love and proceeds to joy, peace, kindness, and self-control. Then Paul adds that there is no law against such virtues because the Spirit, not the law, produces such fruit. Paul ends the section by referring again to the theme of 2:20: those who belong to Christ have crucified the flesh along with its evil desires and impulses.

This section answers the question of how the Christian, freed from the tyranny of the law, lives a Spirit-directed existence in every aspect of daily life. To bear another's burden fulfills "the law of Christ." This infrequent formulation of the new life in the Spirit returns to the theme already sounded in 5:13-14. Through love become servants to one another, for the whole law is fulfilled in one word: "You shall love your neighbor as yourself." That the phrase "law of Christ" is not without its interpretive problems becomes clear from the controversy within the subsequent history of interpretation when it was rendered as *nova lex*.[59]

3. The Canonical Relation of Romans 8 and Galatians 5

To pose the exegetical issue in this manner is to call into question a widespread axiom of modern biblical studies that attention to the chronological relationship between two parallel texts provides the key to understanding a text's growth and thus its theological meaning. Because chronologically Galatians precedes Romans, the sense of the latter parallel is determined by its advance over the former, whether in terms of correction, modification, or rejection. The position being defended here is that the formation of the Pauline corpus altered the relationship between the two letters and assigned Romans as the canonical norm in the light of which the other letters were to be interpreted. Of course, a canonical interpretation is not to be identified with a simplistic harmonization.

59. Franz Mussner, *Der Galaterbrief* (Freiburg: Herder, 1974), pp. 284, 288.

The first thing to note is the highly contingent context of Galatians 5. The exposition of the role of the Spirit is set within the ongoing crisis in Paul's Galatian churches. Freedom in Christ is gained apart from the observation of the law demanded by the troublemakers. The attempt to achieve justification by the law is "to fall from grace." In contrast, Romans 8 is shaped in accordance with a literary context and culminates the apostle's lengthy argument in chapters 5–7 that pursued the theological effect of justification by faith for the Christian life of righteousness.

Thus, the style and purpose of the two passages vary greatly. Romans 8 is largely discursive, but intensifies its emotional power to culminate in a resounding confession in praise of the all-encompassing love of God in Christ whose victory is assured. In Romans 8 Paul explores his understanding of the role of the Spirit in a depth and scope unmatched within the rest of his letters. By offering a highly systematic exposition he explains in detail freedom by the Spirit from the inadequacies of the law, contrasting a life of the flesh as death with a life in the Spirit as true life. He then carefully joins the Spirit's role with the resurrection of Christ with the same Spirit that gives life to the believer (v. 11). He next moves to our adoption as heirs and concludes with the eschatological hope of the church, interpreted within the broadest cosmological scope, whose members are experiencing the reality of God's universal reign as the firstfruits of the new age.

In contrast, Galatians 5 remains highly specific and particular in its intention. Its major focus lies in applying the law of Christ to the practical, everyday life of the Christian within a community of faith. Freedom from the law is not, however, lawlessness, but is characterized by love of neighbor. His listing of specific sins of the old life in contrast to the acts of love is not a turn to conventional Hellenistic moralism but is to view the latter as products of the new life in Christ.

Both Romans and Galatians are in substantive agreement in many of their formulations, even with considerable overlapping of language. Christ has set us free from the yoke of slavery (Gal 5:1; Rom 8:2). The Christian is led by the Spirit and no longer subject to the law (Gal 5:18; Rom 8:14). The flesh and the spirit stand in continual opposition (Gal 5:16; Rom 8:5-7). The law of Christ is realized by love of neighbor (Gal 5:14; Rom 13:9). The Spirit is witness to our adoption as children of God (Gal 4:5; Rom 8:15). Both speak of the firstfruits of the Spirit (Gal 5:22; Rom 8:23). Nevertheless, there are some important differences between their handling of the role of the Spirit. According to the canonical model being suggested, biblical interpretation calls for further theological reflection by the reader in order to relate the diverse witnesses of the various parallel passages according to coherence or lack of such with the substance of its subject matter.

A major issue emerges in relating Galatians 5 to Romans 8 concerning the relation of the law to the Spirit. Throughout Galatians the law is deemed overwhelmingly a negative force unable to provide rectification before God through its observance. It is the enemy par excellence, and being led by the Spirit means complete rejection of its demands. However, the problem arises that suddenly in Galatians 5:14 the law is given a positive role in the context of Paul's describing the Spirit-filled life of the liberated community. We read in 5:14: "The whole law is summarized in a single commandment: you shall love your neighbor as yourself." Or again in 6:2: "Bear one another's burdens, and thus fulfill the law of Christ."

The issue is further complicated by the function of the law in Romans. Not only does Romans 8:4 speak of the "just requirement of the law to be fulfilled in us," but also in Romans 13:8-10 there is a close parallel to Galatians 5:14. The commandments are "summed up in this sentence: You shall love your neighbor as yourself." Because this problem has been treated thoroughly in the Galatians commentary of J. Louis Martyn, much of the following discussion will be with his position.

Martyn argues that the term "law" describes two different aspects or voices. This reading is illustrated from Galatians 5. In verse 3 "the whole law" is used in the negative sense of that opposed to the Spirit, whereas in verse 14 the whole law is interpreted in a positive sense and designates the law of Christ, which is love for one's neighbors. As a warrant for this distinction, Martyn argues that the original law was the promise given to Abraham that preceded the Sinaitic law of Moses (Gal 3:6-9), and was God's intended will. This promise to Abraham was fulfilled in Christ, the one seed (Gal 3:16), and thus Christ redeemed us from the curse of the Mosaic law in order that we might receive the promise of the Spirit through faith. Martyn lays great stress upon the singularity of the promise in contrast to the plurality of the laws of Sinai. Accordingly, there is no linear history of promise in the patriarchal generation.

Furthermore, Martyn is much concerned with the translation of Galatians 5:14, which he renders: "the whole law has been brought to completion in one sentence: 'you shall love your neighbor as yourself.'" The bringing of the law to completion can only be the one act of Christ. He brought the law to an end when he made it the law of Christ. Accordingly, the Christian life is not in any sense controlled by the law, but by the one imperative: love your neighbor.

According to Martyn, it is therefore inaccurate to translate Galatians 5:14 as a fulfillment of the law because it leaves the wrong impression that one can meet the many requirements of the law by performing the one requirement of love for one's neighbor. The passive voice of the verb *pleroō* shows that someone else completes the law, and it is not an exhortation because fulfillment has already been accomplished by Christ. Therefore, the Christian is to be led by the Spirit alone, which results in serving one's neighbor in love.

However, there is a major problem with this interpretation, which Martyn recognizes and seeks to overcome. In the Romans parallel (13:8-10) Paul recites the commandments of the law from the second tablet of the Decalogue: "You shall not commit adultery, not kill, not steal, and any other similar commandments." Then he concludes by affirming that these commandments (plural) are "summed up" in the sentence: love of neighbor. The verb used here is *anakephalaioō*. The plain sense of the word implies that all the commandments of the Decalogue are not brought to an end in completion, but rather are encompassed in the one word of love.[60]

What is at issue is the meaning of the law of Christ (Gal 6:2), and how it relates to the laws of the Old Testament. Various attempts have been made following Hartmut Gese's distinction between Zion-Torah, which is positive, and Sinai-Torah, which is negative,[61] but this distinction cannot be exegetically sustained. Rather, according to Martyn, the real distinction lies between the pre-Sinaitic promise to Abraham and that of the later Mosaic law. The law of Christ is the bringing to completion of the original law to Abraham. Conversely, Martyn judges the Mosaic law to be a false voice (Gal 3:12); it is the voice of slavery. The main point of Galatians is to emphasize that Christians living the Spirit-filled life have no positive relation to the Mosaic law since Jesus Christ has completed the promise made to Abraham.

In my judgment the parallel with Romans 13 as well as the plural commandments of 1 Corinthians 7:19 point in a different direction. The

---

60. Danker et al., *Greek-English Lexicon*, p. 65.

61. Hartmut Gese, "Vom Sinai zum Zion," in *Beiträge zur biblischen Theologie* (Munich: Kaiser Verlag, 1974), pp. 49-60.

law of Christ is not a narrowing of the law,[62] nor does the plural of 1 Corinthians 7:19 imply that not all the Mosaic commandments come from God,[63] but rather the law of Christ is a transformed understanding of the Mosaic law. Not only has the law of Moses been shown to be provisionary (Rom 5:20; Gal 3:23-27), but also the law of Christ is qualitatively different because of the event of Christ's death and resurrection. It is not an extension of the Mosaic law; the entire grounds for which the law was established by God for his elect people have been altered by the Christ event. It is not only a fulfillment of the Abraham promise — indeed, God is faithful to his promise — but, according to Romans 13, it is also an ontological transformation of the Mosaic law. The law of Christ stands in an analogical relationship to the law of Moses only in one respect. The law of Christ remains a divine imperative for Christian behavior. It covers the entire spectrum of human existence over which God is sovereign. The Christian lives under this transformed law, in the sense not of a *nova lex* but of the active presence of Christ's Spirit leading the Christian, both individually and communally, in obedience. The Christian is admonished to pursue the law of Christ in loving behavior toward all persons. It is directed toward the future, and manifests the fruits of the Spirit in overcoming the curse of the old law.

Lying behind this debate is the larger theological issue central to biblical theology. In what sense are the commandments of the Old Testament the expression of the true will of God for Israel and the church? Is there no continuity between the old covenant and the new? The resolution requires careful theological formulation and is far from simplistic in nature. Aspects of the relationship can be formulated both eschatologically in terms of *Heilsgeschichte* and ontologically in the form of its substance. The subject matter of both biblical witnesses is ultimately christological, but the relationship is best formulated dialectically rather than in abstract terms of typology. In the light of God's action in Jesus Christ, the just demands of the law (Rom 8) have been fulfilled; however, the "just demands" are still God's will for his creation. Because of Christ's act in overcoming sin, the law, which is "holy, just and good" (Rom 7:12), is no longer held captive to pervert the Old Testament law by turning it into a false avenue toward rectification (7:13). For this reason the Christian still hears the true voice of

---

62. Martyn, *Galatians*, p. 505.
63. Martyn, *Galatians*, p. 519.

God in the Old Testament, but it is a Scripture that has been transformed because of what God in Christ has done.

One final note is in order. Martyn has forcefully raised the canonical question in the debate over the law of Christ. When interpreting Romans 13:8-10, which speaks of the law of Christ summarizing that of the Decalogue, Martyn concludes his exegesis with a canonical observation. In the light of the ambiguity and tendency for misunderstanding of the law, he concludes with the suggestion that it would be better to interpret Romans 13:8-10 in the light of Galatians 5:14 rather than the reverse.[64] My thesis represents the exact opposite conclusion. The need for interpreting Galatians in the light of Romans arises because of the canonical function of Romans within the Pauline corpus. In the case of the law, the letter to the Romans brings the earlier letter to the Galatians into conformity with the larger subject matter undergirding the entire Christian Bible. In its profound and comprehensive wrestling with the problem, it provides a theological rationale for the Old Testament in the Spirit-filled life of the New. Finally, for canonical reasons I would agree with Nils Dahl's interpretation of Galatians 3:19-29.[65] Despite the continuing tension in these verses, it is quite impossible to interpret the law "ordained by angels through an intermediary" as hostile to God and never intended as divine.[66]

4. 2 Corinthians 3:1–4:6

a. The Structure and Content of the Chapter   In 2 Corinthians 3 the apostle Paul enters into a very different aspect of the treatment of the Spirit when he contrasts the old and new covenants in terms of a written code that brings death with that of the Spirit written on the heart that brings life. In his exposition Paul enters into the subject of the relation of the Spirit with that of Scripture.

The importance of this chapter for Paul's understanding of the Spirit is acknowledged by all. However, it is also true that its interpretation remains one of the most controversial within the entire Pauline corpus. Cer-

---

64. Martyn, *Galatians*, p. 488.

65. Nils A. Dahl, "Contradictions in Scripture," in *Studies in Paul* (Minneapolis: Augsburg, 1977), pp. 159-77.

66. Martyn, *Galatians*, p. 354, "God is absent."

tainly as yet, no broad consensus has emerged.[67] What makes the passage so difficult is that a host of topics, not in themselves directly related to the numerous specific exegetical problems of the chapter, has been anchored to the chapter by its *Wirkungsgeschichte.*

Often in the complex history of interpretation 2 Corinthians 3 has been isolated from its wider context within the letter, for example, to become the focus of the debate over "letter versus spirit." Yet, initially it is important to see that this material is fitted within the larger structure of Paul's description and defense of his apostolic ministry. As pointed out in the earlier chapter on Paul's apostolate, Paul discounts any need for letters of recommendation commending him to the Corinthians. Rather, he tells the Corinthian congregation that its very existence is his best evidence for the supporting of his apostolic ministry. Its members represent a "letter" revealing their transformation through the Spirit of the living God, written on the tablets of the human heart. The Old Testament reference is of course to Ezekiel 36:26. Then in 2 Corinthians 3:6 he speaks of a new covenant, a new divine economy of the Spirit in contrast to an older dispensation that was given in a written document chiseled on stone. The language of the new covenant stems from the Greek translation (LXX) of Jeremiah 31:31-33, and speaks also of a divine law written upon the heart. The written law *(grammatos)* stands in sharpest contrast with that of the Spirit *(pneumatos).* The written code kills, but the Spirit gives life.

What follows is a biblical exposition used to elaborate the difference between these two dispensations. Verses 7-11 of 2 Corinthians 3 appeal to the Mosaic account of Exodus 34:29-30, whereas verses 12-18 focus on the story's continuation in Exodus 34:33-35. Of course, an initial exegetical problem turns on identifying the relation of Paul's argument with the biblical passages to which it refers. Interpreters differ on whether Paul's approach could be styled an exegesis in a more formal sense or should be characterized as a loose appeal, named by Richard Hays "an allusive homily based on biblical incidents."[68] Even more controversial is the view, espe-

---

67. The reader is referred to the standard commentaries on 2 Corinthians by Hans Windisch, Alfred Plummer, Adolf Schlatter, Charles K. Barrett, Victor Furnish, Margaret E. Thrall, and Murray J. Harris. In addition, an exhaustive bibliography of all the modern secondary sources is provided by Scott J. Hafemann, *Paul, Moses, and the History of Israel* (Tübingen: Mohr Siebeck, 1995).

68. Richard B. Hays, *Echoes of Scripture in the Letters of Paul* (New Haven: Yale University Press, 1989), p. 32.

cially pushed by Hans Windisch,[69] that the biblical text has been filtered through a prior form of rabbinic interpretation, at times called midrash, later *pesher.* By and large, Windisch's proposal has not been widely accepted by more recent commentators, although it has been well documented by Otfried Hofius[70] that the cultural influence of rabbinic traditions, such as the Targums, is present in the background of Paul's interpretation. Of course, there is agreement that the Exodus texts have been read according to various Greek versions. Yet the alterations have been of minor significance in terms of its essential meaning, and serve largely to provide the Greek terminology for Paul's reading, such as *diathēkē* for the Hebrew *berit.*

b. Paul's Use of Scripture in Recent Debate   At this juncture, before turning to the actual exegesis of 2 Corinthians 3, it is necessary to address a larger methodological issue of how Paul interprets Israel's Scripture. The issue has been raised with great force by Scott Hafemann and Francis Watson.[71] We begin with Hafemann's proposal before focusing on Watson's interpretation.

In his chapter on the ministry of Moses as portrayed in Exodus 32–34, Hafemann seeks to establish the proper context from which the Old Testament is to be read. He contrasts two different ways of reading these chapters. The first is according to a historical critical approach, shared by most modern biblical scholars. It is characterized by an atomistic investigation of variously construed traditions lying behind the present text, and generally results in failure ever to take seriously the larger biblical narrative in which Exodus 32–34 is anchored. Once so dismembered, the biblical narrative is devalued in an academic search for religious interests behind or beyond the text.[72]

In contrast, Hafemann proposes that the Exodus texts can be read as a narrative, often denigrated as "precritical," but which is the way Paul must have read them. Accordingly, the biblical texts are understood as a work of

---

69. Hans Windisch, *Der Zweite Korintherbrief* (1924; reprint, Göttingen: Vandenhoeck & Ruprecht, 1970), pp. 112-31. See also Anthony T. Hanson, "The Midrash in 2 Corinthians 3: A Reconsideration," *Journal for the Study of the New Testament* 9 (1980): 2-28.

70. Otfried Hofius, "Gesetz und Evangelium nach 2. Korinther 3," in *Paulusstudien* (Tübingen: Mohr Siebeck, 1989), pp. 88-107.

71. Hafemann, *Paul, Moses, and the History of Israel,* and Francis Watson, *Paul and the Hermeneutics of Faith* (London: T. & T. Clark, 2004).

72. Hafemann, *Paul,* p. 191.

literature whose aspects of plot, theme, structure, and contextual setting are pursued as providing the essential ingredients of the intended meaning. Hafemann's concern is to highlight the "theological meaning of the text *as it now stands*."[73] He writes, "Once we join Paul in positing the Mosaic authorship, historical accuracy, and above all, divine authority of Exodus 32–34, we must read the text as a narrative with direct theological import."[74] Lying behind this approach is Hafemann's major thesis that when 2 Corinthians 3:7-18 is read with this understanding of the Exodus narrative, it becomes clear that Paul has not deviated from the original meaning of the Old Testament narrator in its canonical form, but is providing a sober contextual interpretation.[75]

Our time is too restricted to demonstrate in detail that Hafemann's description of the historical critical method is an extreme caricature and seriously misunderstands its aims and methods. One only needs to study with an open mind the exegetical works of the great New Testament scholars of the past generation (Schlatter, Bultmann, Jeremias, Bornkamm, Schürmann, and Schnackenburg), or read in the articles of the *Theological Dictionary of the New Testament,* edited by G. Kittel and G. Friedrich, to see that their critical aim was primarily to understand the theological meaning of the biblical text. Still, I readily agree that Hafemann's criticism contains a modicum of truth that, because of the extravagance of his caricature, runs the danger of being lost. An excessive focus on the history-of-religions content and background can indeed divert attention away from the biblical text's theological witness. However, a deeper problem lies in Hafemann's failure to understand the hermeneutical problems at issue, and the need to grasp the dialectical interaction between a history-of-religions approach and a kerygmatic, confessional one. These two dimensions of the biblical text cannot be identified — the danger of liberalism — nor separated — the danger of conservatism.[76]

Moreover, I am particularly concerned to offer a critical assessment of Hafemann's thesis of how to read the Exodus text as a narrative, or as he expresses it, "as it now stands." I admit to being especially sensitive at this point because my own proposal for a "canonical approach," voiced in sev-

73. Hafemann, *Paul,* p. 194, my emphasis.
74. Hafemann, *Paul,* p. 194.
75. Hafemann, *Paul,* pp. 310-13, 263-429, etc.
76. See Brevard S. Childs, *The Struggle to Understand Isaiah as Christian Scripture* (Grand Rapids: Eerdmans, 2004), pp. 199-322.

eral monographs,[77] has often been misinterpreted as being identical with that represented, for example, by Hafemann. My criticism of his position can be briefly summarized in the following points:

First, Hafemann's description of the Exodus text as a unified narrative, "as it now stands," has little understanding of the elements of modernity that are encompassed in his construal of the Old Testament. To suggest that "we join Paul in positing Mosaic authorship, historical accuracy, and divine authority" is not to understand that terms like "authorship" and "historical accuracy" carried a far different connotation in the period before the Enlightenment and bore none of the technical intensity assumed by Hafemann. Indeed, the very term "narrative" to characterize portions of the Old Testament is a modern term certainly not used in Hafemann's sense by the Reformers. When Karl Barth once said: "Liberal Modernists and conservative Evangelicals are both children of the same Enlightenment father," he signaled an issue that is as relevant today, especially in North America, as when it was first spoken.

Second, Hafemann uses Hans Frei's *The Eclipse of Biblical Narrative* as a warrant for his statement. He writes: "It is assumed that there is no distinction between the literal meaning of Exodus 34 and its historical referent."[78] But Hafemann has misunderstood Frei's major point, according to which the Reformers, in a "precritical" period, were still able to *assume* the coherence of the biblical text with its putative referent. The eclipse of the biblical narrative came about when, following the Enlightenment, a precritical assumption was no longer possible. The post-Enlightenment interpreter became by necessity either critical or anticritical, but the option of a precritical assumption was no longer available once Pandora's box had been opened.

Third, Hafemann bases his interpretation on Exodus as a unified narrative "as it now stands." However, the Old Testament, and especially the chapters of Exodus, is not a unified narrative[79] but is filled with literary and historical tensions. Compare, for example, the Decalogue in chapter 20 with chapter 34, or the tent of meeting in 33:7-11 with the tabernacle in chapters 35–40, or the golden calf story of 32:1-6 with the golden calves set

77. Brevard S. Childs, *Introduction to the Old Testament as Scripture* (Philadelphia: Fortress, 1979); Childs, *The New Testament as Canon: An Introduction* (Philadelphia: Fortress, 1984).

78. Hafemann, *Paul*, p. 192.

79. See Brevard S. Childs, *The Book of Exodus* (London: SCM, 1974), pp. 553-624.

up by Jeroboam in 1 Kings 12:25-33. These tensions are not just history-of-religions problems, but the theological witness of Exodus is structured with these tensions. The closest parallel is found in the early church's rejection of Tatian's attempt to unify the tensions among the four canonical Gospels by means of a single harmonization (diatessaron). The church rightly rejected this harmonization and confessed the one gospel, whose apostolic witness was testified by four different Evangelists. When Hafemann speaks of Exodus 32–34 as a unified narrative, he has provided the glue for his seamless garment by introducing various logical, psychological, and speculative motivations beyond that provided by the biblical text itself.

Fourth, the hermeneutical consequences of his narrative construct prove to be of fundamental importance in his interpretation of 2 Corinthians 3. Constantly his interpretation of the New Testament finds a warrant in an alleged reading of the Exodus text "as a whole," or that "Paul is simply following the flow of the Old Testament narrative,"[80] or that Paul's intention was to read Exodus 34 "within its larger context."[81] The effect is that Paul's argument in 2 Corinthians 3 is constantly being rendered by a massive tour de force. Thus, such interpretations of 3:13b as "in order that the sons of Israel might not gaze into the outcome"[82] or of "glory rendered is operative in its effect" are evaluated even by a conservative evangelical commentator such as Murray Harris as "unusual and awkward, if not impossible."[83] Lying behind Hafemann's exegesis is the explicit dogmatic claim that in no case does Paul's exegesis of the Old Testament deviate from the original meaning (!) of the Old Testament text. However, in my opinion, it is difficult to find a Pauline text that runs in the face of this claim more than 2 Corinthians 3.

Fifth, there is one final issue to debate with Hafemann. Often he identifies his narrative construct of Exodus as its "canonical form." Of course, he has every right to use this terminology in his own way, yet at the same time it is disappointing that he has little awareness of the present hermeneutical debate over the issue of the canonical shaping of the Bible

80. Hafemann, *Paul*, p. 279.
81. Hafemann, *Paul*, p. 281.
82. Hafemann, *Paul*, p. 365.
83. Murray J. Harris, *The Second Epistle to the Corinthians: A Commentary on the Greek Text*, New International Greek Testament Commentary (Grand Rapids: Eerdmans, 2005), p. 298 n. 23.

that is using the term in a very different sense. The issue becomes relevant when Hafemann cites a sentence from Hartmut Gese: "The Old Testament as a literary work developed itself out of kerygmatic intentions."[84] What is meant by kerygmatic intentions? The basic hermeneutical point being made is that the New Testament — and the Old — has been shaped by the recipients, and that the biblical witness has a diachronic dimension reflected by its history of reception. Its witness cannot be read "on the flat," but is shaped by its apostolic tradents in such a way as to preserve and instruct future generations of believers in its proper understanding in accordance with its kerygmatic content. Thus, for example, each of the four Gospels has subsequently been supplied with a title *(euangelion kata NB)*, which identifies its content as gospel. The fourfold corpus bears witness to one gospel, which is its kerygmatic content, but it is recorded by four different Evangelists. Likewise, the Pauline corpus of letters has been received, treasured, and shaped to emphasize the universality of the gospel, while at the same time preserving the particularity of each witness.

The fact that the Christian church is the vehicle by which the Word was transmitted does not mean that the Word is subordinated to church tradition. The church did not control the Word, but only responded to its creative pressures. Although this issue separated Protestants from Catholics in the sixteenth century, there is now in general an ecumenical agreement on the priority of the Word that called into existence the church. However, as Irenaeus instructed the early church, Word and apostolic tradition belong inseparably together, and the church is the divinely appointed vehicle of its transmission. Above all, it is the church's confession of the role of the Holy Spirit as the divine presence at work that continues to enliven and transform the written Word of Scripture into the living Word for today.

We turn next to the important recent methodological contribution of Francis Watson.[85] In his impressive exegetical and hermeneutical reflections he argues that Paul's interpretation of the gospel has been constructed from his careful reading of the Jewish Scriptures. It is not based on a "neutral," historical critical reconstruction of the biblical text, but is a reading according to its canonical context. Moreover, Paul's use of Scripture does not just focus on isolated texts, but encompasses the entire Pen-

---

84. Gese, quoted in Hafemann, *Paul*, p. 194.
85. Watson, *Paul and the Hermeneutics of Faith.*

tateuch as a canonical entity in a holistic reading shaped by its Jewish recipients. Still, its coherence is not a monolithic one, but filled with breaks, tensions, and gaps.

Watson objects strongly to a widely held critical consensus (A. Schweitzer, E. Käsemann) that Paul's reading of Scripture is a secondary proof-texting of a prior Christian dogmatic stance. Rather, he insists that his scriptural reading is constitutive for his entire theology. Paul is aware of a variety of alternative possibilities when interpreting a given text (Rom 4:1-2). Watson exploits this fact by continually contrasting Paul's rendering with three important contemporaneous interpretations — those of Philo, Josephus, and Jubilees — as providing strikingly different understandings of the biblical text from his.

Paul's approach is characterized by Watson as seeking out "the semantic potential of a complex and polysemic text"[86] that he finds in the anomalies and gaps within a narrative that provides him with a warrant for his Christian reading. For example, his reading of Abraham's being justified by faith, not by works of the law, stands in sharp contrast with the contemporary Jewish interpretation that emphasizes his many good works as a model of virtue according to Genesis. Watson mounts a case for Paul's interpreting Abraham in the light of the programmatic theme of Genesis 15:6 (and 12:3). Using these texts as the determinate point for his exegetical interpretation, he can subordinate Abraham's deeds of obedience to his own evangelical reading of God's promise in reckoning Abraham's faith as righteousness apart from works.

Watson sets forth a twofold hermeneutic in describing Paul's rereading of Jewish Scripture. He distinguishes between a scriptural interpretation that proceeds "deductively" on the basis of the scriptural text (e.g., Gal 3:6-9) and one that proceeds "inductively" on the basis of the actuality of Christ (e.g., Gal 3:14a). These two approaches complement each other and cannot exist in a pure form apart from one another.[87]

When Watson then interprets 2 Corinthians 3, he is concerned to demonstrate that Paul's interpretation of Moses' veil (mask), which conceals the fading glory of the old Mosaic dispensation, is not just a Christian interpretation imposed on the Exodus text from a prior dogmatic posture. Rather, Paul pursues the anomalies of the text from which to construe his exegesis.

---

86. Watson, *Paul*, p. 183.
87. Watson, *Paul*, p. 190.

He observes that the veil serves to conceal Moses' shining face when he is *not* fulfilling his role as God's mediator (Exod 34:33-35), which is the reverse of what one would expect of the mask's ritual function. Thus, Paul concludes that Moses is presented in Exodus 34 as actually concealing something he has recognized from his encounter with God in the tent, namely, the fading of the glory of the old dispensation. Paul's interpretation of this textual anomaly thus stands in striking contrast to his contemporary Jewish commentators who see the splendor of the divine manifestation of glory as permanent and eternal. The effect of Paul's interpretation is that the story of Moses has become a parable or allegory of Torah that has been replaced by the more splendid glory of the new covenant.

Watson's interpretation is impressive; indeed, he is one of the first New Testament scholars who deals seriously with the canonical shaping of the whole Scriptures as the context for Paul's reading rather than assuming the need for a prior historical critical reconstruction as its context, or seeing just metaphorical echoes from isolated biblical texts. Nevertheless, I have one significant caveat to register. Watson speaks of interpretation as a three-way conversation between the Pauline letters, the scriptural texts to which they appeal, and the non-Christian Jewish literature of the Second Temple period.[88] What I miss is another crucial partner in this interpretive conversation, namely, the voice of a historical critical, history-of-religions understanding of the text's diachronic, compositional growth. In a word, what is omitted is the continuing dialectic between a historical critical and a canonical reading of the biblical text.

One can illustrate the problem on the basis of 2 Corinthians 3. Some of the anomalies of Exodus 34 derive from its compositional growth from diverse oral traditions and literary sources. In addition, the role of a ritual mask worn by a priest with its references to a divine glory has its history-of-religions parallels from the ancient Near East that have most probably influenced the shape of the Exodus account.[89] Although I do not suggest for a moment that a historical critical reconstruction replace the final canonical context when reading the biblical text, this historical dimension cannot be disregarded as done by Watson.

88. Watson, *Paul*, p. 2.

89. See Childs, *The Book of Exodus*, pp. 607-19. It should be recalled that in Exod 34:29 the verb *qrn* is a denominative of the noun *qeren* (horn), and it was translated literally by the Vulgate as "Moses' horns" until modern comparative Semitic philology proved decisively its meaning was that of a ray symbolizing divinity.

The hermeneutical significance of my argument is that not every gap in the biblical narrative belongs a priori to its canonical shaping involving a theological intentionality. Attention to the historical critical dimension serves as a check against an exegetical overinterpretation of 2 Corinthians 3. The canonical function of the mask as a hiding of the fading glory of the old covenant remains a Christian understanding of this Old Testament text. Whether this reading derives from Paul's exploitation of a tension within the biblical text itself, or stems from his prior Christian theological understanding, is not crucial and often impossible to determine. I am more content to emphasize that there is a fusion between interpretation deductively derived from gaps in the text and interpretation inductively derived from Paul's understanding of the impact of the Christ event in rendering a transformed Old Testament as truthful biblical witness to the glory of the Spirit-filled new covenant.

c. An Exegesis of 2 Corinthians 3 Our focus is first on verses 7-12. Already in verse 6 the contrast between the two dispensations has been made. There is a new covenant in the spirit and an old order of a written code. The new one brings life, the written code death. The Corinthian passage is obviously not speaking anachronistically of a New Testament over against the Old, but of the difference between two divine economies. Paul is also not contrasting the gospel with the law *(nomos)*, and the language is very different from that of Romans and Galatians.

To further elaborate on the differences between the old order and the new, Paul first makes reference to the account in Exodus 34:29-30 of Moses coming down from Mount Sinai with the two tablets in his hands. The Exodus account explains that Moses was unaware that his face shone because he had been talking with God, and that, when Aaron and the people saw his shining skin, they were afraid to approach him. Paul's account abbreviates these features, and using the rabbinic technique of *qal waḥomer* (a fortiori), he describes the incident to compare the superiority of the splendor *(doxa)* of the new order to that of the old. The apostle reasons that if the people could not tolerate the glory of a dispensation carved in stone, how much greater then would be the glory of the Spirit. However, in his description of the glory of Moses, Paul makes a startling alteration of the Exodus account. The glory of Moses that overwhelmed the people by its splendor was characterized by him as *katargoumenēn* (v. 7).

Just how this term is to be interpreted has continued to evoke great controversy, especially during the last decades. What is the meaning of the verb? What is the significance of its form and tense? What is the effect on the larger imagery being portrayed?[90] The verb is a favorite of Paul, and all but two of its twenty-seven biblical occurrences are within the Pauline corpus. Its form is participial, but its tense is uncertain since the present has the same form as the middle and passive voices. Still, the passive is most likely, as indicated by the parallels from Paul's other usages (Rom 6:6; Gal 5:4). Barrett translates: "was in the process of abolition." Thrall offers two similar choices: "being abolished = coming to an end." Harris prefers the aorist: "was in fact faded away." Furnish argues that the present participle expresses action contemporary with the main verb ("was being annulled"), but Hays contests this point and judges that the tense should be made on the basis of the surrounding context.[91]

Hays builds much on his insistence that the verb does not mean "fade," but rather "annul," which arose out of the context of a legal process rather than being a visual image. However, because the entire imagery of the ascent of Moses is dominated by the visual ("see," "brightness," "splendor"), Hays is forced to describe the event not as a narrative but as "a retrospective theological judgment."[92] In my opinion, the terms in the context of 2 Corinthians 3 contain nuances of a legal judgment, but one reflected in a visual form such as "fading to extinction."

However, regardless of how exactly one translates the verb, the major point is that Paul is providing a Christian theological interpretation that runs in the face of Jewish interpretive tradition. Meeks has correctly noted from several midrashic passages that the radiance of Moses' face continued forever.[93] Similarly, Hofius cites a Targum in which the glory of Moses' face did not change, in spite of living 120 years, and still reflected its splendor.[94] In verse 11 Paul summarizes his comparison of the superiority of the new over the old. Not only does the new surpass the old in splendor, but the new order is permanent while the old is transient.

In the verses that follow in 2 Corinthians 3:12-18, the focus shifts to an

90. See the discussion by Hofius, "Gesetz und Evangelium," pp. 96-99.

91. Hays, *Echoes,* pp. 122-36.

92. Hays, *Echoes,* p. 134.

93. Wayne A. Meeks, "Moses as God and King," in *Religions in Antiquity: Essays in Memory of E. R. Goodenough,* ed. Jacob Neusner, Supplements to Numen, no. 14 (1970), pp. 363-64.

94. Hofius, "Gesetz und Evangelium," pp. 99-102.

interpretation of Moses' veil in Exodus 34:33-35. When Moses came down from Mount Sinai, he gave the people the commandments he had received from God. When he had finished speaking with them, he put a veil on his face. But whenever he went into the tent of meeting to speak with God, he took off the veil. Then when he came out, he again put the veil on his face, which still shone. Several points are to be noted. Nowhere in the Exodus account is an explicit reason given for the putting on of the veil, but the implication was not difficult to draw that "their eyes could not continue to stand the gleaming brightness that flashed from his countenance, like the rays of the sun."[95] However, before Paul offers his interpretation he continues the larger theme of the chapter, namely, that his apostolic ministry was very bold and open *(parrēsia)* in contrast to Moses, whose role was one of concealing something from the people.

Much controversy continues to revolve on how to understand Paul's brief explanation of the reason: so that the Israelites might not see "the end of what was being abolished" *(telos tou katargoumenou)*. Both of the key words are difficult and open to various translations. Thrall renders the phrase, "(they) should not gaze upon the end of what was in the process of effacement." Harris still prefers "the end of what was fading away." Finally, Hays understands *telos* to be the "aim or goal" (cf. Rom 10:4),[96] but this rendering of verse 13 seems unlikely. In addition, much speculation occurs in trying to elaborate further on Paul's understanding of the reason for Moses veiling his face,[97] but the various proposals seem largely speculative and peripheral to the movement of the chapter. What is, however, significant is that Paul is offering a Christian theological interpretation of the role of the veil that finds no obvious warrant in the Exodus account itself in spite of Watson's valiant attempt to discover textual support from the anomalies in the story.[98]

In the verses that follow (2 Cor 3:14-18), the full christological implications of Paul's reading of Exodus are developed. The Israelites were unable to understand because their hearts were hardened. Then Paul extends the role of the veil in a metaphorical application. "To this very day, whenever the old covenant (the law of Moses) is read, that same veil remains

---

95. Philo, *Life of Moses* 2.70 (cited by Harris, *Second Epistle,* p. 283).
96. Hays, *Echoes,* p. 136.
97. See Harris, *Second Epistle,* pp. 278-79.
98. Watson, *Paul,* pp. 291-96.

unremoved because only through Christ is the veil taken away." Then the apostle adds in verse 16: "But whenever he turns to the Lord, the veil is removed." Unfortunately, the verse contains a number of ambiguities. First, who is the subject of "turns to the Lord"? It is possible that Moses is the subject and the allusion is a citation from Exodus of his removing the veil when he left off speaking to the people and returned to the Lord. Thrall prefers this solution and sees Moses serving as a type of the Christian convert. Yet this interpretation seems to me less likely. The LXX of Exodus 34:34 reads "enter," and not "turn" as in 2 Corinthians 3:16. Moreover, the context of verse 15 is already of a metaphorical application of the veil in terms of the present ("to this day"). Therefore, I would opt for reading an indefinite subject: "whenever anyone (e.g., any Jew) turns to the Lord the veil is removed." (See Harris for further support of this reading.)

However, now an even more difficult interpretive problem arises in verses 16 and 17. Who is meant by "the Lord"? Is it Christ or is it God, who has manifested himself as YHWH in the Jewish Scriptures? Both Windisch and Bultmann argue that this is a typical conversion formula of the New Testament (Acts 9:35; 11:21; 14:15; 1 Thess 1:9). In contrast, initial credit for mounting a strong case that the referent in verses 16 and 17 is God (YHWH) redounds to J. D. G. Dunn,[99] who presents several arguments for this reading. First, when the noun *kyrios* appears without the article (anarthrous) in Pauline usage, YHWH is meant, whereas when *kyrios* refers to Jesus Christ, it appears with the article. Second, the article in verse 17 is anaphoric (repetitive), referring back to verse 16. "Now this 'Lord' is the Spirit, and where the Spirit of the Lord is, there is freedom." Third, the context of these verses continues to be an interpretation of the Exodus text. Of course, there is a larger hermeneutical issue at stake. If the text is read in terms of YHWH, it signifies that when the veil of the old covenant is removed through Christ (v. 14) by turning to YHWH through his Spirit, then there is freedom. This freedom is unqualified for Paul. The implication shortly to be pursued is that there is now the possibility of a Spirit-filled reading of Moses without the veil that now covers the Jewish Scriptures when read apart from the Spirit.

In verse 18 Paul expands his thought to include all Christian believers ("we all"). Formerly, only Moses could glimpse God's glory, but now all

---

99. James D. G. Dunn, "2 Corinthians III.7 — 'the Lord Is the Spirit,'" *Journal of Theological Studies*, n.s., 21 (1970): 309-20.

Christians are given unveiled access to the Lord's presence. Verse 18 serves to climax Paul's argument in respect to the new covenant in chapter 3. The glory of the Lord is God's glory as manifested in the image of Jesus Christ. In the history of interpretation, verse 17 has engendered some confusion when it is read in terms of a fully developed trinitarian theology. Such an approach fails to reckon with the particularity of Paul's argument in 2 Corinthians 3, which focuses on the effect of the divine Spirit, who is not distinct from Christ, in bringing to an end the old covenant with its obscuring veil and providing freedom within a new spiritual order for all to grow into the image of Christ, which is God's glory. However, I would fully agree with C. Kavin Rowe,[100] that there is a "trinitarian pressure" in these verses not to be overlooked.

5. Richard Hays and Ernst Käsemann on 2 Corinthians 3

Two further topics are closely related to the subject of the Spirit in an interpretation of 2 Corinthians 3. The first addresses the issues raised by Richard Hays in his book *Echoes of Scripture in the Letters of Paul,*[101] which we touched on briefly in a prior chapter. In chapter 4 of his book he offers a detailed analysis of 2 Corinthians 3. He does not argue that the chapter provides a specific hermeneutic for interpreting the new covenant, but rather that Paul offers a strategy with profound hermeneutical implications for today's church. The ministry of the new covenant is not of the "script," which is his translation of *gramma* (letter), but of the Spirit. It is a ministry that is not centered on texts, but on the Spirit-empowered transformation of the human community (p. 130). Although Hays admits that Paul's rejection of the letter *(gramma)* does not mean a rejection of the *graphē* (written Scripture) (p. 251), in actual practice he does not pursue this distinction in formulating his hermeneutic.[102]

---

100. C. Kavin Rowe, "Biblical Pressure and Trinitarian Hermeneutics," *Pro Ecclesia* 11 (2002): 295-312.

101. Hays, *Echoes,* pp. 122-92. Page references to this work are placed in the text during this discussion.

102. For the importance of the distinction, see Gottlob Schrenk, "graphō," in *Theological Dictionary of the New Testament,* vol. 1 (1964), pp. 742-73; E. Kamlah, "Buchstabe und Geist," *Evangelische Theologie* 14 (1954): 276-82; Dietrich-Alex Koch, *Die Schrift als Zeuge des Evangeliums* (Tübingen: Mohr Siebeck, 1986).

Rather, his focus is on the stark contrast between *gramma* and *pneuma*. Where the Spirit reigns, there is freedom of interpretation. The Christian is no longer fettered by the letter. In place of the Mosaic covenant engraved in stone, through the Spirit God writes his will on the fleshly hearts of believers according to Jeremiah 31:33 and Ezekiel 36:26. In the eschatological community of the new covenant, texts will no longer be needful, but Scripture will be subsumed into the life of the community, an embodiment of the Word (p. 129). "Revelation occurs not primarily in the sacred text, but in the transformed community of readers" (p. 144). Under the guidance of the Spirit, "the community of the church becomes the place where the meaning of Israel's Scripture is enfleshed" (p. 149). Later on, Hays further argues that Paul's "ecclesiological hermeneutic" should be normative for the modern Christian church as well. Since I have pursued this issue in an earlier chapter, I shall now concentrate on other aspects of Hays's theory.

A major criticism of Hays's hermeneutic is that, although his initial emphasis falls on the freedom of the Spirit in freeing the Christian from reading Scripture according to the slavery of the *gramma* (its letter), as the argument progresses a Spirit-filled reading is one also freed from the *graphē*. The transformed community is not restricted by concerns over Scripture's "original intention," but is solely guided by the immediate promptings of the Spirit. Scripture is now construed metaphorically as a giant tapestry of latent promises that are now recovered by interpretive strategies. "True interpretation depends neither on historical inquiry nor erudite literary analysis, but on attentiveness to the promptings of the Spirit" (pp. 130, 156).

Hays calls it a paradox that Paul's careful reading of the sacred biblical text (Exod 34) reveals that revelation occurs not primarily in the sacred text, but in the transformed community of readers (p. 144). Our reading of 2 Corinthians 3 points precisely in the opposite direction. "When one turns to the Lord," then the veil of the *gramma* (letter) is lifted, and the Scriptures *(graphē)* can be read without an obscuring veil. In Romans 15:4 Paul makes this same point. "Whatever was written in former days [in the Old Testament], was written for our instruction, that by the steadfastness and encouragement of the Scripture we might have hope." The Christian church is transformed through a Spirit-filled reading of its Scriptures. The role of the written Word is not replaced by an "embodied community," but continues to provide for continual guidance through the work of the Spirit of the church of Jesus Christ.

The second issue to be addressed is the essay of Ernst Käsemann, "The Spirit and the Letter."[103] Not only does the essay provide an exegesis of 2 Corinthians 3, but no discussion of the role of the Spirit in Paul would be complete without attention being paid to this brilliant and classic essay. Herein he mounts his thesis that, in spite of the seemingly narrow textual basis provided by Romans 2:27-29, 7:6, 10:4, and 2 Corinthians 3:6, Paul sets forth a theological hermeneutic in these verses that provides the key to his whole approach to justification by faith in terms of the antithesis between the Spirit and the law.

For Paul the letter of Scripture is the Mosaic Torah in its written documentation. The antithesis between the letter and the Spirit has nothing to do with an inner and outer existence, but rather concerns two spheres of power. The point coincides with that of the old and new covenants and their universal spheres of influence. The stone tablets of the law have been replaced through the action of the divine Spirit. The church is the eschatological charter that replaces the Mosaic Torah. The two cosmic forces are locked in a struggle between life and death. The letter kills because it forces generic man into the service of his own righteousness whereas the Spirit *(pneuma)* is the power that sets the human in the presence of the exalted Lord, into a new eschatological aeon, freeing him from striving after his own righteousness. Käsemann finds a scriptural warrant for the radical discontinuity in 2 Corinthians 3. Here one sees the two possibilities diverging, either to see the Old Testament under the veil of the Torah in its demand for good works, or to understand the Old Testament in the light of the lifting of that veil through Christ. The doctrine of justification is the criterion that decides between Spirit and letter, both of which can be derived from Scripture.

As a test case to support this thesis, Käsemann appeals to Romans 10:4. Two quotations, from Leviticus 18:5 and Deuteronomy 30:11-14, are juxtaposed. According to Leviticus 18:5, the righteousness of the law demands works and promises eternal life for those performing these works. This represents the letter. Conversely, Deuteronomy 30:11-14, citing from the same Moses, makes exactly the opposite affirmation. The righteousness of faith says: "The Word is near you on your lips and in your heart, that is, the word of faith which we preach."

---

103. Ernst Käsemann, "The Spirit and the Letter," in *Perspectives on Paul* (London: SCM, 1971), pp. 158-66. See also Stephen Westerholm, "Letter and Spirit: The Foundation of Pauline Ethics," *New Testament Studies* 30 (1984): 229-48.

Käsemann then draws his hermeneutical conclusion. The dividing line between letter and Spirit runs through Scripture. Paul plays off Scripture against Scripture in "a canon within the canon." Thus, the letter and Spirit remain in a dialectical tension, and only the doctrine of justification in faith of the ungodly provides the key for distinguishing the true voice of the gospel within the Scriptures. It is the criterion for identifying the "near" Word.

Obviously the challenge mounted by Käsemann is too profound and important to address in any brief response. We shall return to the interpretation of Romans 10:4 in a later chapter. However, in the light of our understanding of 2 Corinthians 3, I would again make the case that the dialectic between letter and Spirit is not one caused by Scripture's ambivalent witness of both supporting and then denying the function of the law. Rather, as we sought to demonstrate in chapter 4.II, the law of Moses remains for Paul good and holy, but because of human sin has been misconstrued as "letter," causing Israel to stumble. Thus the law functions on both sides of the great divide between letter and Spirit. When Israel turns to the Lord, who is Spirit, then the veil covering the reading of Scripture is removed and the law becomes the goal reaching out through Christ toward the eschatological redemption of God's entire cosmos.

In sum, it is obvious that Käsemann's view of the Spirit and Scripture has profound implications for his understanding of the role of the Christian canon. These he has spelled out in boldest detail in his famous article directed to the assembly of the World Council in 1950 concerning the canon and the unity of the church.[104] Whether or not one agrees with him, his position remains a powerful challenge to every Christian community that does not see Spirit and canon as opposing forces locked in a struggle for authentic Christian identity.

IV. Community Gifts and Worship

In the previous chapter the close link in the Pauline letters between the Spirit and spiritual gifts has been pointed out (1 Cor 1:7; 2:10-15; 12:1-3; Eph

104. Ernst Käsemann, "The Canon of the New Testament and the Unity of the Church," in *Essays on New Testament Themes* (London: SCM, 1968), pp. 95-107. See also Käsemann's essay "Paul and Early Catholicism," in *New Testament Questions of Today* (Philadelphia: Fortress, 1969), pp. 236-51.

4:11-16). Nevertheless, largely for strategic purposes, there are several reasons for treating the subject of "spiritual gifts" *(pneumatika)* in a chapter initially apart from that of Spirit.

First, the importance and sheer complexity of the subject matter place several demands on the interpreter for a clarity of presentation, which task is simplified if the focus is at first primarily on the gifts of the Spirit. Of course, in the end the organic unity of the Spirit and its gifts (a subject pursued in an excellent essay by Heinz Schürmann)[105] will have to be addressed.

Second, the overlap between Romans 12 and 1 Corinthians 12–14 provides a good example by which to test our thesis of the canonical shaping of the Pauline corpus that affects how the parallel texts are to be interpreted.

Third, the issue of spiritual gifts has been a central factor in the larger question of the nature and order of the Christian community. Specifically, what is the relation of the church as a charismatic community to the emergence of particular "offices" *(Ämter)?* The different evaluations of the charismatic, Spirit-led Christian communities and a hierarchical structure of the church have long divided Protestants and Catholics. Is the move from charismatic communities to one with permanent offices of specially endowed persons to be judged negatively as a betrayal of Paul? (The pejorative term usually used is *Frühkatholizismus* = early Catholicism.) Or is there a legitimate theological coherence between the apostolic and the postapostolic church? In this debate the evaluation of the function of the Pastoral Epistles is crucial.

We analyze 1 Corinthians 12–14 before turning to Romans 12.

1. 1 Corinthians 12–14

A wide modern consensus has emerged concerning the literary unity of chapters 12–14. Of course, the topic of spiritual gifts was already introduced in 1:4-9, and many of the themes were further developed in 8:1–11:1.

---

105. Heinz Schürmann, "Die geistlichen Gnadengaben in den paulinischen Gemeinde," in *Ursprung und Gestalt* (Düsseldorf: Patmos, 1976), pp. 236-67; reprinted in *Das kirchliche Amt im Neuen Testament*, ed. Karl Kertelge (Darmstadt: Wissenschaftliche Buchgesellschaft, 1977), pp. 362-412. See also the basic essay by Ernst Käsemann, "Ministry and Community in the New Testament," in *Essays on New Testament Themes*, pp. 63-94.

Scholars continue to debate whether chapter 13, a poetic encomium to love, was first composed apart from the letter to the Corinthians, but the issue is hardly to be definitively settled, and is actually of minor hermeneutical significance. The chapter has a clear beginning and ending, and is organically linked in content with chapters 12 and 14. The beauty of its poetic style only adds to its crucial function within the letter. Chapter 12 introduces the topic of spiritual gifts, stressing the variety of gifts that all stem from the one God who inspired them. Paul then employs the imagery of the body, first as a common Hellenistic metaphor to illustrate the unity of its various members within the one body, each having need of one another. The metaphor is then applied to the body of Christ and the individual apportionments of different gifts. Next, chapter 13, introduced in 12:31b, sets forth the quintessential attribute of the Christian life that governs all the gifts of the Spirit. Then finally in chapter 14, after having established the theological groundwork, Paul addresses in great detail the problem of the Corinthian worship arising from the failure to grasp the nature, function, and role of the gifts of the Spirit, specifically the proper role for the speaking in tongues (glossolalia).

The first three verses of chapter 12 establish Paul's basic christological stance toward spiritual gifts. The subject matter is introduced with the recurrent formula characteristic of his earlier responses to a series of questions posed by members of the Corinthian congregation: "Now concerning . . ." *(peri de)*. However, it is uncertain whether the subject of spiritual gifts (the plural of *pneumatikon* can be read as either spiritual things or persons) was perceived as a problem by some Corinthians, or was one demanding correction by Paul. The general tone the apostle uses to attack the various parties clearly is an attempt to correct abuses arising from feelings of spiritual superiority, pride, and self-centered behavior that result in disorder and chaos within the worship services. In these initial verses Paul sets forth the christological criterion from which he establishes the norm for proper use of the gifts of the Spirit. He does it in a strikingly bold fashion. All Christians are charismatic. The Spirit alone empowers the confession that Jesus is Lord.

Next he focuses his attention on the variety of spiritual gifts. Significantly, he does not continue to use the term *pneumatikon*, but switches to speak of *charismata*. The semantic difference is between using a history-of-religions category marking the widespread phenomena of ecstatic and supernatural manifestations common to the Hellenistic world, and treating the subject from a theological perspective. Paul does not denigrate this phenomenon, but immediately seeks to bring it directly in relation to the inspiration of God in endowing spiritual gifts for the common good of the church.

He lists a variety of charismatic gifts without any particular order. One can utter wisdom through the Spirit, while another can offer rational utterances of knowledge. One can work miracles, another can prophesy, and another can speak in tongues. The emphasis falls on the variety, each inspired by the same Spirit, and each gift is individually apportioned. The stress on the variety is then carefully balanced by an appeal to the metaphor of the human body. All members of the body, although many, constitute a whole. Just so in Christ. Through baptism Christians enter into the one body of Christ. In verse 14 Paul returns to the analogy of the human body, stressing the special function of the various parts, with one not being superior to another. The mention of the membership in the body of Christ shows that the metaphor has taken on an ontological dimension that receives much more development in his later letters (e.g., Ephesians). The summary of the various types of spiritual gifts reflects now a particular order of importance. Paul speaks of first apostles, second prophets, third teachers, followed by other gifts including speaking in tongues. The stress falls on God's purposeful intent in apportioning these various offices with charismatic gifts. None can claim an exclusive role within the community through an appeal to special spiritual powers. In the background one can hear the note of competitive and rival claims within a disruptive worshiping community.

Suddenly Paul changes his tack and urges the Corinthians earnestly to pursue a more excellent way. It is the path of love from which all the competing gifts can be measured. The many allusions to both chapters 12 and 14 strongly suggest that the chapter relates immediately to Paul's major concern in reforming the role of spiritual gifts in the community's worship. Although there is no explicit reference to God's love in Christ in chapter 13, the christological framework has already been securely set in 12:1-3.

Paul begins his description of the Christian community by emphasizing the meaningless show of spiritual religiosity. His example of false piety picks up notes that clearly lay at the heart of the Corinthian church's misuse of its spiritual gifts: pride in speaking the language of angels, use of prophetic powers and understanding of divine mysteries, and willingness to accept the honor of martyrdom. Then Paul turns to characterize the behavior of love: patient, kind, selfless. Love is not self-inflated, but generous to others and long-suffering. It does not rejoice in the pain of others, but is joyful in celebrating truth. It never tires or loses faith and its hope is never exhausted. These are exactly the qualities missing within the Corinthian community. Although never stated in chapter 13, the Christian reader of the Gospels could not help from seeing in the life of Jesus the complete personification of Paul's description of true love reflected in the larger canonical reverberations.

After a comprehensive review of modern analogies of glossolalia, Anthony Thiselton concludes that Paul used terminology available to him for pursuing the depths of the human self that may today be described in the more developed language of modern psychology.[106] He cites with approval particularly the writings of Gerd Theissen and Krister Stendahl, who concluded that glossolalia is largely the unconscious language capable of probing the dimensions of the subconscious. Several implications can be drawn from this modern study of glossolalia that parallel some of our earlier hermeneutical conclusions.

The phenomenon of glossolalia mentioned by Paul can be studied with the critical tools of modern scientific analysis. Much like our earlier study of Hellenistic Greek language and literary conventions, there is an overlap between secular analysis and its application within the biblical witness. The two accesses to the phenomenon cannot be simply identified, nor can they be fully separated. Thus, for example, the crisis produced in Corinth by the practice of glossolalia can be better understood by applying Dale Martin's sociological analysis of the status symbolism attributed to the practice.[107]

However, the task of biblical exegesis turns on pursuing the theological function that Paul assigns to the speaking in tongues as a gift of the Spirit. Clearly there are sociological and psychological forces at work unknown to Paul. These factors can at times bring the historical crisis in Corinth into sharper focus, such as the threat of arrogance and superiority exercised by some, but they cannot replace or overshadow Paul's theological attempt to reshape the phenomenon to function as a genuine gift of the Spirit for the upbuilding of the community. Nor can sociological categories substitute for Paul's interpretation of the phenomenon as "sighs too

106. Thiselton, *The First Epistle*, p. 985; see also the discussion by Wolfgang Schrage, *Der Erste Brief an die Korinther*, 3 vols. (Zürich: Neukirchener Verlag; Düsseldorf: Benzinger, 1999-).

107. Dale Martin, "Tongues of Angels and Other Status Indicators," *Journal of the American Academy of Religion* 59 (1991): 547-89.

deep for words" (Rom 8:26) and of the "whole creation groaning in travail" for the coming new eschaton (8:23).

What is particularly significant in chapter 14 is Paul's acceptance of glossolalia as a genuine gift of the Spirit, but one whose divine purpose has been misunderstood and abused by some members of the Corinthian community. The apostle first contrasts the function of prophecy with that of speaking in tongues. This form has the role of proclaiming the Word of God to the outside world in clear and unmistakable language. In contrast, like prayer, the speaking in tongues is directed to God and for the task of evangelism. Since love is the criterion by which all the gifts of the Spirit are measured, the gift of tongues must function for the building up of the community. Love is a concern for the unity and welfare of the church. It offers a check on all forms of personal gratification and restricts speaking in tongues from the public realm. Above all, love functions to engender joy and edification, for "God is not a God of confusion, but of peace" (1 Cor 14:33).

2. Romans 12:1-21

Our next exegetical task is to turn to Romans 12, where again Paul sets forth his understanding of the gifts of the Spirit.

Romans 12:1-21 is set within a larger hortatory context that extends to 15:13. Paul's letter marks a shift in focus from the largely doctrinal arguments of chapters 1–11 to one of practical ethical application. This division is often found in the apostle's letters (see Galatians, Ephesians, 1 Thessalonians). That a link between the earlier sections is intentional is indicated by the use of the Greek adverb "therefore" *(oun)*. This move to the moral and practical exhortation serves to make concrete the manner of life demanded of Christians that results from God's act of rectifying the ungodly (4:5).

Paul begins by appealing to his readers from his divinely appointed role as an apostle ("by the grace given me") to present their whole selves as a "living sacrifice" in conformity to a worthy spiritual worship. This complete surrender to God is described as loving since it marks the end of an older life and the transformation in an ongoing daily practice of obedient response. His language of the sharp break from the evil age of the past, and the beginning of a new creation of the future, reflects the radicality of Paul's apocalyptical perspective, which is here not spelled out as in Galatians but is rather assumed as understood. The goal of the new life in the Spirit is toward the goal of discerning *(dokimazō)* what is "the good, acceptable, and perfect will of God." The purpose of God for his church is not acquired from a list of static rules, nor is it attained by means of legal casuistry. Rather, the Christian is called upon to be zealous in searching out the ever new purpose of God by testing and proving what is the good and perfect response. In this new life there is no hiatus between the sacred and the profane, but the obedient life inspired by the Spirit encompasses them both.

In verses 3-8 the proper use of the spiritual gifts (the *charismata*) is set forth without any closely structured order. Paul begins by establishing the proper mind-set. Christians are not to think too highly of themselves, but in a sober act of sensible reflection are to recognize the boundaries of the gifts assigned to each individual. Again Paul appeals to the metaphor of the body. There are many members, but the function of each is not the same. Then Paul moves beyond the metaphor to apply the imagery to the body of Christ, and thus integrally to members related to one another. The various gifts of the Spirit are listed: prophecy, service, teaching, without any ranking implied in the order. The emphasis falls on the manner by which the gifts are employed: literally, joyfully, enthusiastically.

In verse 9 love for one another is singled out. It is the means of holding to the good. Then further qualities of the new life of the Spirit are quickly enumerated: never grow weary in well-doing, but continue to "glow" in service to others. The litany of faithful conduct is continued with virtues long recognized in the classical world as worthy of behavior: patience, modesty, and prudence.

Finally, in verses 14-21, lest it be thought that the right use of the divine gifts of the Spirit be confined only to those within the household of faith, Paul expands the range beyond those of the community of faith. Live in harmony with one another. Never repay one evil by another. Never avenge yourself, but leave such matters with confidence to God. Instead, your task is to feed and give drink to those in need, and thus to overcome the evil of others by your acts of kindness.

In the chapter that follows, Paul moves away from the explicit reference to the gifts of the Spirit and expands the theme of the Christian's relationship to those outside the faith with specific attention to the Christian's duty to the governing authorities. However, in 13:8-10 the apostle offers a summary of his description of the new life by focusing on love as the foundation of all Christian conduct. By returning to the theme of fulfilling the law through love, Paul joins again the major topics of the earlier chapters of Romans (1–11) with their appropriation in the daily life of the church in chapter 12.

3. Canonical Shaping of Romans 12 and 1 Corinthians 12

a. The context of 1 Corinthians 12 focuses on specific, highly contingent problems within the Corinthian community that have arisen from the abuse of spiritual gifts with attitudes of arrogance and superiority, causing dissension and fracturing the life of the church. In contrast, Romans 12, which is literarily linked with a larger unit (chapters 12–15), functions in outlining a practical application of the earlier doctrinal sections of Romans 1–11. As we discussed earlier, many commentators have sought to relate Romans 12 to specific contingent problems within the Roman church. We have rejected this move, which not only rests on speculative reconstructions, but also fails to reckon with the canonical function of Romans within the larger corpus. In chapter 12 Paul reflects on his past crises from his earlier missionary mission to offer his mature, and comprehensive, summary of his entire ministry. Whether or not Romans should be classified as a last will and testament (so Bornkamm), the letter has been assigned a particular function within the corpus. It is our present task to pursue this function initially in relating Romans 12 to 1 Corinthians 12–14. Later in this chapter we shall include parallel chapters from Ephesians 4 in relation to the gifts of the Spirit.

b. First, it is important to note that many similar themes are shared by both books. Paul is not offering random suggestions, but instructions and admonitions in both chapters in a conscious exercise of his apostolic office (1 Cor 14:37; Rom 12:1-3). A christological focus is implicit. Only because of the Spirit of God at work can the Christian confession be made: Jesus is Lord (1 Cor 12:3). Moreover, in both letters the beginnings of a triadic formulation of the identity of God can be observed (1 Cor 12:4-11; Rom 8:9-11).

Then again, the nature of the church's charismatic gifts is outlined. Each individual is allotted a special gift to be used according to its measure, not toward self-interests, but for the building up of the community in a unity, like to the diversity of functions within a human body. Then in both chapters the quality of the Spirit-filled life is described. It is characterized by patience, hospitality, zeal. Various offices are mentioned, but without any special ranking or established hierarchy. Rather, the community as a whole is deemed charismatic, and is guided by the Spirit in obedient conduct. In both chapters love is the criterion by which moral action is measured, which is described in greatest detail in 1 Corinthians 13, but also paralleled in Romans 13:8-10.

Finally, in both chapters an eschatological hope is expressed. 1 Corinthians 13:8-13 contrasts the provisionary character of most gifts of the Spirit with the permanence of love, being the greatest of all. Romans 12:2 speaks of the transformation of the Christian life from the old age of the past to a new mind-set, indeed a new creation. In Romans 8 the fuller dimension of the eschatological hope of the entire cosmos has been portrayed with the church as the firstfruits of the Spirit groaning for its redemption, and the admonition given to keep alert, for "the night is nearly over; the day is almost here."

c. However, the two chapters also have important differences. 1 Corinthians 12–14 deals with a series of topics introduced by the phrase "now concerning . . . ," which accords with the pattern of Paul's responses established earlier in his letter (7:1; 8:1). His following directives address specific problems arising from the abuse of spiritual gifts, especially the effect of the gift of tongues as a cause for the disruption of the church's worship. In Corinthians Paul does not call into question the legitimacy of these special manifestations of the Spirit, but seeks to reorder them for the upbuilding of the church, concluding with the admonition that all be done "decently and in order."

In contrast, Romans 12 offers initially a theological reflection on the "spiritual worship" of the church. The community is not to conform to the ways of the old age, but be transformed. Then he presents a profound theological formulation of the role of the spiritual gifts, touching on the imagery of the one body in Christ, a theme later greatly expanded in Ephesians 4. It is significant that his reflection on the spiritual gifts in Romans does not arise out of abuses, but is encompassed within the theological framework of a transformed existence. Paul does not mention the topic of tongues, but his description of the expression of Christian love in terms of "being aglow on fire" with the Spirit (v. 11) could well be a theological affirmation of "high-voltage religion" (Stendahl's expression).[108]

---

108. Krister Stendahl, "Glossolalia — the New Testament Evidence," in *Paul among Jews and Gentiles* (Philadelphia: Fortress, 1976), pp. 109-24.

Another difference between the two chapters turns on the issue of how one ascertains the will of God. In Corinthians Paul points out the need of developing maturity of judgment. One moves also in the faith from being a child to being an adult (13:11). However, largely Paul offers rational arguments for distinguishing between the role of prophecy and that of speaking in tongues. What would a stranger think if he encountered an incomprehensible babble? Thus, the apostle offers practical advice on letting each person speak in turn, but then adding an interpretation. In contrast, in Romans 12 Paul probes the crucial issue of perceiving the true will of God by employing the verb "discern" *(dokimazō)*. One is to test the Spirit to determine what is the good, acceptable, and perfect divine intention. Paul's approach is highly theological and reckons with a struggle of faith rather than a rigid set of ethical rules. The proper attitudes of the Spirit-filled life are inseparable from the concrete acts of contributing to the needs of the poor and the practice of hospitality to all.

Finally, although 1 Corinthians 14 is well aware of the presence of strangers and of outsiders in their midst, the theme of harmony with others and restraint against those who have acted with evil deeds against the Christian is paramount. Evil is not to be repaid with evil, but rather overcome with good. Then in Romans the apostle addresses the Christian's relationship to the governing authorities and the duties to the state. The passage is concluded with an appeal to love, which is the means of fulfilling the demands of the law.

If one now seeks to characterize the effect of reading 1 Corinthians 12 and Romans 12 within the canonical structure of the Pauline corpus, several hermeneutical insights emerge that influence the exegetical task of reading Scripture. It is not the case that the function of Romans is simply to generalize or abstract the particulars of 1 Corinthians. Romans continues to speak of the gifts of the Spirit with a concrete particularity, but there is a change. Romans focuses no longer on the specific historical crises facing the church at Corinth. Now the addressee is the Christian church at large. The theological interpretation of Paul now moves into a deeper plane of reflection on the gifts of the Spirit in the church's spiritual worship. This reflection no longer anchors the subject to the abuses within one historical context, but probes more deeply into the heart of the divine reality being manifested in the life of the people of God.

In one sense the move is from the contingency in 1 Corinthians to the theological coherence in Romans. Yet the dialectic is not always in this direction. The particularity and theological depth of 1 Corinthians 13 continue to inform the charismatic community of faith depicted in Romans. Moreover, for the subsequent reader of the Pauline corpus, the hermeneutical guide for the appropriation of Paul's gospel to the new and ever-changing crises within the postapostolic church derives from both the coherence of Romans and the particular contingencies of 1 Corinthians. Romans does not replace 1 Corinthians, but continues to demonstrate fresh theological options in applying the divine words of Scripture from the past into a living Word for the future. The context from which the ancient biblical word is applied to the present is not reconfigured by introducing external values in order to "update" the ethical sensitivity so as to match the new demands of modernity (contra Frances Young).[109] Rather, the Christian church struggles to discern the living will of God by a continual, and prayerful, wrestling with all of Scripture in the confidence that the Holy Spirit, which is the Spirit of the resurrected Christ, will reveal in God's time a fresh and faithful application of the gospel suited to the challenges of a changing world.

4. Ephesians 4:7-16

It has long been obvious that there can be no serious discussion of the gifts of the Spirit without close attention to the letter to the Ephesians, and particularly to 4:7-16.[110] This passage is set in a context that focuses on the unity of the Spirit. "There is one body and one Spirit" (v. 4), indeed, "one Lord, one faith, one baptism, one God and Father of us all" (vv. 5-6). Then on the basis of this unity, the author turns to the subject of divine grace being given to "each of us." The shift to the plural is noticeable when speaking of the measure of Christ's gifts to us (v. 7). The close parallels with 1 Corinthians 12:27-31 and Romans 12:6-8 indicate that the subject is not new to the Pauline corpus. However, equally significant is that the imagery of the one body and one Spirit in Ephesians reflects a much more developed theology of the church as the body of Christ in which all things are held together. In

109. Frances Young, "The Pastoral Epistles and the Ethics of Reading," *Journal for the Study of the New Testament* 45 (1992): 105-20.
110. See the bibliography on Eph 4:7-16 in Rudolf Schnackenburg, *Ephesians* (Edinburgh: T. & T. Clark, 1991), pp. 169-70; also the extensive literature in Helmut Merklein, *Das kirchliche Amt nach dem Epheserbrief* (Munich: Kösel-Verlag, 1973).

Christ the fullness of God dwells bodily and the church is knit together and encouraged in its growth, holding fast to its head (Col. 2:19).

What is particularly important in Ephesians 4 is the subtle shift in the accentuation of the theme of gifts. In contrast to the charismatic lists in 1 Corinthians and Romans, which focus on the diversity of the manifold gifts, in Ephesians the emphasis falls on the goals of all divine gifts toward the building up of the one body of Christ in order to attain the unity of the faith (4:13), on putting off the old nature, and on living in harmony as the one body of Christ. Still, it is significant that the bestowal of divine gifts as the special endowment of those equipped for upbuilding the church is not mentioned.

However, in any attempt to analyze the unique contribution of the author of Ephesians, one must guard against becoming trapped in the heated controversies over chapter 4, which long have divided Protestant and Catholic interpreters. Briefly stated, Heinrich Schlier first threw down the gauntlet by suggesting that the gift bearers announced in verse 7 and listed in verse 11 (apostles, prophets, evangelists, pastors, and teachers) held special ecclesial offices *(Ämter)* equipped toward the specific service of caring for the church in an official capacity.[111] Schlier's position was further sustained and expanded in the dissertation of Helmut Merklein.[112] He argued that there were several exegetical reasons for holding this interpretation.

First, the major thrust of Ephesians shows a consistent and profound development in the nature of the church. The church is no longer a local congregation of believers, but has been theologically universalized and given a cosmological dimension (2:6). Second, the imagery of Christ's body in 1 Corinthians 12 as a metaphor to illustrate a unity in its diversity has been transformed into the ontological reality of the church as Christ's body into which the church is incorporated. Third, the church has a history that is grounded on the foundation of earlier apostles and pneumatic prophets, thus linking it to a covenant with Israel. Fourth, Paul the apostle has received the revelation of the divine plan for the church, the mystery realized in Jesus Christ to unite Jew and Gentile within the one household of God with Christ as its chief cornerstone. It is in the light of this massive expansion of ecclesiastical reflection that Schlier and Merklein argued that the charismatic gifts of the early church, described by Paul in his undis-

---

111. Heinrich Schlier, *Der Brief an die Epheser* (Düsseldorf: Patmos, 1957), pp. 177-209.
112. Merklein, *Das kirchliche Amt*, pp. 57-117.

puted letters, have given way to a permanent structure suited to the post-Pauline era. Moreover, Merklein has correctly insisted that the charismatic gifts and the permanent offices should not be set in opposition to one another. The latter is an expansion of the former, not its replacement.

However, in spite of the important theological reasons advanced by Schlier and Merklein, the exegetical issues of the interpretation of Ephesians 4:7-16 have not been fully settled. Indeed, in his ecumenical commentary on Ephesians (Evangelisch-katholischer Kommentar), Rudolf Schnackenburg[113] allowed his Protestant partner, Eduard Schweizer, to outline the traditional Protestant objections to this interpretation of Ephesians 4 as a warrant for permanent ecclesiastical offices. Accordingly, Schweizer questions whether special, permanent offices can be distinguished from ministries given to each of the believers, and argues that no one form of institutional offices has been designated. However, even more astonishing is that Schnackenburg, the teacher of Merklein, announced in his Ephesians commentary that he no longer supported Merklein's interpretation of 4:7-16.[114] For strictly literary reasons, he would now agree that the transmission of the gift in verse 7 relates to the totality of the faithful believers rather than being a special group who held offices. Of course, Schnackenburg still supported Merklein's larger theological arguments for a newly expanded reflection on the nature and function of the church in a post-Pauline setting.

Perhaps the wisest word toward resolving the exegetical impasse respecting the interpretation of Ephesians 4:7-16 has been expressed by Nils Dahl.[115] He notes that the exegetical problem lies in the fact that the measure of spiritual gifts is given to each individual in 4:7, 16 while in verse 11 the gifts are identified with special leaders and preachers. Both themes have been joined, and the unique gifts for the building of the body of Christ seen with all its individual parts (4:11, 16). The exegetical difficulty lies in the fact that for the author of Ephesians the issue whether the leaders are charismatic or permanent ecclesiastical office bearers seems irrelevant to his major point, and thus remains unresolvable.

There is general agreement, however, that the portrayal of the church and Paul's apostolic role has taken on a profound transfiguration. The cru-

---

113. Schnackenburg, *Ephesians*, pp. 191-92.

114. Schnackenburg, *Ephesians*, p. 175.

115. Nils A. Dahl, *Studies in Ephesians*, ed. David Hellholm et al. (Tübingen: Mohr Siebeck, 2000), pp. 70-72.

cial theological issue turns on how the modern interpreter evaluates this development in the post-Pauline period. Dahl avoids the theological issue by resorting to a history-of-religions description of how the profile of Paul in Colossians and Ephesians was reached. He argues that there emerged two different trajectories. The one led toward the second-century Catholic church, to the monarchical episcopate of Ignatius and the succession of bishops of Irenaeus. The other developed into a pneumatic and gnostic understanding of the church and the female *syzygos* of the heavenly *anthropos*.[116]

While Dahl's historical description of two different ways of receiving the Pauline portrait of Ephesians may be correct, in my opinion Dahl has not addressed the theological problem with his reading. Above all, he has not pursued the canonical issue of how the Christian church received and appropriated Ephesians into the Pauline corpus of the New Testament. In this regard, the exegetical and hermeneutical shaping of both Colossians and Ephesians was effected, according to Merklein,[117] by the process of a conscious "Paulinization" *(Paulinisierung)* of his material. In a word, there is a trajectory within both letters that demonstrates the concern, not simply to harmonize the earlier charismatic Paul with a later institutional form, but rather in bringing the fresh ecclesiastical shaping of the faith in the post-Pauline era into conformity with the larger witness of the apostle, which was communicated in both its written and oral forms.

If this is the case, then the central theological issue remains to be addressed. Is the growing institutionalizing of the church through permanent office bearers to be understood only as a historical expediency, evoked by the crises of the new era of the church's history, or are there theological warrants for its growing institutional form that lay claim to a doctrinal norm? Another way to pose this question is to raise the issue of the canonical function of Ephesians within the Pauline corpus.

Some indications of an answer had already been broached when the relation between Colossians and Ephesians was touched upon. In spite of the difficulty of being able to determine with precision whether the dependency is literary, oral, or more probably both, the effect however is quite clear. Ephesians has eliminated most of the highly particularized historical contingencies of Colossians and resorted to a highly universalized

---

116. Dahl, *Studies in Ephesians,* p. 462.
117. Merklein, "Paulinische Theologie," pp. 25-69.

theological context addressed to the church at large. The vocabulary of Hellenistic philosophy has been demythologized and replaced with a far more explicit christological formulation. But above all, the ecclesiastical reflection already begun in Colossians has been greatly expanded, particularly the relation to the nature of God's mystery in joining together Jew and Gentile within the household of God. Canonically speaking, the relation between Colossians and Ephesians has a rough parallel to that between Galatians and Romans.

It is remarkable to see in Nils Dahl's last two essays, published posthumously in the final collection of his works,[118] that he is frustrated by his inability to recover a historically contingent, particularized setting for the letter to the Ephesians. First, he describes what he characterizes as its "fictional setting," which contains largely information gleaned from a straightforward reading of the text. He surmises a probable addressee, discusses the letter's apodictic rhetoric, and judges that the elementary character of the ethical instructions suggests the letter's role of recalling a catechism for neophytes. He then lists the problems with such a "vague" context. Ephesians is as much utopian as it is temporal. The letter speaks in terms of a cosmic topography, not of earthly locality. Virtually no names appear. The author has nothing to say about relations between Christians and Jews. He then conjectures that the admonitions (4:14) about coming heresies are actually part of the author's present social reality.

Dahl then reconstructs what he names "the real setting." On the basis of his larger history-of-religions reconstruction of the post-Pauline period, he seeks to determine the genuinely historical content of the "many winds of doctrine" (4:14), which is a combined form of revealed wisdom and encratistic practice. He infers that Ephesians presupposes a state of diversity and fragmentation within the Christian community. He notes the gnostic background of the idea of unification of the opposites as a way of overcoming cosmic dualism that the author applies to Jews and Gentiles (2:14). In sum, the utopianism is a consequence of the tension between a fictional and a real setting.

In his final essay, "Interpreting Ephesians: Then and Now," Dahl attempts to offer some hermeneutical advice on how to apply the letter of

---

118. Nils Dahl, "The Letter to the Ephesians: Its Fictional and Real Settings" and "Interpreting Ephesians: Then and Now," in *Studies in Ephesians*, pp. 452-59 and 461-73 respectively.

Ephesians in today's world. He is aware that the so-called utopian quality of the letter could lead to nourishing pride and self-satisfaction over the church's achievements. Therefore, he suggests that the book's value does not lie in some abstract doctrine of the church, but rather should be received in the spirit of gratitude for the sum total of what has been given to us. What each interpreter remembers will depend on each one's experience in attempting to understand the implications for everyday life. Much depends on the attitude of the reader and how we listen. Ephesians can serve as a challenge to live up to the calling we have been given.

Any criticism of my esteemed teacher's final essays on Ephesians is made with the greatest hesitancy. Few have been his rival as an incomparable teacher. Still, my hope is that there is a far more robust theological application possible, the articulation of which is the purpose of this entire monograph. It is a continuation in wrestling with this same set of problems that we next see how the issue of the church's order and its offices was handled by the Pastoral Epistles.

V. The Order of the Church and Its Offices

1. Introduction: The History of the Debate

The modern debate regarding the shape and the offices of the apostolic and postapostolic church was first launched in the English-speaking world by Joseph B. Lightfoot in his essay "The Christian Ministry," which appeared in his commentary on Philippians.[119] Very shortly thereafter, in the late nineteenth and early twentieth centuries, there followed a series of learned articles from Edwin Latch, Adolf von Harnack, Rudolf Sohm, and Hans Lietzmann,[120] among others. Then, beginning in the late 1940s, in part responding to the provocative essay of Ernst Käsemann,[121] there was a

---

119. Joseph B. Lightfoot, "The Christian Ministry," in *Saint Paul's Epistle to the Philippians* (London: Macmillan, 1868).

120. For the sake of convenience, these articles have been collected and reprinted by Kertelge, ed., *Das kirchliche Amt im Neuen Testament.*

121. Käsemann, "Ministry and Community," pp. 63-94. Rudolf Bultmann's position concerning the rise of church order is not much different from Käsemann's, but less polemical in formulation, *Theology of the New Testament*, part 3, §59 (New York: Scribner, 1955), pp. 95-118.

virtual explosion of essays on the subject. These came from, on the one hand, Protestants largely supporting Käsemann's thesis of the charismatic ordering of the Pauline churches (Eduard Schweizer, Heinrich Greeven, Martin Dibelius, among others),[122] and on the other hand, Roman Catholics who sought to establish a biblical basis for the church's establishment of its institutional offices (Heinrich Schlier, Heinz Schürmann, and Karl Kertelge).[123]

At first the major defense of the Catholic position was carried on largely by traditional systematic theologians who assumed a direct continuity between the teachings of Jesus and the establishment of the episcopacy in the late first and early second centuries, evidenced by the writings of Ignatius. Initially it was argued that the priestly offices of the Old Testament were simply extended by the Christian church in a spiritual form. Then a more sophisticated position was mounted by relating all the various forms of charismatic services to the body of Christ and his eternal priesthood. However, even the sophisticated form of an eschatological priesthood of Christ as the source for the offices defended by Schlier[124] proved to be unpersuasive even to many Catholics.

A change came about when Catholic New Testament scholars entered the debate (H. Schürmann, K. H. Schelkle, R. Schnackenburg, J. Gnilka, and K. Kertelge). The full impact of the modern critical approach to the New Testament was increasingly accepted, and an uncritical fusion of passages from the four Gospels, Acts, and the Pauline letters was no longer assumed. In the early period of this new exegetical debate, two scholars in particular served as representative of the new Catholic understanding of the biblical basis for the church's offices: K. Kertelge and H. Schürmann.

In his many essays, Kertelge[125] began with the assumption that a direct line from the teachings of Jesus to the church's offices could no longer be de-

---

122. These essays have also been collected by Kertelge in *Das kirchliche Amt im Neuen Testament.*

123. In addition to the articles of Schlier and Schürmann in the collection, Karl Kertelge has written two of his own monographs on the subject: *Gemeinde und Amt im Neuen Testament* (Munich: Kösel, 1972) and *Gemeinde. Amt. Sakrament* (Würzburg: Echter, 1989).

124. H. Schlier, "Die neutestamentliche Grundlage des Priesteramts," in *Der priestliche Dienst,* vol. 1, *Ursprung und Frühgeschichte,* Quaestiones Disputatae 46 (Freiburg: Herder, 1970), pp. 81-114. See the reviews of the Catholic reaction in J. Hainz, *Ekklesia* (Regensburg: Pustet, 1972), pp. 1-28.

125. Kertelge, *Gemeinde und Amt im Neuen Testament.*

fended. Rather, he spoke of an indirect relationship in which the witnesses of the New Testament were invoked, including the role of the Twelve, the apostolic office of Paul, the missionary imperatives of Matthew, and a plurality of secondary functions within separate Christian communities. He pursued the evidence for a role of elders adapted from the Jewish synagogue, and its later extension to the Hellenistic churches. Then he focused special attention on the apostolic office of Paul and its role in his development of coworkers who extended his missionary activity to the Gentiles. In the end, Kertelge recognized the force of historical contingencies (e.g., the challenge of the gnostics) in shaping the developing structures of the church, but he continued to defend vigorously the ultimate force of the church's understanding of the gospel of Jesus Christ that gave the church offices an ontological grounding in Christ's will for his church.

Perhaps even more influential in the debate from the side of Catholic scholarship was the essay of H. Schürmann.[126] His essay is a masterful exposition of the Pauline letters respecting the "gifts of the Spirit" and offers a major Catholic response to Käsemann. Schürmann first pursued the various forms of charismatic gifts, distinguishing between different classifications and diverse vocabulary of overlapping charismata. He stressed the unity of the divergent gifts led by the Spirit, all of which were given for the upbuilding of the church. He also distinguished between the daily life of the early apostolic church and the missionary activity that called forth special gifts such as those of "signs and wonders." The ordering of the various charismatic gifts was regulated by the principle of love and led by the apostolic tradition. Schürmann made a strong case for the presence of both official offices and charismatic ones that were not carefully distinguished by Paul. However, the ordering of the church remained a living application of the apostolic traditions. Schürmann emphasized that the free gifts of the first generation of Pauline communities and the post-Pauline period of the church with its developing official forms should not be played against each other, but both arose from the divine presence of Father, Son, and Spirit in the continuing guidance of the church. Finally, in a footnote he responded directly to Käsemann's dilemma in not finding a charismatic order in the post-Pauline era apart from Protestant sectarians. Schürmann found it ironical since he believed that Käsemann had dug for himself this hole.

126. H. Schürmann, "Die geistlichen Gnadengaben in den paulinischen Gemeinde," in *Ursprung und Gestalt,* reprinted in Kertelge, *Das kirchliche Amt,* pp. 362-412.

2. The Pastoral Letters in the Debate

The purpose of this brief review is not to attempt to resolve this complex set of issues, or to pursue the ongoing theological debate between Catholics and Protestants regarding ecclesiastical offices. Rather, it is to focus on the role of the Pastoral Epistles in this continuing debate. In one sense, two extreme positions that shortly emerged are represented by Ernst Käsemann and Heinrich Schlier.

Käsemann defended the view that the relation between the community and its offices in the early church was treated by Paul exclusively on the basis of a concept of charisma.[127] All Christians were endowed by the divine gifts that did not allow the possibilities of sacred space, sacred time, or sacred persons. Thus, Käsemann argued that there developed in early Christianity an antithesis to Paul's charismatic understanding, which he identified in Luke's writings, in Colossians and Ephesians, and especially in the Pastoral Epistles. Accordingly, the church is no longer seen in the context of Paul's missionary activity. Nor is it understood as the result of divine grace invading the world; rather the church has moved to a defensive posture and its appeal is to other ecclesial connections. It has established specially endowed officers who receive the Spirit to administer the deposit of faith of 1 Timothy 6:20. As a result there developed offices that became the real bearers of the Spirit. The letter of 2 Timothy is in reality a picture of the developed office of bishop, and the Pastorals provide the link between the apostle Paul and the monarchical bishop within the sequence of apostolic succession. This early Catholicism, as interpreted by Käsemann, marked the abandonment of the Pauline gospel and its replacement with a principle of tradition and legitimate successors.

In striking contrast, Heinrich Schlier argued that the Pastorals stand in a direct continuation of Pauline theology.[128] The *parathēkē* (the sound doctrine) that the Pastorals seek above all else to maintain is the apostolic tradition passed on to the next generation of Paul's coworkers. In fact, Schlier contended that the office of apostle has been continued by Timothy and Titus, and confirmed by a rite of ordination. These offices are the

---

127. Käsemann, "Ministry and Community," pp. 85-89; Käsemann, "Paul and Early Catholicism," in *New Testament Questions of Today,* pp. 236-51.

128. H. Schlier, "Die Ordnung der Kirche nach den Pastoralbriefen," in *Die Zeit der Kirche* (Herder: Freiburg, 1956), pp. 129-47.

legitimate extension of Paul's theology, and the spiritual gifts have been now assigned to these office bearers. The ecclesiastical office has its authoritative source in the will of Jesus Christ, who established the principle of apostolic succession that culminated in the establishment of the monarchical episcopacy.

What is remarkable in this debate between Käsemann and Schlier is that both scholars actually agreed in describing the Pastorals as having departed from Paul's charismatic ordering of the church in a post-Pauline form of monarchical episcopacy. The only real difference in their interpretations was in their sharply conflicting evaluations of this departure. For Käsemann the Pastorals are a betrayal of genuine Pauline theology and the beginning of the church's fall into early Catholicism. For Schlier the Pastorals correctly adumbrate the offices of the hierarchical episcopacy, and afford a biblical warrant for the developing Catholic theology of the third century and thereafter through the Middle Ages.

I think it is a fair assessment of the direction of modern critical New Testament scholarship over the last fifty years, including the exegesis of both Protestant and Catholic scholars, that neither the position of Käsemann nor that of Schlier has been sustained without serious modification. Käsemann's description of an exclusive charismatic order of the Pauline churches apart from any established offices is not historically or theologically defensible, and underestimates the diversity and complexity of the evidence for local offices performing different ecclesial functions. Moreover, Käsemann's category of *Frühkatholizismus* (early Catholicism) has not proved useful as the key to the church's growth. Conversely, Schlier's interpretation of the Pastorals as a legitimate adumbration of monarchical episcopacy, virtually identical with the Church Fathers' position after the second century, suffers from a reading back into the New Testament forms of church order that are not yet present in the New Testament itself. Indeed, a comparison of the Pastorals with Ignatius and Clement of Rome from the mid–second century serves to confirm the differences in respect to established ecclesiastical offices.

3. The Broadening of the Discussion

In the period that followed the highly polemicized debate between Käsemann and Schlier, the approach of both Protestants and Catholics was characterized by an attempt to analyze the issue of the offices of the church in the Pastorals within the larger spectrum of post-Pauline Hellenistic religion using the tools of historical critical reconstructions of early Christianity.[129] The fragmentary nature of the sources was freely acknowledged by both sides.

From the Protestant scholars, a representative approach is offered by Jürgen Roloff in his early monograph, articles, and impressive commentary on 1 Timothy.[130] In his article in the *Theologische Realenzyklopädie*, he sought to trace the diverse development of offices from the Gospels and Acts that spoke of a circle of the Twelve, then of the leadership roles of elders in Jerusalem, and finally of the initially important role of wandering prophets. Among the Hellenistic churches centered in Antioch, a variety of differing leadership roles emerged that often exercised specific societal functions. Roloff then described the decisive influence of Paul, who for the first time offered a theological interpretation of offices, christologically based, and the charismatic role of leadership shaped by spiritual gifts such as prophecy. No clearly defined offices could be recognized, but there was an intermingling of functions between free-formed charismatic and quasi-institutional forms inherited from Judaism.

When Roloff came to discuss the Pastorals, he recognized a sharp change in direction largely caused by the death of the first generation of Christians and the growing threat of gnostic-like heresies. Roloff insisted that there was no clear theological formulation of ecclesiastical offices, but the focus fell on the practical task of preserving doctrinal continuity within the community. He saw no indication of the Pastorals having developed a hierarchical order adumbrating an established order of the subsequent monarchical episcopacy.

129. Representative of a history-of-religions approach is the classic commentary of Martin Dibelius and Hans Conzelmann in Hermeneia; the latest critical commentary of Lorenz Oberlinner in Herder TKNT; and Luke T. Johnson in Anchor Bible. Norbert Brox, "Amt, Kirche und Theologie in der nachapostolischen Epoche — Die Pastoralbriefe," in *Gestalt und Anspruch des Neuen Testaments,* ed. Joseph Schreiner (Würzburg: Echter, 1969), pp. 120-33, makes a valiant effort to deal seriously with the Pastorals in a largely positive evaluation. See also Hans-Martin Schenke, "Das Weiterwirken des Paulus und die Pflege seines Erbes durch die Paulusschule," *New Testament Studies* 21 (1974/75): 505-18.

130. Roloff, *Apostolat–Verkumundigung–Kirche;* Roloff, "Amt/Ämter," in *Theologische Realenzyklopädie,* 2:509-33; Roloff, *Der erste Brief an Timotheus,* Evangelisch-katholischer Kommentar zum Neuen Testament 4 (Zürich and Neukirchen-Vluyn: Neukirchener, 1988).

However, in his later article of 1985,[131] Roloff shifted his emphasis from attention to the specific intent of the author respecting the subject of offices to an analysis of the sociological assumptions indirectly reflecting institutional structures within the Pastoral Letters. Although the description of the moral qualifications for the leadership of the bishop was foremost in 1 Timothy 3:1-7 and Titus 1:6-9, actually the portrait revealed the ideal profile of an institutional bishop sharing traditional patriarchal features. Likewise, the image of the church as a household (*oikos*, 1 Tim 3:4-5, 12) reflected the structure of the larger family with the overseeing function of the father in an assumed hierarchical order. The church had become a protected society in which its members were separated from the world of outsiders like a well-constructed building with sturdy pillars. Thus, Roloff offered an objective, historical analysis of the change that had occurred in the postapostolic age, but without offering the pejorative theological evaluation of Käsemann. He simply noted that in the changing historical conditions the charismatic leadership of Paul could not be sustained.

4. The Contributions of German Catholic Scholarship

From the side of Catholic New Testament scholarship, Norbert Brox[132] is a representative who wished to distance himself from the earlier position of Schlier. Brox was one of the first Catholic scholars who aggressively embraced the pseudepigraphical authorship of the Pastorals while at the same time seeking to exploit this position in a positive interpretation of the letters. In a noteworthy article,[133] he mounted an argument for reading Paul's request for his cloak and parchments (2 Tim 4:13) in a figurative, typological manner by which Brox sought to rob the defenders of the direct Pauline authorship of a major warrant for historicity.

Brox argued that an *Amtprinzip* (principle of ecclesial order) domi-

---

131. Roloff, "Pfeiler und Fundament der Wahrheit. Erwägungen zum Kirchenverständnis der Pastoralbriefen," in *Glaube und Eschatologie, Festschrift Werner Georg Kümmel*, ed. E. Grässer and O. Merk (Tübingen: Mohr Siebeck, 1985), pp. 229-47.

132. Brox, "Amt, Kirche," pp. 120-33; Brox, *Die Pastoralbriefe*, Regensburger Neues Testament 7.2 (Regensburg: Pustet, 1969).

133. Norbert Brox, "Zu den persönlichen Notizen der Pastoralbriefe," *Biblische Zeitschrift* 13 (1969): 76-94.

nated the Pastorals.[134] The earlier charismatic, dynamic element of the genuine Paul had been replaced by an institutional understanding of the church in which the charisma was channeled by means of ordination and clerical succession of its officers, addressed as Timothy and Titus. The Pauline office of apostle was elevated to the role of overseer of right belief and provided the grounds on which the true church was established against the inroads of heresy. However, perhaps the most characteristic feature of Brox's pseudepigraphical interpretation was his understanding that these fictive letters served to "update" *(auslegen)* the Pauline tradition to make it apply to a new and later historical situation in the life of the post-Pauline church. Brox freely admitted that the level of theological reflection of the Pastorals was considerably lower than that of the historical Paul, but he attributed this necessity of reinterpretation of the old as constitutive to the church's being in the world. The appeal to the continuity of Christian piety *(Frömmigkeit)* aided somewhat to effect a useful transition.

To summarize up to this point. It is noteworthy that in this period of the interpretation of the Pastorals — roughly from the 1960s and 1970s — both Protestants and Catholics recognized a serious decline in the theological contribution of the Pastorals in comparison with the historical Paul. Although the causes of this alleged decline were explained in different ways, Brox's theory of the historical need to update or actualize Paul's original message in order to address new circumstances became one of the most frequently used hermeneutical theories, which continues to be adopted in different forms by both liberal Protestants and Catholics.[135]

From my perspective, it is extremely fortunate that beginning in the late 1970s and climaxing in a brilliant collection of essays,[136] German Catholic New Testament scholars developed a very different approach to the post-Pauline letters. Suddenly a very different set of questions — historical, literary, theological — was raised, and fresh answers began to emerge.

My concern in the context of this chapter is not to attempt to summarize comprehensively the full range of articles included both within and outside this volume, but rather to select a number of the most important

---

134. Brox, "Amt, Kirch," p. 124.

135. J. Christiaan Beker, *Heirs of Paul: Paul's Legacy in the New Testament and in the Church Today* (Edinburgh: T. & T. Clark, 1992).

136. Kertelge, ed., *Paulus in den neutestamentlichen Spätschriften.*

hermeneutical issues basically shared by the authors. It remains to me astonishing how little modern Anglo-American biblical New Testament scholarship seems even aware of this material. All the essays in Quaestiones Disputatae 89 focus on the topic of its title: the reception of Paul in the late New Testament writings. Alexander Sand, Gerhard Lohfink, Helmut Merklein, and Peter Trummer all begin their essays, not with a theoretical debate over pseudepigraphy, but with the shape of the Pauline letters that by the early second century at the latest had been formed into a *corpus Paulinum* (see the earlier discussion in chapter 1.II). They explore the problem of the forces at work in this process of canonical shaping, the roots of which can be seen already within the New Testament. The research of Nils Dahl,[137] among others, had noted the process of overcoming the high level of particularity of Paul's letters, and the redactional evidence of a universalizing tendency. Paul's letters, however, occasional in nature, were received as apostolic, authoritative directives and were soon circulated among his churches (Col 4:16). The hermeneutical effect of the formation of a corpus was in creating a holistic reading reflected in the early post-Pauline reception.

In several of his articles, Lohfink then focuses on the reception of the Pastorals.[138] He addresses the issue of whether the relation of the Pastorals to the undisputed letters was only a literary one, or an orally transmitted history of traditions. He argues persuasively that both of these alternatives were at work. First, he makes a convincing case of a direct literary connection by citing selected passages, many of which have long been recognized: Romans 1:8-17//2 Timothy 1:3-12; Galatians 4:3-7//Titus 3:3-7; Romans 6:8// 2 Timothy 3:11-13; Romans 14:20-21//Titus 1:15; 1 Corinthians 15:9-10; Galatians 1:13-16//1 Timothy 1:12-17. He concludes that with the greatest probability the author of the Pastorals knew the letters of Romans, 1 Corinthians, Galatians, and Philippians. But then he concludes that the Pastorals as well as the deutero-Pauline epistles (Colossians, Ephesians) transmitted a variety of broader Pauline traditions in a living communal process far beyond the literary relationship. This relationship between the

---

137. Nils A. Dahl, "The Particularity of the Pauline Epistles as a Problem in the Ancient Church," in *Neotestamenta et Patristica, Festschrift Oscar Cullmann,* Novum Testamentum Supplement 6 (Leiden: Brill, 1962), pp. 261-71.

138. Gerhard Lohfink, "Paulinische Theologie in der Rezeption der Pastoralbriefe," in *Paulus in den neutestamentlichen Spätschriften,* pp. 70-121; Lohfink, "Die Vermittlung des Paulinismus in den Pastoralbriefen," pp. 169-88.

corpus Paulinum and a growing Pastoral corpus is further pursued by Peter Trummer,[139] who presents the evidence that the Pastorals did not develop as isolated letters, which were then separately attached to the Pauline corpus, but were a well-structured collection that developed within a canonical process in a living continuity with the ongoing growth of Paul's legacy for the early Christian church.

In his contribution to the Quaestiones Disputatae, Lohfink addresses the basic problem of the relation of Pauline theology with that of its reception in the Pastoral corpus. He covers many of the controversial issues in evaluating the theological content of the Pastorals, particularly in relation to the so-called genuine letters. He focuses first on the central role played in the Pastorals of Paul's office as apostle. Paul has become the unique and definitive teacher of the church, the *didaskalos* of the nations in faith and truth (1 Tim 2:7). He has become the source of "sound doctrine," which is identified with the gospel. This emphasis on the uniqueness of Paul's office is further expanded to include the concrete life of Paul, the church's model for understanding the gospel and guarding against heresy. Through his letters to his coworkers Timothy and Titus, the presence of Paul (his *parousia*) is now actualized,[140] precisely when Paul can no longer be physically present with his churches. In a word, the Pastorals show not only the closest continuity with the theology of Paul, but at the same time, through a careful selection, they also illustrate a crucial shift of accent in their reception.

The effect of this understanding of the reception process involved an overcoming of the distance between the "historical Paul" and the Paul of the Pastorals in that a wholly different understanding of the term "pseudepigraphy" has emerged. The loose parallels cited from classical and Hellenistic religions have little in common with the unique growth of the Pastorals within an evolving inner-Christian development in receiving, shaping, and incorporating the Pauline legacy for the future life of the church. Conversely, the continuing defense of the direct authorship of the Pastorals by conservative scholars (e.g., Fee) fails to understand the

---

139. Peter Trummer, *Die Paulustradition der Pastoralbriefe* (Frankfurt: Peter Lang, 1978); Trummer, "Corpus Paulinum — Corpus Pastorale," in *Paulus in den neutestamentlichen Spätschriften*, pp. 122-45.

140. Robert W. Funk, "The Apostolic Parousia: Form and Significance," in *Christian History and Interpretation: Studies Presented to John Knox*, ed. William R. Farmer et al. (Cambridge: Cambridge University Press, 1967), pp. 249-68.

diachronic, internal growth of meaning reflected in the transmission process involved in the canonical reception of this apostolic material.

There is one more important side to this topic that relates to the issue of ecclesial offices *(Ämter)* with which this chapter began. Once again, a basically new hermeneutical insight was projected in a brilliant article of Lohfink entitled "The Normativity of the Concept of Office in the Pastoral Letters."[141] Lohfink begins by returning to the issue of offices in the Pastorals raised so vigorously by Käsemann and Schlier. He seeks to address the problem by an exact philological study of two crucial words: *parathēkē* and *didaskalia.*

Parathēkē derives from the ancient laws of deposit (Lev 6:2), and denotes that which is entrusted to someone else's care. In the Pastorals it is used in 1 Timothy 6:20 and 2 Timothy 1:12, 14. Timothy is admonished to "guard the *parathēkē*" entrusted to him against the false teaching of the heretics. Likewise, Paul confesses that he has been able to guard that entrusted to him until the end of time. What is the content of that which has been entrusted? According to Lohfink, the answer is fully clear and unequivocal. The content of the *parathēkē* is the gospel that has been entrusted to the guardianship of the church forever! Then Lohfink notes: the issue of the church's offices *(Amtstrukturen)* is not part of the *parathēkē.*

Next, Lohfink turns his attention to the term *didaskalia* (teachings). It is the most important normative concept in the Pastorals, occurring fourteen times. It appears most frequently in two adjectival phrases: "sound doctrine" (1 Tim 1:10; 2 Tim 4:3; Titus 1:9; 2:1) and "true teaching" (1 Tim 4:6). The teacher of the *didaskalia* is of course Paul, whose apostolic authority guarantees his role as the instructor par excellence. Paul's *didaskalia* denotes not only the gospel that it incorporates, but also his apostolic commands, directives, and concrete ethical advice in the shaping of the life of his churches. His *didaskalia* is the gospel he proclaimed, that is, the concrete realization of its content in practice.

Finally, Lohfink draws the theological implications from his philological analysis. There are only two normative categories demanded of the faithful church by the Pastorals: *parathēkē* (the gospel entrusted) and *didaskalia* (his teaching of sound doctrine). This means that even though mention is made in passing of the presence of various offices within the

---

141. Gerhard Lohfink, "Die Normativität der Amtsvorstellungen in den Pastoralbriefen," *Theologische Quartalschrift* 157 (1977): 93-106.

Pastoral corpus, such as bishops, presbyters, and deacons/deaconesses, these offices do not belong to the normative categories of the letters, but are left open and fluid. Even the succession scheme (2 Tim 2:2; 1 Tim 4:14) is not a succession of ecclesiastical offices, but a succession of doctrine.[142] Lohfink does not dispute the legitimacy of the church's developing in the late second and third centuries a system of ecclesial ordering by means of a monarchical hierarchy. However, this development remained only one option and did not rest upon a normative biblical warrant. The author concludes with a broad and timely observation that such biblical evidence should serve to promote genuine ecumenical dialogue between Catholics and Protestants in healing the divisive doctrinal controversies of the past.

5. Hermeneutical Implications of the Debate

Before concluding this section on the Pastorals, I would like to draw some further hermeneutical implications that address the wider issue of the canonical function of the Pastorals within the Pauline corpus. Although it should be obvious from this review of the critical research of German Catholic New Testament scholars that the role of a developing canon was central to the Pauline reception of the Pastorals, I suggest that additional hermeneutical insights can be gained by pressing further the canonical function of the Pastorals.

In a previous section (chapter 3) I sought to explore the nature of the canonical shaping of the Pauline corpus with Romans serving as its introduction and the Pastorals as its conclusion. However, up to now the crucial canonical role of the Pastorals for affecting the entire corpus has not been fully explored. Rather, the widespread practice remains when using the initial categories of scientific, historical research, of describing the features constituting the religion of the Pastorals. Since an allegedly objective historical projection is used when reaching an evaluation, the result is that the Pastorals are measured in relation to the undisputed Pauline letters and judged as largely theologically inadequate.[143] Various elements are highlighted as indication of their failure and their lack of a serious grasp of

---

142. Lohfink, "Die Normativität der Amtsvorstellungen in den Pastoralbriefen," p. 104.

143. Jouette M. Bassler, *1 Timothy, 2 Timothy, Titus* (Nashville: Abingdon, 1996), pp. 30-34; see p. 31.

Paul's theology. Accordingly, the dynamic, imaginative dialectical theology of Paul's situation-oriented theology has been altered into a static, institutional set of rules (so J. C. Beker). Paul's eschatological understanding of the church has been turned into the rigidity of a Hellenistic bourgeois society. Finally, hierarchical offices have absorbed the charismatic gifts of the Spirit shared by all in the earlier Pauline communities. Such negative evaluations are representative of both Protestant and liberal Catholic appraisals. In my judgment, these interpretations offer a basic misunderstanding of the canonical function of the Pastorals.

Fortunately, a key to moving in a new direction has been offered by Lohfink's essay on "normativity." He makes a crucial distinction between normative categories laid upon the church and cultural features of religion that are present, even at times useful, but not deemed normative. In a real sense, there is an analogy between his categories and those of Martin Kähler between *Geschichte* and *Historie*. *Geschichte* is the historical reflections on events and conditions carried on within a confessing community of faith. *Historie* is the attempt to understand events from an objective, scientific analysis, applying ordinary human experience, apart from any confessional content, as the measure of its credibility.

Although it is possible to analyze the religion of the Pastorals in such a way that at times is helpful, such an approach is often tone-deaf to the theological forces within the confessing community that shaped its understanding. Specifically in terms of the Pastorals, they have arisen not as a deceptive manipulation of Paul by an unknown author in order to support his own differing ideology, nor by the application of pseudonymity in order to update Paul's time-constrained limitations to evoke a fresh appeal to its message (so Brox). Rather, the shapers of the Pastorals stood within a canonically growing process that first included the reception of the deutero-Pauline letters (Colossians and Ephesians) and culminated in a "trito-Pauline" corpus of the Pastorals. Above all, the Pastorals set forth the normative categories by which the Pauline material was preserved and studied by coming generations of believers toward the goal of maintaining what had been entrusted, and to guard Paul's sound teaching of the gospel.

How is this to be accomplished? The shaping process took various forms:

a. The active Paul engaged in missionary activity for the conversion of the nations has become the passive Paul, whose apostolic legacy became the norm by which to measure sound doctrine. The Paul who speaks in the

Pastorals is no longer active in forming new churches, but his ministry has been consigned to his coworkers (Timothy and Titus) and his presence *(parousia)* is now manifested in his letters. Paul has become the church's teacher par excellence, and the normative model for reading the gospel through his *didaskalia* forever. The apostle has been personalized, and his suffering has become an integral part of his gospel teaching.

b. Paul's letters have been collected into a unified corpus, and a new context has been established for discerning their material coherence. Moreover, his letters have now been received along with the Old Testament as Scripture. The church is advised to study the Scriptures, the sacred writings, which are able to instruct for salvation through faith in Jesus Christ (2 Tim 3:15). The practical goal is further spelled out: this God-breathed Scripture is profitable for "teaching, for reproof, and training in righteousness." The Scriptures are not a dead, static letter, or rule book, but the living Word of God, who directs his church by his Spirit into the future.

c. The central hermeneutical role of the Pastorals within the Pauline corpus lies in their providing an access to Paul's letters, now understood as sacred Scripture. The central point to emphasize is that Paul's so-called genuine letters have not been replaced by the Pastorals. Even in their less than brilliant style of conventional Hellenistic writing, the Pastorals do not function as a substitution of Paul, much less of his rival, but like John the Baptist, they serve as a pointer to the real source of continuing revelation, to the Scriptures, to Paul, and to the rest of the New Testament's evangelical proclamation.

d. The reading of Scripture as emphasized by the Pastorals is addressed to the practical, spiritual needs of the church, already faced with the threats of divisive heresies. How then is the future post-Pauline church to find instruction from the highly contingent letters of the apostle? The hermeneutical move being suggested is not complex or theoretical. When facing new crises, the Christian community turns to Scripture, to Paul's letters, and seeks to discern through the Spirit analogies by which to move from its new contingency to Scripture's coherence, and conversely, from Scripture's coherence to newer forms of contingency. The normative grounds on which the church stands remain the *parathēkē* (the faith entrusted), but in Paul's *didaskalia* the Christian seeker is offered a normative guide in one fruitful way of applying the gospel. Clearly, the model offered by the Pastorals is fundamentally different from the suggestion that to be relevant to a changing world the church must adapt its message to the shifting cultural sensibilities of its environment. Above all, what is missing in this frequently suggested model is any serious grasp of the reality of the Holy Spirit, whose presence as a living divine instructor has been promised by the Lord of the church in the reading of Scripture.

VI. The Weak and the Strong

1. *1 Corinthians 8:1–11:1*

It has long been noticed that 1 Corinthians 8:1–11:1 and Romans 14:1–15:13 share strong parallels in style, vocabulary, and content concerning the subject of the weak and the strong. (See Charles Cranfield, *Romans,* and Wolfgang Schrage, *1 Korinther.*)[144] However, in contrast to the clear coherence of Paul's argument in Romans, 1 Corinthians 8–10 seems to present major difficulties in the presentation of his response to the issues raised by the Corinthian letter concerning food offered to idols. On the one hand, in 6:1-13 and 10:23-30 Paul seems to dismiss the threat of eating meat offered to idols as harmless in itself, but calls for mutual respect between the two conflicting groups. On the other hand, in 10:14-22 the apostle appears to prohibit categorically any contact with meat associated with idols. However, starting with the essay of Hans von Soden in 1931,[145] there has increasingly emerged a broad consensus among scholars regarding a basic literary coherence of these chapters despite a host of exegetical problems that remain perplexing.

The initial problem in understanding the issue respecting the eating of meat offered to idols turns on the historical and cultural contexts that formed the background of the debate. Again there is a broad consensus that the issue did not emerge as a conflict between Jews and Christians, but was an inner-Christian debate set in the highly syncretistic Hellenistic culture of Corinth. Apparently one group of Christians, probably the majority, named by Paul "the strong," were caught up in an enthusiastic embrace

144. Charles E. B. Cranfield, *The Epistle to the Romans* (Edinburgh: T. & T. Clark, 1979), 2:691-93; Wolfgang Schrage, *Der Erste Brief an die Korinther,* II (Zürich: Benziger; Neukirchen-Vluyn: Neukirchener, 1995), pp. 211-15.

145. Hans Freiherr von Soden, "Sacrament und Ethik bei Paul" (1931), in *Das Paulusbild in der neueren Deutschen Forschung,* ed. Karl H. Rengstorf (Darmstadt: Wissenschaftliche Buchgesellschaft, 1969), pp. 338-79.

of their newfound freedom derived from the gospel, and confessing that idols had no real existence and posed no threat, chose freely to eat meat offered to idols. Conversely, other Christians, named "the weak," appear to have been recently converted to Christianity from paganism — verse 7 speaks of those "being hitherto accustomed to idols" — and were offended in seeing the "stronger" Christians partaking of food tainted by pagan practices.

The text of the Pauline letter to the Corinthians provides little information on the exact cultic background behind this conflict. However, extrabiblical sources indicate that a variety of forces seems at work influencing the conflicting scruples of meat offered to idols.[146] First, it has been pointed out that the cultic practice of sacrifice and eating of meat was a central feature of everyday communal life in Corinth, and was the setting for weddings, funerals, and virtually every social interaction of life. It functioned as an all-pervasive convention within the civil religion. Yet in addition, class distinctions played a significant role in determining its societal function. The eating was not shared by the lower strata of Hellenistic society, especially not by the poor, the slaves, and the marginalized, many of whom composed the Corinthian house communities. One of the implications to be drawn from this sociological reconstruction is that it would be far more natural for the "strong" to have been from a more affluent society in which idol meat was an assumed way of life than those impoverished who remained on the edge of normal communal life.

In his initial response to the Corinthians' questions, Paul appears to identify with the strong. "We know" that idols have no real existence. "There is no God but one." In this conventional creedal statement, one can hear reverberations of the Old Testament Shema, which has been christologically expanded: "For us there is one God . . . and one Lord, Jesus Christ, through whom all things exist" (8:6). Then Paul sketches the restraints to this knowledge. There are those who do not possess this knowledge, whose self-identity is weak, and the eating of idol meat is a defilement. Paul is concerned that the liberty of the strong works as a stumbling block to the weak. By their eating, the weak among the community are led astray: "lest a weak brother is destroyed, a brother for whom Christ died" (8:11).

146. Gerd Theissen, *The Social Setting of Pauline Christianity* (Philadelphia: Fortress, 1982), pp. 121-44.

Therefore, Paul seeks a balance between the freedom of the strong and the scruples of the weak. He offers advice, not a command. Yet in so doing he relativized completely the significance of the meat offered to idols. One is no worse off by not eating, and no better off by eating. What is important is that one does not sin against Christ by causing a fellow Christian to fall on account of this action. Both sides are to show respect to each other for the sake of the gospel. In chapter 9 the apostle presents a different aspect of the same general topic. According to common sense and according to Scripture (Deut 25:4), a worker should be paid for service rendered. How much more then should he as an apostle share this same right of honest compensation for his labor. Yet for the sake of the gospel, Paul has refused to exercise his right. His reward lies in making the proclamation of the gospel free of charge and not exercising his right. The thrust of this autobiographical illustration is to bring home his concern for the larger good of the community. He has adjusted his own needs for the sake of others in order that he might exercise the greatest influence for the sake of the gospel. Then he returns to the vocabulary of chapter 8: "To the weak I became weak, that I might win the weak." By forgoing his own rights, he identifies with those who do not fully share the knowledge of God's freedom in order to bring unity to a diverse community of faith.

Next, in chapter 10 Paul seems to interject a very different note into the discussion. He offers a typological reading of Israel's history that recounts the exodus through the Red Sea and Israel's divine sustenance in the wilderness by means of divine food (manna) and supernatural drink (water from a rock). Paul renders these events in sacramental language. Israel was "baptized in the sea," and ate and drank the supernatural elements provided by God.

Then Paul draws the implications. These things happened to Israel as a warning, but they were written down as Scripture "for our instruction upon whom the end of the ages has come" (10:11). His admonition is that neither the sacrament of baptism nor the Eucharist offers an unassailable form of divine protection, a guarantee against the virulent threat of demons. Those who flirt with idolatry — those "craving" for food tainted by idolatry — will suffer disastrous consequences. Those "strong" within Corinth who are secure in their own sense of freedom are courting imminent danger to their faith.

Hans von Soden first understood the significance of the shift into sacramental language.[147] Eating meat within the context of a pagan cultic sacrifice involves an issue far deeper than respecting the scruples of fellow Christians. Von Soden sought to reconstruct the sacramental function of pagan sacramentalism in which the participant was joined ontologically to the process of evil. In contrast to this pagan ceremony, the Christian partakes sacramentally of the cup of blessing, the blood of Christ, and through the loaf of the body of Christ. There can be no joining of these totally incomprehensible sacramental activities to pagan sacrifices. They are offered to demons and not to God. You cannot drink the cup of the Lord and the cup of demons. Such idolatry can only evoke the full wrath of God and lead to catastrophic destruction. Therefore, Paul utters a categorical imperative: "Flee from the worship of idols" (10:14).

Before von Soden's probing analysis of the role of cultic sacramentalism involved in temple sacrifice, modern commentators found Paul's responses to the eating of idol meat fully inconsistent (see Johannes Weiss).[148] Some even spoke of a "liberal" and a "conservative" Paul, the one being flexible, the other rigid. What was especially missing in such a caricature was an understanding of Paul's dialectical theology. On the one hand, he could dismiss idols as lacking existence and thus harmless. On the other hand, he could recognize the continuing powers of evil emerging from idolatry in the temple cult that could continue to arouse temptations causing danger and destruction of Christian faith (see Thiselton).[149]

In the conclusion of chapter 10, Paul returns to his earlier discussion of the weak and the strong. "All things are lawful, but not all things are helpful." He reaffirms his earlier position that one should not seek his own good, but that of his neighbor. Then he offers a specific illustration of the exercise of one's freedom when invited to dinner. If the issue of conscience is raised, the Christian should refuse to eat in order to honor the scruples of another. But overriding this freedom that he leaves to each individual to exercise is the basic rule: do all to the glory of God, that the unity of the church be enhanced.

Briefly to summarize chapters 8:1–11:1 of 1 Corinthians. One is struck by the contingent specificity of the problem raised by the Corinthian letter to Paul concerning the eating of meat offered to idols. The modern reader

147. Von Soden, "Sacrament und Ethik," pp. 355-70.

148. Johannes Weiss, *Der erste Korintherbrief*, 2nd ed. (Göttingen: Vandenhoeck & Ruprecht, 1910).

149. Thiselton, *The First Epistle*, pp. 715-76; Richard B. Hays, *First Corinthians* (Louisville: John Knox, 1997), pp. 143-44.

of Paul's response is left without much help as to the exact details of the complex historical, cultural, and religious background out of which the problem arose. We have seen that information obtained from extrabiblical sources (especially sociology and history of religions) has aided in sharpening the issues at stake. Particularly a partial recovery of some of the sacramentalism involved in the cultic activities of the temple has helped greatly in bridging between chapters 8 and 10.

Yet it is also the case that despite a somewhat blurred background, Paul's response has not been rendered incomprehensible to later generations of readers. It is noteworthy that Paul continues to draw out the theological grounds on which he has offered his advice, and leaves his readers with a coherent formulation for Christian action: shun idolatry; do all for the glory of God; seek the good of one's neighbor rather than those of self-interest.

2. Romans 14:1–15:13

In Romans 14:1–15:13, despite the strong parallels in language and content with 1 Corinthians 8–10, one observes immediately the strikingly different contexts of the two. The setting of Romans is discursive and hortatory, not controversial as in Corinthians. There is no mention whatever of idol meat. Moreover, the language of Romans is general and the contrast between the weak and the strong has lost its sharp contours. To illustrate the person who is weak, Paul chooses an extreme example of a religious scruple: someone eats only vegetables (14:2). Then he turns to another typical example of religious scruples: the observance of the sanctity of certain days over others. (Contrast Colossians 2:16.) Moreover, the terminology of the "strong" is delayed until chapter 15.

I judge therefore that it is a basic exegetical error to assume that Paul is addressing specific contingent events in Romans 14–15 in accordance with his approach in Corinthians. The majority of modern commentators are misled when they extrapolate from a few vague hints in chapters 15–16 to posit that Paul's use of weak and strong reflects a specific controversy in Rome between Jewish and Gentile Christians. An extreme example of such an approach is found in Paul Minear's *Obedience*.[150] Rather, I think Sanday

---

150. Paul S. Minear, *The Obedience of Faith: The Purpose of the Epistle to the Romans* (London: SCM, 1971), pp. 121-43.

and Headlam are correct in rejecting the attempt to reconstruct specific parties within the Roman community.[151] In Romans Paul is writing in a general style and is merely selecting a typical instance of religious scrupulosity in these examples.

Paul then moves quickly from the issue of the scruples of the weak to develop a more comprehensive theological criterion for Christian behavior. Initially, he returns to his earlier formulation: "Let every one be fully convinced in his own mind," thereby continuing his advocacy of individual freedom. Whatever the decision, it must serve to "honor the Lord and give thanks to God." Then Paul probes even deeper. Our lives belong fully to God, whether in life or death. This theological certainty is then grounded in the death and resurrection of Christ. In 1 Corinthians Paul had urged a harmony between the weak and the strong. "Let neither despise the other." In Romans Paul grounds his earlier advice on the theme of the coming apocalyptical judgment of God. Each person will have to give account of himself to God, who alone has the right to judge.

In Romans 14:13-23 the apostle returns to the Corinthian theme of not acting in such a way as to cause the ruin of a neighbor. Again he cites the refrain "one for whom Christ died" (v. 15//1 Cor 8:11). He again asserts the fundamental irrelevance of food in commending us to God (1 Cor 8:8), but in Romans he generalizes his earlier point into a theological principle that reverberates with a Gospel logion of Jesus (Mark 7:14-19): "I know . . . in the Lord Jesus that nothing is unclean in itself." But here the context is not the debate with Judaism over kashrut, but rather the grounds for Christian freedom. The effect of this section is that Paul is redefining what is right and wrong. "The foundation of right action in every case is a right relationship to God of trust."[152]

In the penultimate section (Rom 15:1-6) Paul brings up again the theme of the strong bearing the failings of the weak in not trying to please oneself. However, this time Paul does not use his own example (1 Cor 9) of refusing to exercise his rights for the larger good of the community, but

151. William Sanday and Arthur C. Headlam, *The Epistle to the Romans* (Edinburgh: T. & T. Clark, 1895), pp. 384-85, 399-403. See also Paul Sampley, "The Weak and the Strong: Paul's Careful and Crafty Rhetorical Strategy in Romans 14:1–15:13," in *The Social World of the First Christians,* ed. L. M. White and O. Larry Yarborough (Philadelphia: Augsburg Fortress, 1995), pp. 40-52. Sampley argues that Paul's language is "figured speech, oblique address, suggestion," in order to encourage the readers to apply the rhetoric to themselves.

152. Meyer, "Romans: A Commentary," p. 214.

rather chooses a christological warrant: "Christ did not please himself, but bore the reproaches of others." From this Paul draws the hortatory implication: "live in such harmony with one another in accordance with Christ Jesus that together you may with one voice glorify God."

Finally (Rom 15:7-13), Paul concludes the theme of welcoming one another for the glory of God by focusing his theme of overcoming friction in the relation of Jew and Gentile. The passage picks up many of the themes of Romans 9–11, and uses this age-old friction to demonstrate how it disappears before God's intention for a unified people. Citing Scripture, he reminds Gentiles that their faith rests on God's faithfulness to the Jews, and the Jews that the divine purpose was always for the inclusion of the Gentiles in Israel's messianic election.

3. Comparison of Corinthians and Romans

Paul W. Meyer[153] speaks of the temptation to read Romans 14 in the same terms as Paul's advice to the Corinthians, which is the approach usually followed. Meyer suggests that a closer reading of Romans reveals that Paul is modulating his Corinthian experience to fit the larger argument of Romans. It is these subtle changes that will play a role when we seek to pursue a canonical interpretation of Romans in relation to Corinthians. Still, it is important not to overinterpret some of the minor changes. In Romans Paul does not use the term of conscience found in 1 Corinthians 8–10, but the parallel expression in Romans 14:1 is not much different in substance.

The first point to note is that Paul's handling of the topic of the weak and strong in Romans is structured in relation to the larger coherence of the entire letter. One notices that the continuation of the use of a catena of Old Testament verses (15:9-12) follows the pattern set in 9:25-29 and 10:18-29. The exhortations of chapters 14–15 continue also to develop the basic appeals of the preceding chapters 12 and 13 as an intentional shift from primarily doctrinal discourses to ethical and practical exhortations. Of course, Paul's central argument that the gospel is a revelation of God's righteousness assumes that doctrinal exposition is integrally joined with its moral implications. Thus, themes that run throughout the earlier chap-

---

153. Meyer, "Romans: A Commentary," p. 213.

ters are continually picked up without full elaboration and subtly played upon, such as the reverberations of the baptismal formula in 13:14: "put on the Lord Jesus Christ," in the exhortation to harmony in accord with Jesus Christ (15:5). Then again, the sovereignty of God as judge of his creation is also a theme of Romans 1–3. Also in the final section (15:7-13), numerous themes from Romans 9–11 are struck such as the confirming of God's faithfulness to the patriarchs, and salvation first to the Jews and then to the Gentiles, which provide serious grounds for not attempting to reconstruct alleged contingencies with the Roman church as Paul's motivation for his letter.

Another major characteristic of Romans in comparison with Corinthians is the extent to which the element of doctrinal coherence has replaced the dominant concerns of the contingent crises dealt with throughout the Corinthian chapters. The specificity by which the weak and the strong are constructed in Corinthians has been replaced by illustrative examples. He now speaks of a "vegetarian" with scruples, or of one esteeming one day above another, but the specificity of, say, Colossians 2:16 or Galatians 4:10 is missing.

Then again, Paul's discourse in Romans reflects a consistent concern to probe to the doctrinal heart that undergirds his practical advice. This is, of course, not to suggest that theological formulations are lacking in Corinthians, but there is a deeper, more comprehensive probing in Romans. So in the confession that "we belong to the Lord, whether we live or die" (Rom 14:8), the apostle grounds this truth in the death and resurrection of Christ, which is a missing feature in 1 Corinthians 8–10, and appears in 1 Corinthians 15 only when the denial of the resurrection provides the contingent event for a full theological elaboration. The relativizing of the importance of food for the church is clearly made in 1 Corinthians 8:8, but a comprehensive and unambiguous theological formulation is offered only in Romans: "nothing is unclean in itself" (14:14).

Finally, there is a distinction in the way Israel's Scriptures are cited. In Corinthians a law of Moses is used as an illustration of a practice of not muzzling an ox. Or again, different events in Israel's history in the wilderness are cited as a warning against idolatry. In both cases in Corinthians, Paul argues that these things were "written down for our instruction," and thus are relevant when an application for Christian behavior is drawn from them. However, in Romans the citations of Old Testament passages are introduced each time by a formal citation formula (14:11; 15:9-12).

Moreover, Paul expands on the significance of these writings being written "for our instruction." The writings are now named "the Scriptures," and their function designated: "by steadfastness and by the encouragement of the Scriptures we might have hope" (15:4). The closest parallel to such a description of the function of Scripture as the vehicle for God's instruction to his church in the future is found in 2 Timothy 3:15, which also speaks of Scripture's role: "to instruct you for salvation through faith in Christ Jesus." The parallel is close enough to caution those who dismiss the formulation from the Pastorals as being a rigid ossification of tradition in contrast to the dynamic expression found in the "genuine" Pauline letters.

4. The Weak and the Strong within the Pauline Corpus

Our attention is first directed to the canonical function of Romans as an introduction to the Pauline corpus. As has already been suggested, the shaping of Romans as the introduction to the Pauline corpus was certainly not the creation of Paul, but those coming after the apostle who collected, received, and treasured his tradition and gave it a specific canonical role within the corpus. Still, the placing of Romans as an introduction was not a tour de force, but was encouraged by the very nature of the letter itself. To suggest with some scholars that if the context of Romans was not related to a specific crisis, then the only other option is to postulate timeless doctrine, completely misses the point. Romans is not a timeless tractate, but an exposition of the gospel, that is, the demonstration of the power of God. Our task is now to demonstrate the canonical effect of the corpus in understanding Paul's understanding of the weak and the strong.

What is initially striking in 1 Corinthians is how Paul reshaped the questions posed by the weak and the strong. Both sides had arguments in their favor. "Have we not been freed by the gospel from such pagan superstitions as idols?" "How can we Christians continue to live like pagans, eating meat that has been polluted by those very rites from which we have been freed?" Paul's response is to change the nature of the debate by relativizing its significance. Whether you eat meat or do not eat meat is irrelevant to the faith. What matters is the mutual respect for each other, as people redeemed by the death of Christ. The harmony of the community can function with members having different understandings of Christian freedom. Both sides are constrained to forgo their personal rights for the good of the church. Thus Paul does not offer a simple straightforward answer to their questions. He does not issue a command, but leaves the decision open within the larger theological context of calling for a behavior that renders glory to God and harmony between all members.

However, then Paul is faced in 1 Corinthians 10 with another problem that remains in some tension with his advice. Paul makes clear that although idols are indeed silly superstitions, yet there remains in paganism a continual diabolic threat. The world God created is still under the power of evil forces, and the Christian lives in a constant battle, in a warfare between the old and the new ages. A particularly dangerous locus for Satan's temptations lies in the cultic rites of the temple. Scripture warns of this continuing danger that caused the destruction of Israel in the wilderness. Therefore, "Put on the whole armor of God that you may be able to withstand the wiles of the devil" (Eph 6:11). Shun the worship of idols.

How then does Romans fit into the search for Christian obedience in such a situation outlined by 1 Corinthians? Romans again addresses the issue of the weak and the strong. Yet Paul now distances himself from the immediate specificity of the eating of meat offered to idols. He generalizes the problem by choosing typical examples of Christians struggling with various religious scruples regarding diet or observance of holy days. Paul affirms his earlier advice: let everyone be fully convinced in his own mind. Whatever he does must be to the glory of God.

Then Paul raises the stakes of the discussion. He reminds his readers of the eschatological dimension of the Christian faith. We have been united with God in life and death, but we also stand accountable before the judgment of Christ when all creatures will appear before the sovereign creator. In his essay on these chapters, Wayne Meeks has made some valuable literary and theological observations.[154] He begins by showing that these latter chapters in Romans are not an unimportant appendix, but integral to the entire letter. The leitmotif of bearing the burdens of the weak without passing judgment is sounded in an apostrophe already in Romans 2:1, and continues throughout the first eleven chapters. Then the whole argument of not judging one's neighbors is grounded theologically in God's restraint in judging us, which relativizes our own propensity for judgments and provides the warrant for his case.

---

154. Wayne A. Meeks, "Judgment and the Brother: Romans 14:1–15:13," in *In Search of the Early Christians* (New Haven: Yale University Press, 2003), pp. 153-66.

The confession of the ultimate triumph of God's justice controls our entire life, not just regarding proper eating or drinking. Therefore, let us pass no judgment on others. We know that because God is creator, nothing of his creation is in itself useless. Rather, what is required is the pursuit of peace and mutual obedience. The ultimate role for Christians has been established by Christ, the Lord of both the living and the dead.

Paul ends his discussion by placing the debate between the weak and the strong in the context of the whole book of Romans, namely, the relation between Jewish and Gentile Christians. Neither are identified with the weak or the strong, but both are reminded how Jew and Gentile, the quintessential example of division, have been reconciled by God and together constitute the divine purpose of God for his creation from the beginning.

In sum, the effect of reading Romans and Corinthians within the context of the Pauline corpus is to establish a dialectical relationship between the contingency of Corinthians and the doctrinal coherence of Romans toward the goal that future generations of Christians are provided instruction for divine guidance through analogies drawn from the ministry of the apostle Paul.

However, lest this proposed hermeneutic be dismissed as an unpersuasive construct, the canonical shaping of the corpus provides, in the closing admonitions of the Pastoral Epistles, an additional warrant. In 1 Timothy 4:1-5 the writer speaks through the Spirit of threats to the faith that will arise in the future ("in later times"). The dangers he foresees show striking similarities to those faced by several of Paul's churches, but especially by the one in Corinth. There will arise those advocating "deceitful spirits and doctrines of demons," "forbidding marriage and enjoining abstinence from foods." The writer then rejects these threats in language closely resembling Paul's in Corinthians and Romans. "Everything created by God is good, and nothing is to be rejected if it is received with thanksgiving." The writer further commends the practice of the public reading of Scripture (4:13). The role of the community's reading of Scripture is further clarified in the Pastorals by 2 Timothy 3:16, which gives a highly practical goal of how Paul's written legacy is to function. These writings were given "to instruct for salvation." Moreover, because shortly the Pauline letters were included within the church's Scriptures (2 Pet 3:15), his writings served to generate the good works commensurate with true Christian faith.

A major point to repeat regarding the canonical function of the Pastorals within the Pauline corpus is not that Paul's earlier "undisputed" letters have been replaced by the later Pastorals. Rather the Pastorals serve to commend the continual study of all of Scripture — the Old Testament and the Pauline letters included — for instruction in righteousness. Whether one calls this study of Scripture "dialectical" is in itself unimportant. But what is being advocated is that from a reading of Paul's letters, the future church will be instructed with a Word from God. Indeed, in the highly particularized contingent-oriented letters, analogies will be revealed by which the church can address both the old and the newer dangers to the faith. Although it is true that much of the unique profundity of Paul's theology is not reflected in the Pastorals, the Pastorals function truthfully to point the church back to Paul's written legacy in its entirety. Indeed, the lesson to be drawn from the history of the church's wrestling with Scripture is that often in times of the greatest crises, the force of Paul's letters has again exploded with fresh power to enliven a moribund church.

VII. Israel and the Church: Romans 9–11

1. Form, Function, and Purpose of Romans 9–11

There are several larger literary questions to be addressed before turning to the exegetical and theological issues of these chapters. The first issue concerns the proper contextual approach to the book of Romans as a whole. Donfried provided a review of the various options by republishing many of the important articles on the subject, a revised edition of which brought an additional bibliography up to 1991.[155] He distinguished between those who believed that Paul dealt with a specific, concrete historical situation in Rome and those who thought the letter's difficulties were largely literary and reflected a complex redactional process. In his own essay, Donfried sought to provide methodological principles by which to proceed in the debate. His basic conclusion was that any study of Romans should proceed on the initial assumption that this letter was written by Paul to deal with a particular historical situation in the Roman church. In sum, he identified himself completely with the first historical option.

155. Karl F. Donfried, ed., *The Romans Debate*, rev. ed. (Peabody, Mass.: Henrickson, 1991).

In my judgment the strongest opposition against this formulation was voiced by Günther Bornkamm in his essay "The Letter to the Romans as Paul's Last Will and Testimony."[156] He argued that the many attempts to relate Romans to a specific, internal historical situation by means of various speculative reconstructions have ended in dead ends. Rather, Bornkamm proposed that the topics of Romans, almost without exception, were a return to issues treated in his earlier letters to his churches, which are characterized by a high level of contingent problems. Then Bornkamm suggested: "What Paul had previously said is now not only set down systematically . . . but gives, for the first time, his mature and considered thought." In my earlier chapter on the canonical shaping of Romans (chapter 3), I accepted his proposal in general (apart from the last will and testament hypothesis) as presenting the most persuasive argument within this debate in characterizing the nature of the letter.

However, there is a major problem that he clearly saw and sought to deal with. The problem is that the issues raised in Romans 9–11 — God's promises to Israel, election, covenant, and hardening of the heart — have no detailed parallels in the earlier Pauline letters, but constitute a unique subject of Romans, about which there were of course a few hints (3:1). Bornkamm attempts to offer a solution to this problem. He argues that "the Jew symbolizes man in his highest potentialities"; he represents the "religious man" whom the law tells what God requires of him.[157] Without pursuing in detail Bornkamm's further expansion of this idea, I feel strongly that this response is inadequate and misconstrued. In the Pauline letters Jew and Gentile were never blurred together as a symbol of universal man. Not surprisingly, Ernst Käsemann,[158] independently from Bornkamm, reached a somewhat similar position in specifying "the devout Jew . . . as the reality of the religious man," who along with the Gentiles is linked in disobedience, when denying God's solidarity only with the ungodly. In my judgment, one must move in another direction in the interpretation of Romans 9–11.

The second major introductory issue turns on the continuing debate concerning the function of chapters 9–11 within the book of Romans. Dur-

---

156. Günther Bornkamm, "The Letter to the Romans as Paul's Last Will and Testimony," in *The Romans Debate*, pp. 16-28.

157. Günther Bornkamm, *Paul* (London: Hodder and Stoughton, 1971), p. 95.

158. Ernst Käsemann, "Paul and Israel," in *New Testament Questions of Today*, p. 186.

ing much of the late nineteenth and early twentieth centuries,[159] these chapters were usually considered to be a peripheral appendix having little importance for Paul's message to the Romans. Fortunately, there has been a striking change in perspective. Initial credit goes to Krister Stendahl, in his well-known lecture "The Apostle Paul and the Introspective Conscience of the West."[160] Stendahl argued that these chapters had been basically misunderstood, especially by Luther and the subsequent exegetical tradition in thinking that its subject matter was addressing the question of how salvation was to be achieved for all of humanity. Luther's answer was not by works of the law, but by faith in Jesus Christ alone. According to Stendahl, this traditional Reformation approach failed to understand that Paul's real question turned on the relation between Jews and Gentiles and how to defend the status of Gentile Christians as honorary Jews. Then he argued that the actual climax of Romans is found in chapters 9–11, namely, Paul's reflections on the relation between church and synagogue. The chapters preceding on justification are only introduction to this highly particularized problem relating to the coexistence of Judaism and Christianity, and not an essential doctrinal component of his missionary enterprise.

While Stendahl deserves credit for his unnerving of the New Testament guild in its reading of Paul, I think it is fair to say that recent scholarship has moved in a different direction when assessing the significance of chapters 9–11. Stendahl not only failed to see how integral chapters 9–11 were to the first eight chapters of Romans, but he also did not recognize that the interpretation of chapters 9–11 is dominated by appeals to the Old Testament, especially to the themes of Isaiah and Deuteronomy.

Increasingly, a wide consensus has emerged that the leading issue of chapters 9–11 focuses on the faithfulness of God to his promises to Israel. In an important article J. Christiaan Beker takes up this issue.[161] How is

159. In a very illuminating brief review of the history of the interpretation of Rom 9–11, E. Elizabeth Johnson in her dissertation, "The Function of Apocalyptic and Wisdom Traditions in Romans 9–11" (Ph.D. diss., Princeton University, 1989), outlined the various options that emerged, especially that of F. C. Baur in the nineteenth century. (I wondered whether she perhaps underestimated the widespread impact made by Stendahl's essay, which was made with his customary rhetorical flair.)

160. Krister Stendahl, "The Apostle Paul and the Introspective Conscience of the West," in *Paul among Jews and Gentiles* (Philadelphia: Fortress 1976), pp. 76-96.

161. J. Christiaan Beker, "The Faithfulness of God and the Priority of Israel in Paul's Letter to the Romans," in *The Romans Debate*, pp. 327-32.

Paul able to maintain both the priority of Israel and the equality of Jew and Gentile in Christ on the basis of justification by faith alone (Rom 3:28-31)? In the end, Beker argues that the theme of Romans is the faithfulness of God in maintaining the integrity of his character and in fulfilling his promises to Israel, both through his saving action. Certainly Beker made an illuminating start especially in understanding the role of chapters 9–11, but much more needs to be said to engage the depth of Paul's line of argument within these chapters.

A very detailed analysis of Romans 9–11 has recently appeared in J. Ross Wagner's monograph, *Heralds of the Good News*.[162] After first providing an introduction to how Romans was interpreted in the first centuries, Wagner offers an exhaustive study of the use of Isaiah by Paul in chapters 9–11. His comprehensive study will serve as a new benchmark from which further study of these chapters will proceed. The author seeks to show the various ways in which Paul reinterpreted the book of Isaiah (and other Old Testament prophets) to provide a scriptural warrant for his understanding of the gospel as the mystery of God's action in reconciling both Jew and Gentile. Isaiah is the herald whose approach Wagner seeks to describe under the rubric: "Plotting Isaiah's Story in the Letter to the Romans." When shortly I turn to a more detailed exegesis of chapters 9–11, my dependence upon Wagner's work will be obvious and is acknowledged with appreciation.

Nevertheless, there is one issue in which I disagree, and it strikes to the heart of my major proposal in this monograph, namely, the issue of canon. Wagner does not address the subject of canon in the form I propose. Rather, he speaks of Paul's understanding of the message of Isaiah as "story," and from this story of Israel Wagner attempts to show how Paul's story is shaped. Initially this use of the term "story" has been derived from Richard Hays,[163] and it provides a similar, if not identical, meaning for Wagner. Story serves as a construct by which to emphasize a coherence that unifies the detailed elements derived from various parts of the Old Testament. It is the glue that keeps Paul's exegesis from becoming lost in an endless citation of individual texts.

---

162. Wagner, *Heralds of the Good News*.

163. Hays, *Echoes*, pp. 95-121. See also Bruce W. Longenecker, ed., *Narrative Dynamics in Paul* (Louisville: Westminster John Knox, 2003), for essays debating the use of the concept of story in Paul. Of the essays, only the concluding one by Francis Watson, pp. 231-39, has any appreciation of the "scriptural context" of its canonical shaping.

From my perspective, the term "story" is inadequate for several reasons. First, it is far too vague and nebulous to register Paul's approach to the coherence of Israel's continuous witness. It arose as a modern hermeneutical device that sought to escape the problems involved with the term "history." During the nineteenth century and earlier, history became the center of a scientific methodology of treating the past according to a correspondence theory of reference.[164] The truth of a text was determined empirically by establishing an ostensive reference set within a diachronic grid. Equally unhelpful was the nineteenth-century attempt to speak of a *Heilsgeschichte* that could not escape the traps of philosophical idealism and abstraction. Thus story became a means of affirming an encounter of truth — either orally or literarily — that found its meaning within its own genre without a direct dependency on external verification. Hans Frei spoke of a history-likeness of a realistic novel. However, the term aroused a new host of problems and was seriously damaged as an exegetical tool from the side of modern analytical philosophy.

My second objection is that story does not do justice to the dominant feature of Paul's interpretation of Israel's role as herald of the gospel, namely, his appeal to Israel's Scriptures. One does not have to look long at Romans 9–11 to see the overwhelming scope of its witness to sacred Scripture.[165] Within these few chapters the expression "as it is written" occurs some seven times (9:13, 33; 10:15; 11:8, 26; 15:9, 21). Paul then speaks of "Scripture says" (9:17; 10:11; 11:2). Again, Moses "writes" (10:5), and Isaiah "says," "cries out," "predicts" (9:27; 10:20; 9:29). There is also the voice of Moses, Hosea, and David (10:19; 9:27; 10:16; 9:25) repeatedly cited, and of God's speaking through the lawgiver and prophets. Finally, after mounting an argument, Old Testament passages are simply cited by Paul as affirming a biblical warrant (10:13, 18). At times it is difficult to distinguish between a direct citation and an allusion, but direct citations number well over forty.

Moreover, Paul's use of Scripture is never that of treating a dead written document from the past. Although Israel's witness is indeed written, which distinguishes it from just a story, it is always regarded as the living Word of God. It has a voice and it speaks. It is the source of life and joy, the

---

164. Hans Frei, *The Eclipse of Biblical Narrative* (New Haven: Yale University Press, 1974).

165. Otfried Hofius, "Das Evangelium und Israel. Erwägungen zu Römer 9–11," in *Paulusstudien*, p. 201.

source from which sacred tradition is continually made alive. It can be re-interpreted, joined with other parts of Scripture, detached from its original moorings to address the present concerns of Paul and his churches. When Beker identified the theme of Romans to be the faithfulness of God to his promises, the element missing in his argument was that the faithfulness of God is manifested by means of Israel's Scripture. The major response that Paul is making in answer to the objection to his message of God's salvific intent toward the Gentiles is to demonstrate that what he is preaching as the mystery of God's purpose in uniting Jew and Gentile has already been announced in Israel's Scripture. It provides the warrant through the living voices of its prophets for the proof of God's faithfulness to his promises to Israel, and at the same time reveals the universal scope of his call to the nations, indeed to the entire creation.

2. Paul's Gospel Grounded on Israel's Scriptures

Paul's argument in chapters 9–11 falls into three different sections: 9:1-29, 9:30–10:21, and 11:1-39 with a climactic doxology in verses 33-39. A second indication of the structure has been noticed in the three rhetorical questions, each of which is then further developed: 9:6, 9:30-32, and 11:1.

The problem of discerning the logical development and inner coherence of these three chapters has long been debated. However, during the last several decades controversy over their interpretation has been greatly exacerbated by the analyses of Heikki Räisänen and E. P. Sanders,[166] whose leads have been followed by many others. According to Räisänen, Paul's personal dilemma regarding his Jewish kinsfolk resulted in an incoherent struggle to relate two or three mutually conflicting perspectives, namely, Israel's irrevocable divine covenant with God, and the impartiality of God in including on the same footing with his promise a special election of Abraham's descendants.

In response, first in her dissertation and second in a highly persuasive article,[167] E. Elizabeth Johnson has made a case that a single argument

166. Heikki Räisänen, "Paul, God, and Israel: Romans 9–11 in Recent Research," in *The Social World of Formative Christianity and Judaism: Tribute to Howard C. Fee*, ed. Jacob Neusner et al. (Philadelphia: Fortress, 1988), pp. 178-206. See also E. P. Sanders, *Paul, the Law, and the Jewish People* (Philadelphia: Fortress, 1983), pp. 192-99.

167. E. Elizabeth Johnson, "Romans 9–11: The Faithfulness and Impartiality of God," in

holds Romans 9–11 together, and even has achieved an internal coherence within the letter to the Romans as a whole. Rather than focusing on three mutually exclusive answers to the problem of Israel's unbelief — an axiomatic reflex for Räisänen — Johnson seeks to show that there is an intentional balance between God's faithfulness and his impartiality that undergirds these chapters. "Paul maintains the tension between divine impartiality and faithfulness to Israel without allowing one to overcome the other."[168] Thus, the genuine contribution of Johnson lies in her recognizing that the crucial issue of God's faithfulness to his promises to Israel cannot be resolved in isolation from the other equally crucial issue, namely, God's impartiality in dealing with Jew and Gentile on precisely the same terms. Nowhere is Paul's dialectical approach more clearly expressed than in Romans 11:28: "In terms of the gospel, they are enemies of God for your sake, but in terms of election, they are beloved for the sake of their ancestors."

Our task is therefore to pursue in more detail Paul's argument in chapters 9–11 as he turns to Israel's Scriptures to make his case. Paul begins in Romans 9:1-29 by expressing his deepest sorrow for his kindred according to the flesh. Why is he anguishing? Several factors are involved. Had he not just written that nothing can separate us from God's love (8:39)? Yet it is clear by now that the majority of Jews have not embraced the gospel. Still far more is at stake for Paul than even his own highly existential feelings. In the light of Paul's central argument in chapters 1–8 that the gospel is the power of God for salvation to everyone who has faith, both Jew and Gentile without distinction, what does this message mean for Israel? According to Paul's announced gospel, the righteousness of God has been manifested toward all his creation regardless of ethnicity. Therefore, the fundamental question arises: What possible advantage does Israel have? Without a moment's hesitation, Paul recites the message of the Scriptures that recounts God's dealing with his elected people: they are the chosen children of God; theirs is the splendor of the divine presence; theirs are the patriarchs and from them, through natural descent, sprang the Messiah (vv. 4-5).

However, more than just an enumeration of Israel's past is needed.

Pauline Theology, vol. 3, ed. David M. Hay and E. E. Johnson (Minneapolis: Augsburg, 1995), pp. 211-39.

168. E. E. Johnson, "Romans 9–11," p. 222.

What good is the past history if the blessings offered no longer have validity in the present? Has God kept his promises to Israel, to those living Jews today about whom Paul is speaking and with whom he identifies himself, "my kinsfolk by race"? The rest of chapter 9 confronts this burning existential issue with the apostle's defense. The Word of God has not failed, and Paul demonstrates the abiding faithfulness to Israel by an appeal to Scripture.[169]

His first appeal is to the patriarch Abraham. Citing Genesis 21:12, Paul shows that not all of Abraham's descendants were the chosen children of God, but divine election was made only from those in the line of Isaac. (Obviously a statement not contested by Jews.) Next, the witness of Moses is called forth to emphasize God's freedom to show mercy on those whom he has chosen. Wagner has convincingly shown how Paul intertwines the echoes of Exodus 32–34 to demonstrate God's mercy even in the face of Israel's unfaithfulness.[170] Then the apostle presents the objections of his imaginary Jewish interlocutor: Why then does God still find fault when no human being can ever resist his will? Paul's response is misunderstood unless one grasps the context of the debate. Paul is not saying: God can do whatever he wants, so be still (shut up) with your logical objections. Rather, Paul is debating with an imaginary orthodox Jew. He, of all people, should know from his own Scriptures that God's relation to his creation is that of the potter with the clay. By linking Isaiah 29:16 (LXX) and 45:9 (LXX), he finds a biblical warrant that God's unique commitment to Israel does not preclude his judging or redeeming the nation.

Then, by further appealing to passages from Exodus (9:16; 33:19), Paul proceeds to show that God has endowed "vessels of wrath" to extend his

---

169. Recently a book has appeared by Brian J. Abasciano, *Paul's Use of the Old Testament in Romans 9.1-9* (London: T. & T. Clark, 2005). The book claims to offer an intertextual and exegetical interpretation of Paul using Richard Hays's intertextual approach by interpreting Paul's allusions in relation to their original Old Testament contexts as providing a typological tapestry from which Paul's full exegetical intentions are discovered. An adequate response would require a lengthy review beyond the scope of this project. However, I do not find his method or its execution persuasive, and I doubt that he has understood the subtlety of Hays's intertextual approach. Rather, the author uses a harmonistic reading of the Old Testament passages (especially Exod 32–34) from which he draws analogies to Paul's meaning that blur rather than illuminate Paul's argument. For example, to conclude that the promises to "ethnic Israel" have been forfeited and fulfilled by the true spiritual Israel, that is, the church, is, in my judgment, a serious misunderstanding of Rom 9:1-5.

170. Wagner, *Heralds*, p. 52.

mercy also to the Gentiles. Appealing further to Hosea and Isaiah, which he conflates, Paul introduces the theme of the great reversal. Those who are not "my people" have become beloved. Wagner makes the acute observation that although Paul's reinterpretation of Israel's Scripture is motivated by the hard realities of Israel's unbelief of the gospel, Paul's intent is to find support in Israel's Scriptures that God had intended this outcome all along.[171]

In the second section of his argument for God's faithfulness to Israel, although extending his mercy to all (9:30–10:21), Paul turns to the central question of Romans 1–8. Why did Israel, which pursued righteousness based on the law, not succeed in fulfilling that law? They did not pursue it through faith, but as if it were based on works (9:30-33). What is, of course, most astonishing in Israel's pursuit (or race) for righteousness is the imagery of her stumbling over a stone placed there by God himself; Paul cites Isaiah 28:16. Precisely what is meant by the stone (Christ, Torah, God?) is still hotly debated, but the effect is clear. Being ignorant of the righteousness that comes from God, and seeking to establish their own, they did not submit to God's righteousness (10:3). "For Christ is the *telos* of the law that everyone who has faith may be justified" (10:4).

In the verses that follow, Paul once again attempts to establish his thesis by appealing to Israel's Scripture as his warrant. The interpretation of 10:5 and 6 remains controversial and no consensus has emerged. The initial issue is how to relate the citation by Moses of Leviticus 18:5 ("the one who practices the righteousness which is built on the law shall live by it") and the quotation of Deuteronomy 30:12-13 in verse 6 ("the righteousness based on faith says . . ."). A majority of commentators have heard the two voices as two contradictory alternatives, and different hermeneutical strategies have been proposed by which to interpret the contradiction.[172] More recently Richard Hays, followed by Wagner, has argued for the continuity between the two voices of Scripture.[173] It is not my intention to attempt to resolve this complex exegetical debate at this time, but rather to pursue the central point of Paul's use of Israel's Scripture in mounting his case. His point is to demonstrate from Israel's Scripture that justification comes from God without distinction between Jew and Gentile. Everyone who

---

171. Wagner, *Heralds*, p. 89.
172. Dahl, "Contradictions in Scripture," pp. 159-77.
173. Hays, *Echoes*, pp. 77-83; Wagner, *Heralds*, pp. 160-65.

calls upon the name of the Lord, that is, God, will be saved (10:13). Deuteronomy 30:12-14 is understood as assuming that the goal of the law has been realized in God's raising Christ from the dead who is the telos of the law.[174] Paul then proceeds in Romans 10:11-13 to offer scriptural evidence to support his claim that believing leads to righteousness (Isa. 28:16).

In response to the question: "How can one believe in Christ, of whom one has never heard?" Paul points to Isaiah (52:7; 53:1) as the herald of the good news. The voice of the psalmist is then also added (Ps 19:4) to buttress the universality of the voice of the gospel. Chapter 10 ends with the theme of God's purpose to make Israel jealous by offering salvation to the nations, a theme on which Paul will elaborate in his final argument. However, chapter 10 concludes with Paul returning to the overarching theme of God's continuing concern for his people Israel, disobedient and rebellious as they are, according to the witness of Isaiah 65:2.

In the third section of his argument (Rom 11:1-36), Paul picks up his original question, but now expanded with the force from chapters 9 and 10. Has God actually rejected his people? Certainly not! Once again the apostle presents himself as evidence. He is an Israelite, a descendant of Abraham (11:1; 9:3). Then turning to Israel's Scripture, he rehearses Elijah's complaint against Israel (1 Kings 19:14) and God's response: "I have kept for myself seven thousand who have remained faithful." Paul draws an analogy between that remnant, chosen by grace, and the remnant of Israel "at the present time." For his imaginary Jewish interlocutor, there is still a remnant chosen by grace.

Next, Paul elaborates on a theme first introduced in Romans 10:19. It was God's intention to harden Israel (Isa 29:10; Deut 29:4; Ps 69:22-23) in order that through their disobedience salvation would come to the Gentiles, thus making Israel jealous. A comparison is made: if Israel's trespasses mean riches for the world, how much more will Israel's full inclusion mean (Rom 11:12)! In verses 17-29 he further extends his argument with a figure of the natural branches of an olive tree being broken off in order to graft a wild shoot in their place. How much greater will be the restoration of those natural branches to their original roots!

However, a basic question still remains central to Paul's discourse. He had spoken of the remnant of Israel, but also of the hardening of the ma-

---

174. Paul W. Meyer, "Romans 10:4 and the 'End' of the Law," in *The Word in This World*, pp. 78-94.

jority of Israel for the sake of the Gentiles. What then is the future of the remaining portion of Israel? Does God's faithfulness extend also to them or only to the faithful remnant? What Paul now articulates with a clarity not found elsewhere in his letters is called a "mystery" (11:25). The spiritual blindness that has come upon the majority of Israel is only temporary. It will last only "until the full number of the Gentiles come in" (v. 25). Then it will be that "all Israel will be saved." A veritable catena of Old Testament verses is intertwined as Paul's scriptural warrant (Isa 59:20-21; Jer 31:31-34; Isa 27:9).

As one would expect, much debate surrounds the exact meaning of Paul's assertion. Wagner observes that Paul had earlier divided the term "Israel" into "the elect" and "the rest."[175] Now in chapter 11 he focuses his primary attention on the rest that had stumbled and made the entry of the Gentiles possible. It would then follow that it is the rest who have been temporarily rendered blind but whose future acceptance and blessing Paul now anticipates. Significantly, the rest who have been hardened extends "to this very day" (11:8; Deut 29:4).

At this point Otfried Hofius offers an important observation on the succeeding verses (26-27) that has seldom been seen.[176] The issue revolves on the manner by which this salvation of Israel is to occur. Usually the debate centers on whether Israel will be "converted" to Christ or will be offered another way to salvation. Hofius argues that neither of these alternatives is intended by Paul. Rather, Israel's salvation derives from a direct word of Christ and occurs in the same manner in which Paul himself came to faith, through an encounter with the resurrected and exalted Lord. Paul sees himself thus as a prototype of the electing God who has not abandoned Israel. Hofius further suggests that this self-manifestation of Christ as Lord does not necessarily imply that "all Israel" receives a direct revelation like Paul's (Gal 1:12), but that the "mystery" of Israel's salvation will be revealed through the Scriptures of Israel, the very source from which Paul found the confirmation of the salvation of "all Israel" (Isa 45:17, 25). Thus, Paul ends his lengthy argument with a resounding doxology praising the wisdom and knowledge of God by using the exalted vocabulary of Job and Isaiah.

A final summation of Romans 9–11 is offered in 15:7-13. Not by chance,

---

175. Wagner, *Heralds*, pp. 277-78.
176. Hofius, "Das Evangelium und Israel," pp. 196-202.

it was formulated by combining passages from Israel's Scripture. Christ became a servant of the Jewish people to maintain the truth of God's making good his promises to the patriarchs and at the same time to give the Gentiles cause to glorify God for his mercy. What to many modern interpreters may seem like a blatant contradiction is for the apostle a carefully balanced tension that reflects the inscrutable wisdom of God's sovereign will as the mystery of his redeeming all his creation.

3. The Hermeneutics of Paul's Use of Scripture

It has been my thesis in the previous paragraphs that the main function of Paul's discourse in chapters 9–11 arose from the painful context of the historical rejection of the gospel by the majority of the Jewish people in response to his Christian missionary proclamation of God's universal salvation of Jews and Gentiles. Paul addresses the situation theologically in defending the faithfulness of God to his covenant people by seeking to demonstrate that the good news of the gospel (the righteousness of God revealed through faith to all) had already been announced in Israel's sacred Scriptures.

For well over a century Paul's interpretation of the Old Testament has been the subject of intense scrutiny. However, within the last few decades several important books have succeeded in stimulating the New Testament discipline to a fresh analysis of Paul's hermeneutics. When I now concentrate my attention on the monographs of Dietrich-Alex Koch and J. Ross Wagner,[177] the choice is not intended to underestimate the important prior research carried on by generations of earlier scholars on which these new syntheses have been built.

Several aspects of Paul's use of the Old Testament have established themselves in a wide scholarly consensus: Paul's use of Israel's Scripture reflects a careful study of the biblical text that shows he was steeped in his material. Although his use was highly selective in most of his letters, in Romans 9–11 his usage covers the full range of the prophecies of Isaiah. His

---

177. Dietrich-Alex Koch, *Die Schrift als Zeuge des Evangeliums: Untersuchungen zu Verwendung und zum Verständnis der Schrift bei Paulus* (Tübingen: Mohr Siebeck, 1986). See also Wagner, *Heralds of the Good News,* and Christopher B. Stanley, *Paul and the Language of Scripture: Citation Technique in the Pauline Epistles and Contemporary Literature* (Cambridge: Cambridge University Press, 1992).

application of the text is exegetical and not simply a pretext or rhetorical decoration.

However, when one turns to the details of his interpretive strategy, there is far more room for debate and disagreement:

a. Wagner's impressive focus on the textual problems has confirmed that Paul's usage, with few exceptions, is dependent on Septuagintal translations that occasionally reflect a Greek text that has probably been revised from a Hebrew text. Textual evidence from the Masoretic traditions, Targums, and Qumran texts indicates that Paul has thoroughly imbibed the interpretive strategies prevalent in the first-century Hellenistic Jewish circles.

b. Both Koch and Wagner have stressed the freedom with which Paul appropriated and applied Israel's Scripture. Not only does he revise and alter the text to aid in mounting his argument, but he also exploits nuances within the Greek to make his case that depart from the Hebrew original.

c. One of the features that Wagner has demonstrated in great detail is Paul's constant conflating of two or more texts to support his exegesis. Although in some cases a conflation may be an inherited factor, usually in Romans 9–11, the conflation reflects an intentional strategy of Paul. The effect is that he can read one prophetic text, such as Hosea, through the lens of another. Often, diverse texts are unified around a single theme by a technique of clustering of texts.

d. Although Paul's use of Scripture never departs from his sense of a written Scripture, his application shows his dynamic understanding of God's Word as spoken. He constantly speaks of the voices of Moses, David, and Isaiah who "cry out," "proclaim," and "confront." These voices are not seen as isolated phenomena, but as part of a chorus of witnesses forming a wave of harmonious testimony. It is also central to Paul's use of Scripture to see how he continually shifts the historical focus from the past to the present. The Israel that rejected Isaiah's message is extended "to this day" (11:8), and for Paul the promise of deliverance of the rest of Israel remains an eschatological hope still unrealized.

e. Paul's freedom is far from arbitrary or without restraint. Rather, Scripture is a divine vehicle bearing testimony to theological reality. Its truth is thus not tied to its linguistic form, but it can be extended to embrace a fuller divine reality only partially manifested in the original form. For Paul, his rendering of Scripture is not an intentional distortion, but a truthful application when judged by its faithful apprehension of its subject matter, namely, the manifestation of God in Jesus Christ.

f. Some modern scholars have described Paul's interpretation of the Old Testament as a "christological misreading,"[178] a term popularized by Harold Bloom.[179] The implication is that Paul has imposed on the ancient Jewish Scriptures his own alien theological construct that runs in the face of its literal, plain sense. Such a characterization would have been incomprehensible to Paul, who would have insisted that his reading was true to an essential christological reality undergirding the biblical text.

The major hermeneutical point I would make is that Paul's intertextual, christological reading is not a misreading, but a truthful witness to the Old Testament when read in the context of the dramatic transformation of reality achieved by the death and resurrection of Jesus Christ. There is no exegetical indication in the Pauline corpus that Paul sets his reading as only a strategy by which to form a dialectic with an alleged plain reading of Israel's Scripture (contra Meeks). As an apostle, he bears truthful witness to Jesus Christ by transforming the Jewish Scriptures to bear testimony to God's new divine activity. To name Paul's reading a misreading is to introduce an inappropriate history-of-religions category that assumes a text's true meaning is only its plain sense determined by its original historical context. Of course, Paul is aware that Israel's Scriptures can be read by the contemporary Jewish audience without its grasp of its true christological referent. Therefore, he is careful in mounting his argument in Romans 9 ("not all of the descendants of Abraham are the children of promise") to develop his case in this chapter according to a common understanding of the text shared by his Jewish interlocutor.

I am fully aware that the Christian Bible consists of two distinct testaments in which the Old Testament retains its canonical authority as a testimony to God's creative activity in electing a people, Israel. This means that the Old Testament continues to sound its own discrete voice, and cannot be rendered into a timeless typological metaphor. For this reason the task of biblical theology arises within the church when the New Testament is heard in concert with the Old Testament, and in a form in which its evangelical witness to Christ has incorporated the voice of a christologically transformed Old Testament.

---

178. Hays, *Echoes*, pp. 16, 74-75, 112-15; Wayne A. Meeks, "On Trusting an Unpredictable God," in *In Search of the Early Christians*, pp. 210-29.

179. Harold Bloom, *The Anxiety of Influence* (New York: Oxford University Press, 1973); Bloom, *A Map of Misreading* (New York: Oxford University Press, 1975).

However, this is a hermeneutical problem that has not arisen in Paul's letters. He does not play his christological reading over against its original plain sense, but as an apostle bears his true witness to the gospel often by reinterpreting the plain sense of the Old Testament text. Even to suggest with Wagner that there is an "undertow" of the original sense in Paul's letters remains largely a subjective modern judgment,[180] not integral to Paul himself, but arising from the *Wirkungsgeschichte* of the church's subsequent interpretation.

4. The Canonical Function of Romans 9–11

One of the major theses of this book has been that the letter to the Romans has been assigned an introductory role to the Pauline corpus. Romans serves to present Paul's mature, systematic theological reflections at the end of his missionary career in which he reviewed many of the burning, contingent events of his churches. Romans provided a coherence to the contingencies of his earlier letters without sacrificing their particularity. The shaping of the Pauline corpus by its apostolic and postapostolic tradents, when received and read by succeeding generations, established an interpretive means by which these once occasional letters were understood analogically as a guide to future church challenges. We also observed how this canonical function of the Pauline corpus was further developed by the Pastoral Epistles, which actualized the normative role of Paul's teachings in his apostolic witness to the gospel for the future generations of the Christian church.

The problem arose in understanding the canonical function of Romans that chapters 9–11 were not primarily a review of contingent events related to a particular church (contra Donfried) that he had faced in earlier critical situations. Rather, there was a lingering theological problem for Paul that increased in intensity as the growth of the Gentile churches only exacerbated the problem raised by the Jewish rejection of the gospel. For Paul, the issue was highly existential (9:1-3). Was God faithful to his promises to Israel? When Paul announced that God showed no partiality, was Israel's special role negated and rendered worthless?

The canonical significance of Romans 9–11 lies in the way Paul uses the Scriptures of Israel — shortly to become the church's Old Testament —

---

180. Wagner, *Heralds,* p. 220.

with abiding authority. In the Pastorals we observed that Timothy and Titus were admonished to continue the reading of Scripture. 2 Timothy 3:16 spoke of its ongoing function as a guide for nurturing and instructing their churches. However, it is only in Romans 9–11 that a detailed model is provided on how the Old Testament is to be read and used in Christian theological reflection.

What then can be discerned hermeneutically from Romans 9–11? Israel's sacred Scripture remains the church's Word of God. It has not been replaced by the evangelical traditions of the gospel, but now christologically understood, it bears continual witness to the creator God whose intent in the election of Israel entered into the history of his covenant people. The Old Testament bears testimony to God's unswerving grace and mercy to all his creation. Israel's history not only points to the fulfillment of the divine promises to Israel, but also testifies to the divine entrance of God's actual presence, an ontological adumbration of the obedient servant who was in the "fullness of time" incarnated in Jesus Christ.

Nevertheless, Israel's witness remains the Old Testament. It is separated canonically from the New, which was not just an extension of the Old. Rather, the Christian church was born anew from the divine impact of Christ's death and resurrection. The significance of this event was only gradually understood from the light of the Old Testament, while conversely the Old Testament received its fuller meaning from that of the New (Augustine).

Paul's use of Israel's Scripture in Romans 9–11 is a model for understanding its canonical function within the Pauline corpus, but also for the New Testament as a whole. The message of the Old Testament is not the same as that of the New. Prophecy is different from fulfillment. Yet in the light of God's full revelation in Jesus Christ, these ancient writings of Israel can now be understood, not only according to their original historical contexts, but also as the living Word of God testifying to the eternality of God as Father, Son, and Spirit. Thus, the church prays, as did Israel, with the words of the Psalter, but instinctively understands that the Lord, who is our shepherd (Ps 23:1), is also the good shepherd of John 10:11. Like faithful Israel who awaited the salvation of its covenant God, we Christians also live in hopeful expectation of our redemption and that of "all Israel" with whom we will be finally united in God's time.[181]

---

181. See the interesting essay of Wilhelm Vischer, "Das Geheimnis Israels. Eine Erklärung der Kapitel 9–11 des Römerbriefs," *Judaica* 6 (1950): 81-132. It is followed in the

VIII. The Apocalyptic Shape of Paul's Theology

The significance of the apocalyptic traditions for the study of the New Testament emerged during the late nineteenth century, but it received its high profile in the twentieth century from the works of Albert Schweitzer.[182] Since the ensuing history of his interpretation has been reviewed many times,[183] it will not be necessary to repeat it in any detail. Initially, Schweitzer's work had a profound effect on the search for the historical Jesus, and did much to undercut the widely prevailing liberal view of Ritschl and Harnack, who regarded the kingdom of God as an ethical goal to be pursued by a continuing social agenda for the Christian church. Shortly thereafter, Schweitzer also applied the concept of apocalyptic eschatology to the study of Paul, which has been an important emphasis ever since.

Beginning in the 1930s, many attempts were made to meet the challenge of Schweitzer and his successors. Within the English-speaking world, the work of C. H. Dodd reflected his lifelong interest in the subject of eschatology/apocalyptic.[184] In Germany, Rudolf Bultmann dominated the field of New Testament in the decades before and after World War II in offering a fresh existentialist interpretation of apocalyptic tradition.[185] Then beginning in the 1950s, from within the Bultmann school, Ernst Käsemann presented a major challenge to the Bultmann consensus in a series of provocative essays that were encapsulated by his famous slogan: "Apocalyptic

---

same issue by an essay of Leo Baeck, "Das Judentum auf alten und neuen Wegen," pp. 133-48. Baeck closes his essay with the affirmation: "Judaism and Christianity are bound together with one another through the mystery."

182. Schweitzer, *The Quest of the Historical Jesus* (1906; reprint, New York: Macmillan, 1968); Schweitzer, *Paul and His Interpreters: A Critical History* (1911; reprint, London: A. & C. Black 1912); Schweitzer, *The Mysticism of Paul the Apostle* (1930; reprint, London: A. & C. Black, 1931). See Norman Perrin, *The Kingdom of God in the Teachings of Jesus* (London: SCM, 1963), for an overview of the responses to Schweitzer with an emphasis on the English-speaking academic reaction.

183. The most recent review is offered by R. Barry Matlock, *Unveiling the Apocalyptic Paul* (Sheffield: Sheffield Academic, 1996).

184. Charles H. Dodd, *The Parables of the Kingdom* (London: Nisbet, 1935); Dodd, *The Apostolic Preaching and Its Development* (London: Hodder and Stoughton, 1936); Dodd, *History and the Gospel* (London: Nisbet, 1938).

185. Bultmann, *Jesus and the Word* (New York: Scribner, 1934); Bultmann, *Theology of the New Testament*, 2 vols. (New York: Scribner, 1952-54); Bultmann, *History and Eschatology* (Edinburgh: University Press, 1957).

is the mother of all Christian theology."[186] Käsemann's influence has continued to expand, especially in North America, and one now speaks of the "apocalyptic Paul" as the center of a new renaissance within the field.

There are several initial problems that every interpreter must face in addressing the subject of apocalypticism. First, what is meant by the term "apocalyptic"? In spite of a half-century of intense debate, its definition remains unsettled.[187] Second, and closely akin, is how the term, both as a literary genre and as a social/theological concept, relates to its history-of-religions' origins and growth. Not only from the Old Testament, but also from its subsequent explosion within Jewish and wider sectarian circles, it is clear that the questions of literary genre and phenomenological manifestations are closely intertwined.

In the light of the complexity of these initial problems, it would be folly to attempt to offer yet another definition. Moreover, my concern with the subject of apocalypticism is far narrower in scope. It focuses on the central question of a canonical reading of the Pauline corpus. Specifically, how does the subject of apocalyptic in its various manifestations — historical, literary, theological — affect the reading of this New Testament corpus? How does one even structure an approach that can address this particular concern without unpacking all the multifaceted topics that have entered into its lengthy debate?

1. The Old Testament Background of Apocalypticism

Initially, I would defend the use of the term "apocalyptic" despite all its continuing difficulties and ambiguities because of its role within the Old Testament. There is widespread agreement that in the late postexilic period, including both the Persian and Hellenistic eras, a new phenomenon, different from that of the prophetic traditions, emerged. The exact

---

186. Käsemann, "The Beginnings of Christian Theology," in *New Testament Questions of Today*, p. 102.

187. See the following works: Richard E. Sturm, "Defining the Word 'Apocalyptic': A Problem in Biblical Criticism," in *Apocalyptic and the New Testament*, ed. Joel Marcus and Marion L. Soards (Sheffield: Sheffield Academic, 1969), pp. 17-48; Martinus C. de Boer, "Paul, Theologian of God's Apocalypse," *Interpretation* 56 (2003): 21-33; Douglas Harink, "Apocalypse: Galatians and Hauerwas," in *Paul among the Postliberals* (Grand Rapids: Brazos, 2003), pp. 67-103.

origins of the change remain debated. In one important sense, it offered a radicalization of prophecy, but it also involved other forces as well, including wisdom, mythology, mathematical speculation, astronomy, and mysticism. Daniel never addresses his hearers with the traditional idiom of the prophets: "hear the Word of Yahweh," but rather he interprets dreams and has visions. Above all, he is concerned with the end of all history, the signs of which are presented in a series of events increasing in evil and apostasy (an "abomination of desolation"). Using the genre of *vaticinium ex eventu,* he portrays in his visions of the last days the imminent denouement of the world as the Most High God, the Ancient of Days (Dan 7:9-10), intervenes from heaven to cut off the wicked rule of Satan's rulers and to establish his everlasting kingdom of the saints. In striking contrast to the prophetic hope of a transformed Zion as the city of God to which the nations flow in peace and harmony (Isa 2:1-4), the apocalyptical writer sees the corruption of the world being so pervasive that a new aeon, discontinuous with the historical past, must be created by direct divine intervention.

Of course, the basic hermeneutical problem facing the New Testament writers was how an apocalyptical message could serve future Christian generations that appeared so securely anchored to the past Maccabean age, particularly one so closely related to the tyranny of Antiochus IV Epiphanes (d. 163 B.C.E.). There is strong evidence that the interpretation of Daniel had been sharply altered by those who read it. Thus, the author of 4 Ezra 12:10-36 was well aware that his interpretation differed from that originally understood by the visions of Daniel when he identified "the fourth beast" with Rome, not Greece. Similarly, the writers of the New Testament Gospels, who also lived in the Roman period and portrayed the Christian communities as suffering under the persecution of the fourth kingdom (Matt 24; Mark 13; Luke 21), provide additional evidence that the book of Daniel was still being understood eschatologically in the post-Maccabean age, as a true witness to the end of the age, which still lay in the future.

It is important to notice how the book of Daniel was reinterpreted. The belief in the coming new age, which would be ushered in by God, was not separated from the end of the fourth kingdom and then projected into the future. Rather, the original sequence of the destruction of the last world power and the immediate entrance of the kingdom of God was retained unaltered. Then both the period of the fourth kingdom and the coming divine kingdom were projected into the future to constitute the end of the age. The policy of Antiochus against the Jews was now understood typologically. Antiochus had become a representation of the ultimate apocalyptic enemy. For the reader of the canonical book, Daniel still spoke apocalyptically of the end of the old age and the expectation of the new.

2. Characteristic Features of Apocalypticism

It is the usual practice of the various introductions to the subject of apocalyptic to provide a list of features that are generally regarded as common to the genre of the phenomenon. Two well-known lists typify the move.

According to Klaus Koch,[188] the following elements are generally present in apocalyptic:

a. the present constitutes the last days,
b. resurrection, world judgment, new aeon,
c. imminent end and fate of the individual,
d. sequence of world kingdoms,
e. periodization of history,
f. invasion of wickedness.

The list of Philipp Vielhauer is as follows:[189]

a. doctrine of two ages,
b. pessimism and transcendental hope,
d. universalism and individualism,
e. determinism and imminent expectation.

Then both authors attempt to expand the lists with more specific characteristics of the literary genre: pseudonymity, visions, ecstatic experiences, and historical surveys. Also a variety of literary forms are frequently seen as prophetic utterances, blessings, symbolic acts, and wisdom apho-

---

188. Klaus Koch, "Einleitung," in *Apokalyptik,* Wege der Forschung 365, ed. K. Koch (Darmstadt: Wissenschaftliche Buchgesellschaft, 1982), pp. 1-29.
189. Philipp Vielhauer, "Apokalypsen und Verwandtes," in *Apokalyptik,* pp. 403-39.

risms.[190] In his article on the social function of apocalyptical language, Wayne Meeks identifies three dualities: cosmic, temporal, and social,[191] to which J. Louis Martyn would add a fourth.[192] Finally, in an attempt to throw a net wide enough to encompass the sheer complexity of the genre being described, John J. Collins offers an expansive definition: "'Apocalypse' is a genre of revelatory literature with a narrative framework, in which a revelation is mediated by an otherworldly being to a human recipient, disclosing a transcendental reality which is both temporal, insofar as it envisages eschatological salvation, and spacial, insofar as it involves another, supernatural world."[193] Despite the care and learning of these various scholars to describe the essence of apocalyptic, when one next seeks to apply these categories to an understanding of the apostle Paul, one is left with a deep sense of uneasiness. In an incisive, probing essay over two decades ago, Leander Keck struck at the heart of some of the difficulties.[194] First, these lists of commonality found in apocalypticism necessarily suffer from abstraction. To speak of different aeons, of world judgment, or of periodization may not be wrong, but the more interesting features that divided the usages of such categories tend to be lost or flattened in the process. If we have all been taught during the last half-century that poetry cannot be successfully paraphrased, does not the same lesson also apply to apocalyptic?

Second, Keck has pointed out that many of the alleged elements of commonality are not found in Paul, but in fact at times represent the very antipathy of his theology. For example, the issue of theodicy (why the innocent suffer) has been fully dissolved through Paul's theology of the cross. Or again, such a feature as "pessimism" is fully inadequate even to

---

190. The most exhaustive collection of the full range of options is still that edited by David Hellborn, *Apocalypticism in the Mediterranean World and Near East* (Tübingen: Mohr Siebeck, 1983). Several more recent attempts at defining and describing apocalyptic material are Martin Hengel, "Paulus und die frühchristliche Apokalyptik," in *Kleine Schriften*, vol. 3 (Tübingen: Mohr Siebeck, 2002), pp. 302-417, and Michael Wolter, "Apokalyptik als Redeform im Neuen Testament," *New Testament Studies* 51 (2005): 171-91.

191. Wayne A. Meeks, "Social Functions of Apocalyptic Language in Pauline Christianity," in *Apocalypticism in the Mediterranean World and Near East,* pp. 667-705.

192. J. Louis Martyn, "Epistemology at the Turn of the Ages," in *Theological Issues in the Letters of Paul,* pp. 89-110.

193. John J. Collins, "Introduction: Toward the Morphology of a Genre," *Semeia* 14 (1979): 9.

194. Leander E. Keck, "Paul and Apocalyptic Theology," *Interpretation* 38 (1984): 229-41.

touch on Paul's description of sin and the human condition. Third, the emphasis of such lists of commonality, viewed from a history-of-religions perspective, while occasionally helpful, runs the serious risk of bypassing the radical transformation of apocalyptic that Paul has effected. Even to assume that inherited imagery always provided the initial force for his thought, rather than being a secondary rhetorical flair, calls for constant critical evaluation. We shall return to this methodological problem shortly when we briefly review some of the major scholarly reconstructions of the twentieth century.

3. Apocalyptic and the Growth of Early Christianity

One of the first things to observe is that each of the major attempts of New Testament scholars to address the subject of apocalypticism involves not only a particular understanding of the terminology; it also provides a larger historical, literary, and theological construct of its place within the development of early Christianity and the New Testament canon. This point can be illustrated by briefly reviewing several of the leading interpretations of Paul that have sought to respond to the challenge of Schweitzer.

a. Charles H. Dodd   Dodd began his early works with a view of apocalyptic much like that of Schweitzer, being a part of Paul's Jewish background. Accordingly, the world was under the dominance of demonic forces. The apocalypticist looked for a new order when God would radically alter the universe by direct intervention. Jesus himself was influenced by such beliefs, but he transformed them by announcing that the eschatological kingdom of God is a present reality. The kingdom of God has come and Jesus' ministry is one of realized eschatology. In Dodd's book on the parables, he sets out this transformation of traditional Jewish eschatology.

In the period after the death of Jesus, the early Christian community, along with Paul, briefly continued to toy with apocalyptic traditions. Dodd finds this illustrated in the Thessalonian letters,[195] but then shortly Paul's thinking took a new turn. Future eschatology is replaced by the insight that the new apocalyptic age has already arisen. The principle of "realized

---

195. Dodd, *Apostolic Preaching*, pp. 31, 37-38.

eschatology"[196] continues the initial ministry of Jesus, but Paul develops it further into a Christ-mysticism. All the expectations of the future have been fulfilled in the death and resurrection of Christ. For Paul, apocalyptic terminology has become a symbolic system manifesting the divine purpose in history. In fact, increasingly for Dodd apocalypticism has become a philosophy of history by which symbolically the true meaning of history is unlocked in the Christ event. The trajectory of the transformation of primitive Jewish eschatology extends from Jesus to Paul and John, and continues to provide a present hermeneutic by which the church understands the new crises arising from future historical events.

b. Rudolf Bultmann Bultmann has been very consistent from the start in setting forth his understanding of the role of apocalypticism in the development of early Christianity. In Bultmann's interpretation Jesus stands in the historical context of the Jewish expectation about the end of the world and of God's new future.[197] The presuppositions are the familiar ones, not unlike those of Schweitzer. There is the pessimistic, dualistic view of the world immersed in demonic corruption. Again, the end of the aeon is approaching and the new is about to dawn with divine intervention. This results in the coming of the divine representative from heaven, and the rewards for good and punishment for evil in a universal judgment. However, Bultmann insisted that Jesus broke out of this traditional Jewish eschatology. He announced that the eschatological "now" has come. God's reign is breaking in. It is not here, but is dawning. Jesus' call is for decision to prepare for its arrival.

In the postresurrection period, Jesus' preaching was retained in its mythological form, but shortly that began to change. This occurred largely within the Jewish Hellenistic communities that formed the background for Paul's message. Because of the experience of the Spirit and the demands exerted from its early missionary activity, various changes occurred along with a continuing apocalyptic expectation. Out of this Hellenistic context,[198] Paul's transformation of apocalyptic emerged. The crucial step was taken when Paul declared that the change from the old aeon to the new did not take place in the future, but in the coming of Jesus Christ.

---

196. Dodd, *Parables of the Kingdom*, pp. 36, 51.
197. Bultmann, *Theology*, 1:4-5.
198. Bultmann, *Theology*, 1:49-53, 173-76, 346-48.

With the resurrection of Christ the decisive event had already happened. The hopes and promises of the prophets were fulfilled when the kerygma was proclaimed and a response of faith was evoked from its hearers.

The process of overcoming the mythology of apocalypticism, roughly akin to that of Dodd, was given a far more precise, philosophical basis in Bultmann's famous program of demythologizing. The obsolete worldview was not simply removed, but reinterpreted to address the basic problems of human existence, and thus provided him freedom from the world of anxiety. It lies beyond this brief presentation to explore the existential philosophical position that undergirded Bultmann's anthropological reading of Paul's kerygma. However, the effect of his reading is that a trajectory is sketched that moved from an inherited worldview of Jewish mythology to an apocalypticism that was initially transformed by Jesus. Then the apocalyptical features were radically reduced as peripheral, first by Paul, and then even more consistently by John.[199] Especially significant for Bultmann is that the development of the Christian church shortly moved in a different direction, first represented by Luke-Acts, and ultimately to the Pastorals in which the dynamic transformation of Paul and John in penetrating to the existential meaning of an outmoded worldview was lost as the church adapted itself to a hierarchical episcopacy and accommodated its faith to a state religion within Roman culture.

c. Oscar Cullmann   The treatment of Oscar Cullmann can be brief because his major work preceded the growing debate over the role of apocalypticism launched by Käsemann. Cullmann's concern was above all to challenge the eschatological picture of Jesus and Paul articulated by Schweitzer. Along with his criticism of Schweitzer, however, he turned his polemic against Bultmann and his understanding of eschatology and history.

Briefly stated, his thesis was that the key to understanding the New Testament as well as the Old was a theology of history *(Heilsgeschichte)*.[200] This particular biblical history was a time line that extended from the creation of the world in Genesis to the fulfillment of God's rule in the final

---

199. Bultmann, *Theology,* 2:183-86.

200. First clearly stated in his *Christ and Time* (1946; reprint, London: SCM, 1951), and further expanded in *Salvation in History* (1965; reprint, London: SCM, 1967). See R. Bultmann's critical review of Cullmann's *Christ and Time* in *Existence and Faith: Shorter Writings of Rudolf Bultmann*, ed. S. M. Ogden (London: SCM, 1985), pp. 226-40.

consummation of the ages. The most significant feature of this time line, which extended from the beginning to the end, was that, in contrast to Judaism, the New Testament shifted its middle point from that of Torah to the death and resurrection of Christ. From this one point, a christological perspective was given by which to understand both Israel's past and the church's future. Cullmann acknowledged that this form of biblical history was indeed at times mythical in nature rather than being strictly historical, but then he argued that the sense of the whole was rendered by the historical fact of the Christ event. This extended time line thus received its eschatological fulfillment from Christ's death and resurrection manifested in this one salvific event: the now of the kerygma, the eternal redemptive purpose of God from eternity.

Cullmann's understanding of a linear time line consisting of different stages within a unified *Heilsgeschichte* was frequently criticized by those who thought he had relativized the uniqueness of Christ's death and resurrection by placing it within a continuous series of other events. Did not this move overlook the radical discontinuity reflected in Paul's dramatic eschatology? In addition, some claimed that Cullmann's thesis had been damaged with the publication in 1954 of Hans Conzelmann's book *Die Mitte der Zeit* (poorly rendered as *The Theology of Luke*), which argued that a concept of "salvation history" was only in Luke's account of the gospel and was lacking in Matthew, Mark, and Paul.

Finally, there is one crucial point in Cullmann's reconstruction of history that did affect his understanding of the growth of the early church. Although Cullmann followed, by and large, a traditional interpretation of the formation of the New Testament canon as a means to protect the apostolic tradition from the heretical attack of Gnosticism according to a *regula fidei*, Cullmann's insistence on a single time line had a deleterious effect on the church's approach to the Old Testament. Rather than to draw out the theological implications of a Christian Bible's consisting of two testaments, an Old and a New, Cullmann's scheme of a single time line left little place for the discrete witness of the Old Testament with both a vertical and horizontal canonical function for the church, in which the two testaments related in a subtle dialectical interaction. Actually the church sought to do full justice to the relation between the two testaments with its christological content, by seeking to ground the Christian faith upon a trinitarian doctrine, which theological development reached its culmination only in the fourth and fifth centuries.

d. Ernst Käsemann In a series of brilliant articles commencing in 1954,[201] Käsemann set forth his understanding of the key role of apocalyptic in the development of early Christian theology that stretched from Jesus to Paul and beyond to the second-century Church Fathers. Beginning with his crucial essay "Sentences of Holy Law in the New Testament," he offered a form-critical study of a particular mode of early Christian proclamation that he set within the context of charismatically endowed primitive Christian prophets. He argued that this legal form arose from apocalyptic and Old Testament prophets. These sentences reflected the heightened eschatological response to the presence of Christ in the Spirit as ruler of the cosmos in the expectation of the imminent return of Christ in judgment during the last days.

Six years later he published his provocative essay "The Beginning of Christian Theology" in which he presented a critical reconstruction of the earliest post-Easter communities. He described this phenomenon with the nomenclature of "enthusiasm," namely, the spirit-filled celebration of the presence of Jesus Christ that was joined with an apocalyptic ceremony announcing Christ's imminent return. Shortly a tension developed within the groups between the strict Jewish-Christian party still grounded in Torah observance and the more liberal Hellenists who formed around Stephen and the seven for a mission to the Gentiles, thus preparing the way for Paul. These Christian Hellenists were rooted in Jewish apocalyptic traditions that they joined with the possession of the Spirit as the pledge of the coming parousia. The heart of this primitive Christian theology was seen in the accession to the throne of heaven by God and his Christ, an event that served as the manifestation of the righteousness of God. It is from this force that Käsemann designated apocalyptic as "the mother of Christian theology."

It is important to observe that Käsemann did not include the historical, earthly Jesus as an apocalyptic figure. Jesus' own preaching did not bear an apocalyptic stamp, but rather he proclaimed the immediacy of God. He himself was not the subject of his message. Instead, he challenged his hearers to prepare for the encounter with the gracious God who comes both to liberate and to judge. Käsemann suggested that this nonapocalyp-

---

201. These articles were reprinted in *New Testament Questions of Today:* "Sentences of Holy Law in the New Testament," pp. 66-81; "The Beginning of Christian Theology," pp. 82-107; "The Subject of Primitive Christian Apocalyptic," pp. 108-37.

tic Jesus explains why the early post-Easter Christian message was not driven by the preaching of the earthly Jesus, but rather from the apocalyptic consequences of his death and resurrection.

The next step in the growth of Christian theology arose from the role of Paul, who found himself fighting on two fronts. He strove against, on one side, those Jewish Christians who continued to insist on Torah observance, and on the other side, the dangers emerging from the ranks of the Hellenistic enthusiasts who failed to understand the needed "eschatological reservation" in their triumphant celebration of heavenly freedom. In response to the errors of both extremes, Paul developed his understanding of God's righteousness as the justification of the ungodly. The centrality of the cross demonstrated forever the inability of the law to break the enslavement from the demonic powers of sin and to redeem not the pious, but the ungodly.

In his debate with Bultmann over the terminology of Romans 1:1-17,[202] Käsemann argued that Paul had radicalized and universalized the divine promise in his doctrine of the rectification of the ungodly. The righteousness of God expressed itself as power *(Macht),* that is, as God's own activity and nature as sovereign ruler. God's gift is never separated from the giver, but God himself has entered the arena and remains within it, subordinating all creation to his lordship. Käsemann therefore sought to undercut Bultmann's anthropological interpretation by making the heart of Paul's proclamation Christ's seizure of power as the Cosmocrator in his reign over the whole universe. Apocalyptic serves the central role in Paul's thinking since it provides the axis on which universal history, the lordship of Christ, and the righteousness of God are joined. It also provides the key to understanding the development of early Christian theology.

Finally, Käsemann's survey of the history of early Christian theology was most clearly formulated in his polemical article entitled "Paul and Early Catholicism."[203] Accompanying the growing loss of belief in the imminent return of Christ, early Catholicism domesticated and even subverted Paul's radical apocalyptic understanding of history. Already in the Gospel of Luke and in Acts, Käsemann perceived the process of an idealization of the church, as its message became a static deposit of doctrine,

---

202. E. Käsemann, "The Righteousness of God in Paul," in *New Testament Questions of Today,* pp. 168-82.

203. Käsemann, "Paul and Early Catholicism," pp. 236-51.

controlled by the sacramentally guaranteed ecclesiastical offices. For his part, Käsemann found his recovery of the apocalyptic beginnings of true Christian theology to be his challenge for the modern church to reclaim its radical, eschatological message for the sake of the church and the world.

It is now time to summarize this chapter on the role of apocalyptic in the development of early Christian theology. In every case the construct being offered involves not only a proposal regarding the origin and growth of apocalyptic within the development of the early church, but also serious implications for the interpretation of the biblical material within the final canonical form of the New Testament. In a word, there are profound implications for the role of the canon and the enduring significance of the phenomenon of apocalypticism in the ongoing life of the Christian church. Dodd's treatment of apocalyptic that focused on a concept of "realized eschatology" rendered the apocalyptic material into a symbolic role as flexible images and proposed a trajectory from Paul to John as the best guide for its practical assimilation within a philosophy of history. Bultmann saw apocalyptic as a peripheral feature from an ancient mythological milieu and submitted it to a process of demythologizing, according to an existentialist reading allegedly found in Paul and John. Cullmann envisioned a single linear time frame stretching from the Old Testament to the New Testament, but he subordinated the rich variety of their usages of apocalyptic material into a rigid geometric construct that largely blunted the exegetical specificity in maintaining a unified continuity of historical events. Finally, Käsemann offered a most challenging proposal in his careful reconstruction of an apocalyptical construct that traced its alleged origin and transformation within a Jewish-Christian, Hellenistic community. From this milieu Paul formulated his understanding of the apocalyptic reign of God by means of a radicalization and universalizing of the activity of God as Cosmocrator of the world by which his sovereign, righteous power was manifested in the death and resurrection of Christ in initiating the dawn of a new aeon. However, according to Käsemann, this apocalyptic understanding was almost immediately misunderstood by the Christian church and lost in the development of early Catholicism. The process by which the church established a fixed New Testament canon was deemed a sorrowful domestication of Paul's theology,[204] and rather than retaining its dynamic charismatic power, the church capitulated to a static institu-

---

204. Käsemann, "The Canon," pp. 95-107.

tion that lay claim to transmitting the spiritual gifts of God through the creation of its ecclesiastical offices.

4. Apocalyptic Traditions within the Pauline Corpus

In the preceding paragraph my concern was to review the continuing difficulties of defining precisely the nature of apocalyptic material. Nevertheless, in the end I have accepted the terminology even with all its remaining ambiguities. The main reason for this decision stemmed from the important function of apocalyptical traditions within the Old Testament when it entered into Israel's history in the Persian and Hellenistic periods, leaving its indelible stamp both on the prophetic books (e.g., Isaiah, Ezekiel, Zechariah) and, of course, on Daniel. In addition, the explosion then of Jewish apocalyptic material in the Hellenistic and Roman periods brings additional testimony of its powerful influence before and after the rise of Christianity.

I also hope to have shown that within the New Testament field, the various proposals respecting its origins, its Jewish milieu, and the Hellenistic adaptations that sought in different ways to trace apocalyptic influence within the larger framework of a developing Christian theology extended through the second century and beyond. Several significant proposals regarded apocalyptical material as unwanted, inherited baggage, peripheral to the essence of Christian faith and prone to sheer fantasy that required it to be rendered innocuous or to be demythologized. In contrast, Käsemann assigned a crucial theological role to apocalyptic, but his understanding of apocalyptic was derived from a highly restricted selection of apocalyptic elements that he used to form an impressive theological construct. (It is of interest to reflect on Gerhard Ebeling's response to Käsemann's 1961 essay, "The Beginnings of Christian Theology," in which Ebeling raised the still unanswered questions on the relation of Käsemann's construct to the larger history-of-religions phenomenon and its multifaceted literary legacy.)[205] The one common element that emerged from our brief review was that in no instance did the issue of canon and its development within the church play a positive role in evaluating the role of apocalyptic within the

---

205. Gerhard Ebeling's response was entitled "Der Grund christliche Theologie," *Zeitschrift für Theologie und Kirche* 58 (1961): 227-44. Käsemann then responded with expanded footnotes in "On the Subject of Primitive Christian Apocalyptic," in *New Testament Questions of Today*, pp. 108-37.

Pauline corpus. At best, canon was assigned a negative role and judged as a sign of the growth of early Catholicism.

My procedure in addressing the canonical role of apocalyptic within the Pauline corpus will be first to identify those elements within the corpus that have been widely described by biblical scholars as apocalyptic. At the outset, it is important to note that there is no formal category within the canon of apocalyptic, such as the law, prophets, and Gospels. This choice, therefore, according to its subject matter, can only be approximate since at times the identification is tied to a particular exegetical reading that is not regarded by others as directly related to apocalyptic tradition. Next, I shall attempt briefly to determine how a specific apocalyptic tradition functioned within a specific Pauline letter. Only then shall I try to draw some theological and hermeneutical implications regarding the role of apocalyptic within the Pauline corpus.

a. 1 and 2 Thessalonians   There are two passages in 1 Thessalonians in which apocalyptic traditions play a major role: 4:13-18 and 5:1-11. Beginning with 4:13, Paul addresses questions raised by some members of his congregation at Thessalonica. The issue does not turn on the truth of the resurrection of Christ, which was assumed as true. Rather, it concerns the fate of those whose Christian family and friends have died before Christ's anticipated return. How will these persons relate to those who are left alive "until the coming of the Lord" (the *parousia*)? Paul writes to comfort those who are grieving. He reassures them that those who are left alive at the time of the parousia — he appears to include himself — will not precede those who died earlier. Paul then delivers his message as "the word of the Lord"; that is, he speaks his message as a Christian prophet. Verses 16-17 share a catena of themes drawn from most probably pre-Christian and post-Easter tradition. "The Lord will descend, at the word of command, at the sound of the archangel's voice and God's trumpet-call." Then those who are still alive shall join them, "caught up together in the clouds to meet the Lord in the air." These apocalyptical themes have loose parallels in the Old Testament (e.g., Zech 12:1-6) and later pseudepigraphical apocalyptic writings.[206] However, the closest parallels are found in the so-called Synoptic apocalypses (Mark 13; Matt

206. See Abraham J. Malherbe, *The Letters to the Thessalonians,* Anchor Bible 32B (New York: Doubleday, 2000), pp. 260-308.

24; Luke 21).[207] The fact that the parousia is still part of the Aramaic-speaking Christian church before Paul is evidenced from the use of the formula *maranatha* ("come Lord," 1 Cor 16:22).

A new section begins in 5:1-11, but it continues to address the issue of the parousia. Paul writes not as if he were bringing some new information to the congregation, but when speaking of the "times and seasons" (a well-known apocalyptical abbreviation) he seeks to remind them of things they know. The parousia is simply identified as "the day of the Lord" *(yom YHWH)*, which served in the Old Testament prophets as a terrifying warning before the coming eschatological judgment (Amos 5:18-20; Isa 2:12; Joel 2:1-2). What follows would suggest that a different issue had arisen. There are some within the congregation who do not expect an imminent return of Christ but counsel an attitude of peace and security. Paul denounces this response as falsehood. They dwell in darkness and will reap God's wrath. Then Paul counsels his church to live with eschatological vigilance: "keep awake and be sober." They are to encourage each other with the hope of salvation. The letter ends with a return to the theme of living without fault until "our Lord Jesus Christ comes" (5:23).

The situation being addressed in 2 Thessalonians has again shifted. The Thessalonian congregation has been greatly shaken — frightened out of its wits — by the allegation from some source (spirit, word, or letter) that the day of the Lord has already come or is now present. Paul is quick to brand such teaching as deceptive. Then he elaborates on why such a rumor cannot be true by outlining a series of apocalyptical events that must precede the parousia: first comes the rebellion, then the "man of lawlessness" is revealed. Next, this "son of perdition" exalts himself, pollutes the temple, and claims to be God. Then and only then will the Lord Jesus appear to destroy him and his satanic powers. This sequence of apocalyptic signs is taken largely from the book of Daniel (8:11-14; 11:31-39) with additional pseudepigraphical expansion and rabbinical commentary. But once again the author does not present this information as something unknown in the community, but he calls upon them to recall what he had said to them when he was still with them (2:5).

Up to this point in surveying the contents of the two letters we have

---

207. See the critical commentaries and essays listed in Maarten J. J. Menken, *2 Thessalonians* (London: Routledge, 1994), pp. 150-55, to pursue these complex and critical issues.

refrained from entering the long-standing critical debate over the Pauline authenticity of 2 Thessalonians.[208] I think it is fair to say that the issue has not been decisively resolved and scholars of repute continue to be divided in their evaluation. However, in recent years the inauthenticity of the letter has probably become the critical judgment of a majority. My intention is not to rehearse the problems once again, but rather to suggest that the canonical effect of the apocalyptical material within the final form of corpus is the focus of our present concern. The rationale for this decision lies in its reception within the Pauline corpus as an apostolic witness. In my New Testament introduction,[209] I have argued that the canonical function of the letter is not to be immediately identified with the historical process of the letter's composition. Frequently within the Pauline corpus there are signs of an indirect relationship to Pauline authorship. "The primary issue from a canonical perspective is not whether 2 Thessalonians accords with a reconstructed portrait of the historical Paul, but rather with the profile of the canonical Paul whose testimony has been preserved within the authoritative collection of the church's scripture."[210]

One of the main canonical functions of the two letters is to affirm for the Pauline communities that the apocalyptic witness of the Old Testament, especially of Daniel, still functions as a truthful witness, of course, in need of interpretation. In 1 Thessalonians the hope of the coming parousia is used to comfort the church grieving over separation from their friends and families. It also serves to instill a way of holy Christian living in the tension caused by life "between the times." In 2 Thessalonians the apocalyptic sequence of events of Daniel continues to form a pattern describing the "signs and times," now reapplied to the present life of the church in the post-Easter period. Although there is evidence from within the Pauline corpus that the hope of Christ's imminent return did not continue with the same intensity as in the two letters of Thessalonians, nevertheless this canonical function remains, which cannot be dismissed or marginalized as though merely a remnant of "early primitive apocalyptic" thinking.

---

208. Kümmel, *Introduction,* pp. 181-90.

209. Childs, *New Testament as Canon,* pp. 358-72, and the detailed discussion in A. J. Malherbe's *Letters to the Thessalonians,* pp. 349-75. The strongest arguments against Pauline authorship of 2 Thessalonians have been mounted by Wolfgang Trilling, *Untersuchungen zum Zweiten Thessalonicherbrief* (Leipzig: St. Benno Verlag, 1972), and Menken, *2 Thessalonians.*

210. Childs, *New Testament as Canon,* p. 368.

b. Galatians   The case for seeing apocalyptic as the dominant theological force shaping the letter to the Galatians has been mounted in its most powerful form by J. Louis Martyn.[211] By his magisterial commentary, supported by a series of probing essays, Martyn has not only made an impressive case for his apocalyptical reading, but he has also clearly effected a decisive shift in the interpretation of Galatians for many decades to come.

Right from the beginning of his commentary,[212] Martyn is aware of an initial problem he must encounter. How can one characterize Galatians as apocalyptic when all the elements of apocalyptic found in 1 Thessalonians (4:13–5:11) are missing: the future return of Christ, the archangel's cry, the blowing of the last trumpet, and the general resurrection of the dead? Martyn proceeds by describing the specific vocabulary of Paul that he feels clearly reflects its apocalyptic milieu.[213]

1. The present evil age (1:4b). To speak of a present age implies that there is another age, and such a tradition has a clear parallel in rabbinic theology, which spoke of "this age" and "the coming age." Thus Martyn concludes that the conceptual frame of reference that posits two ages is a fundamental scheme of apocalyptic thought. Although Paul never speaks literally of "the coming age," he sets "the new creation" over against the old age, thus reflecting an assumption of an eschatological dualism.

2. God's apocalyptic revelation of Jesus Christ (1:12). Martyn defends his translation, instead of the usual rendering of "revelation," as far closer to the radical sense of Paul's call. He even extends the sense of 1:16 to be an event "when God apocalypsed Christ to him." In an earlier essay Martyn argued that this event involved an "epistemological turn of the ages" when a new perception was given to him because of the cross. Thereafter his vision was "bifocal."

3. God's sending of Christ "in the fulness of time" (4:4). The phrase is understood as an apocalyptic motif closely connected with the imagery of an invasion that connected the evil age and the new creation.

4. Flesh and spirit constitute opposites at war (5:16). These two ontological realities are engaged in a continuous conflict that embraces a cosmic scope extending throughout the entire universe.

5. Christ gave his life to liberate from sin (3:13). Jesus' death was the fo-

---

211. Martyn, *Galatians* and *Theological Issues in the Letters of Paul.*
212. Martyn, *Galatians,* p. 105.
213. Martyn, "Apocalyptic Theology in Galatians," in *Galatians,* pp. 97-105.

cus of God's apocalyptic warfare when humanity was freed from the malevolent grasp of the present evil age.

6. The cross of Christ has now been shared (2:20). Paul's identifying his life as one "crucified with Christ" has become paradigmatic for all Christians as the means by which their freedom has forever been won.

Anyone who carefully follows the sheer breadth and depth of Martyn's interpretation cannot but be impressed by the tremendous theological force of his presentation. There can be no question but Martyn has greatly sharpened the profile of Paul's theology through his application of an apocalyptic model.

Nevertheless, in my judgment there remain problems to be addressed in Martyn's interpretation. First, I have the impression that Martyn has, in a sense, "loaded the deck" by his translations. For example, I do not think the Greek term *apokalypseōs* (1:12) can be etymologized and read as "apocalyptic revelation." The lessons learned from James Barr[214] against etymologizing meaning are not easily overcome! The danger lies in transferring a larger construct to a particular linguistic instance. Likewise, it seems to me that the language of warfare, invasion, and battle has introduced too intensive a tone not actually present to the degree implied by this imagery. Second, I would argue that Martyn, much like his mentor Käsemann, has included within the overarching umbrella of apocalyptic, subject matter that is, at best, only indirectly related to apocalyptic, such as the "righteousness of God," justification by faith, participation in Christ's crucifixion, and baptism into Christ. Could not one argue that a phrase such as "the fulness of time" (4:4) derives equally well from the framework of *Heilsgeschichte* and is akin, say, to Hebrews 1:1? Third — and this cannot be pursued here in detail — Martyn's hermeneutical application of a "mirror image" approach[215] to Paul's theology in Galatians based on a reconstruction of the theology of the "Teachers," while at times convincing, remains also highly speculative and shapes his description of Paul's response in terms of apocalyptic.

Finally, there is another hermeneutical problem that is in need of clarification. As is well known, Käsemann spoke of apocalyptic being the

214. James Barr, *Semantics of Biblical Language* (London: Oxford University Press, 1961).

215. See the essay by John M. G. Barclay, "Mirror-Reading a Polemical Letter: Galatians as a Test Case," *Journal for the Study of the New Testament* 31 (1987): 73-93.

"mother of Christian theology." In his various articles he sought to trace theology's origin from a trajectory begun with "holy law," through Hellenistic enthusiasm, until Paul's transformation of theology by his fresh application of apocalyptic. As a result, apocalyptic was assigned a primary force in shaping Paul's theological formulation. In its role in the undisputed letters of Paul it became absolutized and used as a criterion by which to evaluate other uses of apocalyptic traditions, such as in "early primitive apocalyptic" (1 and 2 Thessalonians), and its later alleged ossification in the Pastorals. However, this assumed trajectory of the growth of apocalypticism rests on a highly subjective reconstruction that greatly affects its function within the Pauline corpus.

What I am suggesting is that there is another alternative for interpreting the role of apocalyptic, even within Galatians. It is one that does not start with the hermeneutical assumption that apocalyptic is the primary force in the development of Paul's theology, but rather is an important but secondary use of images that served Paul well in his confrontation with the troublemakers of his Galatian churches. I find it interesting that in Martyn's early essay from 1967,[216] he rarely applies the category of apocalyptic (I find one example in the text and a few in the footnotes), but he speaks of the inextricable connection between eschatology and epistemology. He locates the heart of Paul's theology in a knowledge informed "by the cross" *(kata stauron)*. Does this not imply that Christology is the primary force shaping his theology, rather than apocalyptic?

In the final paragraphs of this chapter I shall attempt to articulate why this understanding of the role of apocalyptic, not as the source but as a secondary vehicle within Paul's developing theology, affects the canonical understanding of the Pauline corpus.

c. 1 and 2 Corinthians   When one turns to the two letters to the Corinthians, one discovers that many of the apocalyptical themes found in Galatians are repeated. The "day of the Lord" will manifest itself with a fiery judgment (1 Cor 3:13). The "end of the ages" has come upon believers (10:11). The saints will judge the world, and even the angels (6:2-3). 16:22 even uses the Aramaic formula "our Lord come" for a benediction. Similar apocalyptical phrases continue in 2 Corinthians. Paul speaks of "keeping Satan from gaining the advantage over us" (2:11); of the "god of this world

---

216. Martyn, "Epistemology at the Turn of the Ages."

blinding the minds of unbelievers" (4:4); of Belial (6:15) and of Satan disguising themselves as angels of light (11:14). However, in both letters these apocalyptical references are fragmentary images that can function within wisdom and forensic contexts (1 Cor 2:7; 6:2).

However, there are several places in which an entire passage is built around apocalyptic themes. The prime example is, of course, in 1 Corinthians 15, in which Paul confronts an erroneous understanding of Christ's resurrection. The chapter begins with the apostle recounting the traditions regarding the resurrection that he had "received" as the confession of the church. This is the content of what "we preach and you believed" (15:11). Then Paul addresses the false understanding of the resurrection that "some" — exactly who is not stated — have been spreading: "How can some say that there is no resurrection of the dead?" Then Paul mounts his rebuttal that if there is no resurrection of the dead, then Christ has not been raised from the dead, and Christian faith is worthless.

Next Paul expostulates in positive terms the meaning of the resurrection: "As in Adam all die, so in Christ all shall be made alive" (15:22). When he then speaks of an order, the sequence and the terminology are clearly apocalyptic. Christ is the "firstfruits" of those who at his parousia belong to him. Then comes the *telos* (the end), which is a technical apocalyptic term, when Christ delivers the kingdom to God after destroying every ruler of authority and power. Then, citing from the Greek Old Testament, he offers a catena of scriptural passages in describing the results. The last enemy death is destroyed, and all things are put in subjugation to God.

Paul continues to address other issues regarding the nature of the new spiritual body, and concludes by unfolding a "mystery." "We shall not all sleep, but we shall all be changed, in a flash, in the twinkling of an eye, at the last trumpet . . . and the dead will rise" (15:51-52). "God be praised, he gives us the victory through our Lord Jesus Christ" (15:57). There can be no doubt but that apocalyptic provides the framework for Paul's exuberant finale.

Turning to 2 Corinthians, we find one passage that stands out as providing an apocalyptic center for a whole theme, namely, of Paul's ministry of reconciliation (5:18-19). Martyn[217] provides a convincing interpretation of this apocalyptic imagery: "if any one is in Christ, he is a new creation, the old has passed away, behold the new has come." The apostle stands at

---

217. Martyn, "Epistemology," pp. 89-110.

the juncture of the ages. The death and resurrection of Christ effects the end of the old and the beginning of the new. From now on, for anyone in the realm of Christ, there is a new creation. The old aeon has passed away; the new has come. When Paul speaks about no longer regarding Christ from a human point of view, he is arguing for a new perspective, a new way of knowing. What separates the old way from the new is the apocalyptic event of Christ's death and resurrection. The new way of knowing is not an appeal to an esoteric knowledge. It is not a mystic trance, but it is a life in the midst of a new creation, within a transformed community that knows the power of the cross to serve one's neighbor in need.

d. Romans   We turn to the last of Paul's undisputed letters. The debate over an apocalyptic reading of Romans has been initiated and dominated by Ernst Käsemann. At first the debate was carried on with Bultmann regarding the interpretation of Romans 1:16-17 and the "righteousness of God." Käsemann broke out of the old impasse over whether the righteousness of God was to be understood as an objective or subjective genitive by insisting that the passage was not to be interpreted anthropologically, but apocalyptically in reference to the power of God in exercising his sovereignty over the whole world in revealing itself apocalyptically in Jesus Christ.[218] Earlier, before this debate had begun, commentators had often noted fragments of apocalyptic traditions, such as found in Romans 13:11-13 ("salvation is nearer to us now than when we first believed") or in Romans 16:25 ("the revelation of the mystery kept secret for ages"). However, Käsemann raised the stakes dramatically in announcing boldly that an apocalyptic understanding of the doctrine of justification reveals the entire purpose of the book of Romans. It turns on God's action in Christ manifested in a universal context in which God became Cosmocrator with his power extending through the entire earthly and heavenly spheres.

It is now a truism to state that Käsemann's commentary has radically changed the debate over the apocalyptical context of Romans.[219] No one can study his interpretation without feeling its sheer power. However, once again, difficult problems emerge. Because Käsemann's understanding of the apocalyptic has been shaped by his earlier theories of the origin and

218. R. Bultmann, "dikaiosynē theou," *Journal of Biblical Literature* 83 (1964): 12-16; Käsemann, "Righteousness of God," pp. 168-93.
219. E. Käsemann, *Commentary on Romans* (Grand Rapids: Eerdmans, 1980).

history of apocalyptic traditions arising first in Judaism, reshaped by the post-Easter Hellenistic community, and finally dramatically transformed by Paul, it is often difficult to distinguish between a mind-set named apocalyptic and Käsemann's theological formulations, which extend the implications drawn far beyond the Pauline text itself.

Moreover, it is necessary in making an evaluation to reflect on what elements, even within the parameters of apocalyptic tradition, have been devalued or omitted. One example comes to mind. In an interesting essay of 1989, Martinus de Boer made the case that one can reconstruct two different tracks of Jewish apocalyptical eschatology.[220] One track provides support for Käsemann's "cosmological" reading of Paul, but the other provides some measure of support for Bultmann's "anthropological" reading. Therefore, de Boer raises the question whether Käsemann's construct for reading Romans has possibly underevaluated some genuine elements of Paul's theology that happened to be defended by Rudolf Bultmann.

e. The Pastoral Epistles   One of the frequent charges made regarding the Pastoral Epistles is that these pseudonymous epistles have lost the genuine apocalyptic message of the historical Paul and have moved into a safe bourgeois accommodation to a Greco-Roman society without a dynamic eschatology. Although few would defend the view that the brilliant and profound Christian theology of Paul found in his undisputed letters is reflected in the Pastorals, it is certainly a serious error to claim that eschatology, indeed even apocalyptic themes, has been completely lost in the Pastorals.

There is frequent mention in these letters of awaiting "the appearing of our Lord Jesus Christ" (1 Tim 6:14), of "our blessed hope, when the splendor of our great God and Savior Christ Jesus will appear" (Titus 2:13). The parousia will occur "at its proper time" (1 Tim 6:14). Timothy is admonished to guard the sacred traditions entrusted to him "until that day," the return of the Lord (2 Tim 1:12). Until then, the Christian is called upon to live a sober life "in this present age" (Titus 2:12). Timothy is to instruct his churches in righteous living lest they be "caught in the snares of the Devil and held at his will" (2 Tim 2:26). Finally, 1 Timothy 3:16 preserves an ancient creedal statement of the "mystery of our religion" that well reflects the ancient, eschatological enthusiasm of the early church:

---

220. Martinus C. de Boer, "Paul and Jewish Apocalyptic Eschatology," in *Apocalyptic and the New Testament*, pp. 169-90.

He was manifested in the body,
vindicated in the Spirit,
seen by angels,
proclaimed among the nations,
believed in throughout the world,
taken up in glory.

5. Theological and Canonical Implications of Apocalyptic

We have attempted to focus on important passages within the Pauline corpus that are generally considered to reflect apocalyptic traditions. We have then sought to investigate the nature of these various aspects of the apocalyptic traditions, to explore the sources and range of the imagery, and to consider briefly their function within each letter.

One of the first implications to be drawn is that in the Pauline letters apocalyptic, however loosely defined, is not a closed system of thought. There is no obvious stylistic coherence to be discerned, but serious elements of apocalyptic have been differently applied to meet the changing contingencies faced by Paul in his various letters.

Second, there is no compelling evidence to suggest a developing trajectory that would establish that the eschatological traditions in, say, 1 and 2 Thessalonians were of a "primitive" nature and thus judged expendable since paralleled apocalyptic elements continue to appear, if in fragmentary form, throughout the corpus (1 Cor 15).

Third, and most important, there is nothing fully persuasive in Käsemann's proposal that "apocalyptic is the mother of Christian theology," that is, its ultimate source. Such a theory not only rests on a highly speculative basis of his form-critical and traditio-historical projection ("Sentences of Holy Law in the New Testament"), but also seems in stark conflict with the very obvious forces at work from the beginning of the church's existence. Above all, the crucial role of the Old Testament in the development of Christian theology has been greatly underestimated in Käsemann's construct. Indeed, it is certainly true that the post-Easter Christian theology was not a continuation of the preaching of the earthly Jesus, nor an extension of biographical traditions of his life. Rather, the New Testament emerged from the explosive force of the death and resurrection of Jesus Christ. As a result, the theological reflection of the early church focused on how to comprehend the full significance of these events. A dialectical move developed that is evidenced especially in Paul's letters.

The Christian churches sought to understand their Jewish Scriptures, usually transmitted in a Greek translation, from the perspective of the exalted Christ, while conversely and at the same time they strove to understand God's action in Christ from the passages of the same Scriptures (see 1 Cor 15:3-11; Rom 15:4; 16:26; Acts 18:28). Of course, from such a reading of the Scriptures Jewish apocalyptic traditions entered into Paul's thinking, but not as the source of the Christian faith, and along with many other Old Testament traditions of wisdom, psalmody, and liturgy.

In my opinion, Günther Bornkamm correctly illuminated this issue when he wrote:

> It is erroneous . . . that his (Paul's) eschatology was a sort of framework taken over, touched perhaps with modification, from Jewish and primitive Christian apocalyptic, into which as into an already given fixed system he set the Christian gospel . . . and even if in fact there is a correlation between apocalyptic inheritance and Paul's gospel, the truth is the reverse: the eschatology which Paul took over he conscripted into the service of the gospel; he did not reinterpret the gospel in the light of tradition; but the latter in the light of the saving event.[221]

What then has been the effect of seeing Paul's apocalyptic theology within the context of the canonical corpus? First, it has enforced the position that Paul's theology has deep Old Testament roots, and is not merely a reformulation of late Jewish Hellenistic themes. Second, it has affirmed a theological connection between Paul's particular apocalyptic application in his undisputed letters and other apocalyptic traditions represented in the Gospels (Matt 24; Mark 13; Luke 21) as well as in 1 and 2 Thessalonians (see 2 Pet 3:8-13). Third, there is a larger structural pattern found in both the Old and New Testaments that offers a canonical context for better understanding Paul's eschatology; namely, just as the prophetic and apocalyptic witnesses within the Old Testament were distinct but often fused

---

221. Bornkamm, *Paul*, p. 198. See, in addition, the profound reflections on the theological centrality of the cross for New Testament theology in Roy A. Harrisville, *Fracture: The Cross as Irreconcilable in the Language and Thought of the Biblical Witness* (Grand Rapids: Eerdmans, 2006).

and intertwined (Jer 4:23-26; Ezek 39:1-23), so also in the New Testament the eschatological traditions of the Gospels were distinct from those of the apocalyptic Paul but nevertheless were also often fused. Thus, the canonical context of the larger Christian Bible provides a much-needed check against playing the "apocalyptic Paul" over against the "Catholic" Pastorals, or the discontinuity of apocalyptic over against the *Heilsgeschichte* of Luke-Acts.

Finally, the Bible's enduring apocalyptical witness, whether from the Old Testament or the New, sounds a confident but also terrifying and haunting note for Christians in every age: Do not grow too comfortable at home in your earthly world because God's kingdom will come in the latter days, not as a result of human moral strivings, performed with the best of will, but when God suddenly breaks off human history and his kingdom descends from above as a radically "new heaven and a new earth" (Isa 65:17-18; Rev 21:1-4).[222]

---

222. For the *Wirkungsgeschichte* of the effect of apocalyptical tradition throughout the whole history of the Christian church, see Günter Lanczkowski et al., "Apokalypten" I-IV, in *Theologische Realenzyklopädie*, vol. 3 (1978), pp. 189-257.

5. The Canonical Framing of the Pauline Corpus

I. Acts of the Apostles

The goal of this chapter appeared initially to be a limited one, namely, to describe the function of the book of Acts in relation to the Pauline corpus. However, it shortly became clear to me that the interpretation of the role of Acts was intertwined with a host of other critical issues that, at the very least, had to be recognized and briefly addressed. Although Luke-Acts is not the storm center it was thirty years ago, many of the same problems remain without a widespread consensus having been reached. Indeed, the interpretive forces seem to be even more centrifugal than before with a variety of fresh literary, historical, and theological options emerging, all of which directly or indirectly affect one's understanding of the material's canonical function. For this reason a very brief outline is needed to provide the larger context for the ensuing analysis.

1. The Debate over the Canonical Role of Luke-Acts[1]

Although the beginning of the modern critical study of Acts is usually assigned to the work of F. C. Baur in the first half of the nineteenth century,

1. Because this history has been reviewed many times, the reader is referred to the following sources: Ernst Haenchen, *Die Apostelgeschichte,* 12th ed. (Göttingen: Vandenhoeck & Ruprecht, 1959), pp. 13-46; Eckhard Plümacher, "Apostelgeschichte," in *Theologische Realenzyklopädie,* vol. 3 (1978), pp. 483-528; Joseph A. Fitzmyer, introduction to *The Gospel according to Luke,* vol. 1, Anchor Bible 28 (New York: Doubleday, 1981), pp. 3-283; Fitzmyer,

our review can begin with the debate between Adolf von Harnack and Theodor Zahn that shaped much of the later debate.[2] The many historical and theological issues turned on whether the development of the New Testament canon was a process governed by the internal force exerted by the authoritative writings themselves (Zahn), or whether it derived from a conscious creation of the church toward the end of the second century. Zahn lay stress on the theological authority leading to a natural process from the oral word of proclamation to its written form of canonization testified to by its usage. Harnack stressed the external factors by which various segments of the church representing diverse theological traditions sought to gain political power in opposing the threats from Marcion and Gnosticism. In the early twentieth century Harnack's position largely gained the upper hand and critical scholarship went through various methodological strategies to modify and expand Harnack's theses (*Tendenz* criticism, source criticism, form criticism).[3]

Then, starting in the late 1950s and continuing through the 1970s, there was a virtual explosion of interest in Luke and Acts, largely led by students and associates of Rudolf Bultmann (Conzelmann, Käsemann, Grässer, Klein, Vielhauer, etc.). They argued that Acts reflected a tendentious ideology of its Hellenistic authors who idealized the early history of the church, badly distorted the theology of Paul, and misunderstood many of the central themes of the Gospels. Particularly in the forceful rhetoric of Käsemann,[4] supported by an impressive group of like-minded Protestants, a case was mounted that starting with Luke, continued by the deutero-Pauline letters, and culminating in Acts and the Pastorals, a biblical warrant was provided for the establishment of "early Catholicism." Fortunately, the extreme nature of this formulation has been increasingly rejected as being unhelpful even by some of its earlier proponents.

---

introduction to *The Acts of the Apostles* (New York: Doubleday, 1997), pp. 47-187; Charles K. Barrett, introduction to *The Acts of the Apostles*, vol. 11 (London: T. & T. Clark, 1998), pp. xix-cxviii.

2. Theodor Zahn, *Geschichte des neutestamentlichen Kanons*, 2 vols. (Erlangen: Deichert, 1888-92); Adolf von Harnack, *Das Neue Testament um das Jahr 200* (Freiburg: Mohr, 1889); Zahn, *Einige Bemerkungen zu Adolf Harnack's Prüfung der Geschichte des neutestamentlichen Kanons* (Erlangen: Deichert, 1889).

3. See Haenchen for the details of this history, *Die Apostelgeschichte*, pp. 13-53.

4. Ernst Käsemann, "Paul and Early Catholicism," in *New Testament Questions of Today* (Philadelphia: Fortress, 1969), pp. 236-52.

During the same period there emerged another shift in the focus on Acts that stressed that the key to understanding this material lay in recovering the unity of Luke-Acts, which insight had been lost due to the canon's separating Acts from "the first book," Luke. The initial emphasis for exploring the unity of the Lukan diptych stemmed from Henry Cadbury,[5] but it was picked up by others in the post–World War II period, and in North America its leading advocate was Paul Schubert,[6] followed by many of his students. During this period the emphasis on the original unity of Luke-Acts often played an important role in describing the history of canonization, and various theories were developed that identified the inclusion of Acts into the canon with its separation from the Lukan Gospel. Only quite recently have a few voices been raised questioning the dominant role that the unity of Luke-Acts has played.[7] We shall return to this issue in a subsequent paragraph.

Then again, one of the most innovative newer approaches to the study of Acts can be roughly characterized as style criticism. Initial credit for this conscious move away from traditional historicism redounds to Martin Dibelius.[8] Dibelius had first established his reputation as an initiator of the form-critical approach to the Gospels along with Bultmann and K. L. Schmidt. However, when his essays on Acts were first published as a collection, it became immediately clear from his initial essay, "Style Criticism of the Book of Acts," that he had greatly broadened his perspective in focusing on the larger literary composition of the material. Quite recently a brilliant new extension of Dibelius's work was written by Daniel Marguerat,[9] who analyzed the whole concept of Luke as Christianity's earliest historian by comparing the style of Acts with the Hellenistic Greek historian Lucian

5. Henry J. Cadbury, *The Making of Luke-Acts,* 2nd ed. (London: Macmillan, 1958; original 1927).

6. Paul Schubert, "The Structure and Significance of Luke 24," in *Neutestamentliche Studien für Rudolf Bultmann,* ed. W. Eltester (Berlin: Töpelmann, 1954), pp. 165-86. See also Schubert's Festschrift, *Studies in Luke-Acts,* ed. Leander E. Keck and J. Louis Martyn (Nashville: Abingdon, 1966).

7. Mikeal C. Parsons and Richard I. Pervo, *Rethinking the Unity of Luke and Acts* (Minneapolis: Fortress, 1993). See also Daniel Marguerat, *The First Christian Historian* (Cambridge: Cambridge University Press, 2002), pp. 43-64.

8. Martin Dibelius, *Aufsätze zur Apostelgeschichte* (1951); ET, *Studies in the Acts of the Apostles,* ed. Heinrich Greeven (London: SCM, 1956).

9. Marguerat, *The First Christian Historian.* See also Stanley E. Porter, *The Paul of Acts: Essays in Literary Criticism, Rhetoric, and Theology* (Göttingen: Mohr Siebeck, 1999).

of Samosata and the Roman historian Dionysius of Halicarnassus. He then sought to identify the book of Acts as a form of theological historiography with important similarities and differences that provide fresh access into Luke's intention and approach when writing Acts. In a subsequent paragraph I shall attempt to show the effect of these literary insights on the study of Acts's canonical function within the New Testament.

Finally, credit should be paid to Robert Wall for his recent attempts to develop a critical methodology when interpreting Acts that is shaped by attention to its canonical form and function.[10] Wall raises many important questions, both in his essays and in recent commentary, that have often been overlooked. While I remain appreciative of his work, especially his valiant effort to overcome the negative legacy of Conzelmann and his school, for various reasons my own canonical approach moves in quite a different direction from his. In a word, I find Wall's appropriation of James Sanders's categories of "canonical criticism" ("monotheistic pluralism," "modern apostolic communities," "the church as counter-cultural") unhelpful, and that they reflect a very different understanding of the history of New Testament canonization and its modern theological appropriation (see below).

There is one important aspect to this history of scholarship that cannot be fitted into any of the discrete stages of the discipline described above because it has been a strong minority voice ever since the rise of historical critical research and has continued so unabated into the present. I am speaking of the profound contributions to the study of Acts and the Pauline corpus by European Roman Catholic scholars. Of course, in the English-speaking world the learned contribution of, say, Joseph Fitzmyer has long been recognized. But what I am suggesting is that German Protestant scholarship, which has clearly dominated the critical discussion of Luke-Acts during the last half-century, has not adequately recognized the important contributions made by certain European Roman Catholic scholars, particularly in regards to the theological dimensions of the issues. I have in mind the writings of Gerhard Lohfink, Karl Löning, Thomas Söding, and P. G. Müller in the long-overlooked volume *Paulus in den*

---

10. Robert W. Wall, "The Acts of the Apostles in Canonical Context," in Robert W. Wall and E. Eugene Lemcio, *The New Testament as Canon,* Journal for the Study of the New Testament, Supplement 76 (Sheffield: Sheffield Academic, 1992) pp. 110-32; Wall, *The Acts of the Apostles,* New Interpreter's Bible, vol. 10 (Nashville: Abingdon, 1994), pp. 3-368.

neutestamentlichen Spätschriften;[11] the brilliant essays of Heinz Schürmann;[12] and the crucial essays of Jens Schröter[13] and Joseph Verheyden[14]
in the recent volume *The Biblical Canons* (Leuven, 2003). In the paragraphs that follow, I hope to exploit some of their crucial insights.

2. The Canonization of Acts

The canonical function of Acts in relation to the whole New Testament,
but especially in relation to the Pauline corpus, can be correctly described
only when one reconstructs the historical process leading to its canonization. There is widespread agreement that the Gospel of Luke and the Acts
of the Apostles were written by the same author. Although the author of
this double work is anonymous, very early it was assumed by the church
that Luke wrote both books. (The historical correctness of this assumption
is questioned by many, but this debate will not be pursued at this juncture
since this identification is tangential to the historical process being traced.)
What is crucial at the outset is the point made by Schröter that Paul's apostolic authority was not derived from his alleged association with Luke, but
rather that the reverse was true.[15] Luke's authority as a witness to the gospel was derived from Paul's prior authority whose revelation of Jesus
Christ had been earlier established: in the church's earliest traditions.

A very strong case can be made that in about the same historical period two independent corpora emerged, a fourfold Gospel corpus and a
Pauline corpus. The age of the Gospel corpus is usually set at the end of the
first century or beginning of the second; the Pauline at the beginning of
the second, if not slightly earlier.[16] A crucial observation in determining

11. Karl Kertelge, ed., *Paulus in den neutestamentlichen Spätschriften. Zur Paulusrezeption im Neuen Testament,* Quaestiones Disputatae 89 (Freiburg: Herder, 1981).

12. Heinz Schürmann, "Das Testament des Paulus für die Kirche," in *Traditionsgeschichtliche Untersuchungen zu den Synoptischen Evangelien* (Düsseldorf: Patmos, 1968),
pp. 310-40.

13. Jens Schröter, "Die Apostelgeschichte und die Entstehung des neutestamentlichen
Kanons," in *The Biblical Canons,* ed. J.-M. Auwers and H. J. De Jonge (Leuven: University
Press, 2003), pp. 395-429.

14. Joseph Verheyden, "The Canon Muratori: A Matter of Dispute," in *The Biblical
Canons,* pp. 487-556.

15. Schröter, "Die Apostelgeschichte," p. 404.

16. Martin Hengel, "The Superscriptions of the Gospels," in *The Four Gospels and the*

the role of Acts has been made by Schröter,[17] whose conclusions were earlier defended by Haenchen, D. Kuck, and C. K. Barrett, namely, that Luke's Gospel functioned independently of Acts. The lack of any significant external mention of Acts until Irenaeus and Tertullian[18] provides important evidence in interpreting the role of Acts in the canonical process. Moreover, when attention did turn to Acts, it was in the context of Marcion's threat in the middle of the second century. This history calls into question Harnack's theory that the book of Acts provided the decisive key in legitimating the link between Paul's letters and the Gospels.[19] Similarly, the assumption that Luke-Acts functioned together in the church as a unified two-volume work until they were separated by the canonization of Acts appears increasingly dubious in the light of Schröter's research.

Fitzmyer's commentary presents well the arguments for dating the composition of Luke about A.D. 80-85.[20] The earlier proposed date of the 60s is refuted by Luke's relation to Mark and his apparent reference to the destruction of Jerusalem in 70. Similarly, a late date in the second century between 100 and 130 is highly unlikely and lacks any alleged dependency on Josephus or Marcion. More difficult is the problem of determining the date of the composition of Acts. Often it has been assumed because of the Luke-Acts hypothesis that Acts shared the same dating as Luke. However, several indices point to a later date for Acts.[21] The description of the church's history covered by Acts extends from A.D. 30 to 60, but the perspective of the writer describes a church that shares features of a later period. For example, the Lukan Paul reflects many characteristics of the Pas-

---

One Gospel of Jesus Christ (Harrisburg, Pa.: Trinity, 2000), pp. 48-53; Graham N. Stanton, "The Fourfold Gospel," *New Testament Studies* 43 (1997): 317-46; Andreas Lindemann, "Die Sammlung der Paulusbriefe im 1. und 2. Jahrhundert," in *The Biblical Canons*, pp. 321-51; finally, see the classic essay of Kurt Aland, *Die Entstehung des Corpus Paulinum im Neutestamentlichen Entwürfe*, Theologische Bücherei 63 (Munich: Kaiser, 1991), pp. 302-50.

17. Schröter, "Die Apostelgeschichte," pp. 398-418.

18. See Andrew Gregory, *The Reception of Luke and Acts in the Period before Irenaeus: Looking for Luke in the Second Century* (Tübingen: Mohr Siebeck, 2003).

19. See J. Schröter's summary and criticism of Harnack's position in "Die Apostelgeschichte," pp. 395-404.

20. Fitzmyer, *Gospel according to Luke*, 1:53-57.

21. See C. K. Barrett, "Acts and Christian Consensus," in *Context: Festschrift Peder Johann Borgen*, ed. P. W. Bøckman and R. E. Kristiansen (Trondheim: Tapur, 1987), pp. 19-33, and Barrett's more recent reflections, *Commentary on Acts*, vol. 2 (London: T. & T. Clark, 1998), pp. xlii-li.

toral Epistles. Again, a terminus ad quem is set by no clear reference in Acts to the presence of a Pauline letter corpus, which took shape at the turn of the century. (I shall avoid the fruitless speculation of the 1930s and 1940s between M. S. Enslin, John Knox, C. K. Barrett, and others on whether Luke knew of the Pauline corpus, and if he knew, why he did not use it.)[22]

It has long been recognized that Acts entered the New Testament canon as authoritative Scripture as an independent witness. Accordingly, Acts was not joined as a part of either the Gospels or the Pauline corpus. The manuscript evidence shows that the position of Acts developed along two different traditional lines.[23] On the one hand, Acts was positioned after the Gospels and before the Pauline corpus in a tradition reflected in the Muratorian fragment, Irenaeus, Tertullian, and Origen. On the other hand, in a second, equally old tradition, it was represented in codices 01, A, and B that Acts was connected to the Catholic Epistles and then followed by the Pauline corpus. Actually this second order remained the dominant one in the manuscript evidence throughout the Middle Ages.

Since the canonical authority of both the Gospels and the Pauline corpus had already been established apart from any appeal to the book of Acts, the crucial issue arises about the forces and purpose that led to its canonical inclusion. The Muratorian fragment (late second century) that joined Acts to the Pauline corpus explicitly explained that Paul's intent, while addressing only seven churches by name, lay in directing his letters to the one universal church. Thus, this same universalizing concern lay behind the second tradition of the ordering of Acts when it was joined directly to the Catholic Epistles. Although scholars continue to differ in describing the purpose, goals, and historical events by which Acts assumed its canonical role, it seems now quite clear that Acts did not enter the canon to provide legitimacy for the Gospels or for the Pauline corpus. Nor did Acts serve as a commentary on the Gospels. The very fact of the remarkable lack of explicit references to the Gospels, including Luke, indicates that its inclusion was not premised on its being an extension of the earthly ministry of Jesus or a commentary on these traditions.

Even the often defended theory that Acts sought to bind Paul and the

---

22. For the literature, see W. O. Walker, "Acts and the Pauline Corpus Reconsidered," in *The Pauline Writings*, ed. Stanley E. Porter and C. A. Evans (Sheffield: Sheffield Academic, 2005), pp. 55-74.

23. Zahn, *Geschichte des neutestamentlichen Kanons*, 2:280-83.

Gospels together (see R. Wall)[24] requires a far more nuanced analysis. Rather, the reconstruction of Jens Schröter is to me the most persuasive explanation. At a period in the early church at the beginning of the second century, long before the threat of Marcion, the book of Acts served to establish the legitimacy of the Pauline interpretation of the gospel, along with the other apostles, as the truthful apostolic witness to the crucified and resurrected, living Lord of the church. Having said this, we now turn to a more detailed exposition that characterizes the goals of the book of Acts.

3. The Goals, Purpose, and Function of Acts

Describing even briefly the major function of Acts, including its literary, historical, and theological aims, is nearly impossible. The sheer scope of the important secondary literature confirms the complexity of entering a field lacking any wide academic consensus on which to build. However, one positive feature is that some of the contentious questions that long occupied scholars of Acts have fallen into oblivion from their own weight and no longer need to be rehearsed. For example, the attempt to recover and reconstruct the various sources used by the author of Acts has been largely abandoned as a misconstrual of the historical genre reflected in Acts (see Marguerat below).

Some thirty years ago Nils Dahl set forth what he considered to be certain aspects of Luke-Acts that many scholars could broadly agree with.[25] First, Luke-Acts is a two-volume work in which the first volume tells how the salvation promised to Israel was realized through the life, death, and resurrection of Jesus. The second volume then tells how his appointed witnesses proclaimed this salvation in Jerusalem, Samaria, and even to far wider circles.

Second, Luke connects this narrative with the ancient biblical history of Israel in a continuous series of promises and fulfillments that Dahl characterized as "proof from prophecy." Third, the author restricts the earthly ministry of Jesus to Israel. However, after the failure of the Jews in Jerusa-

---

24. Wall, "Canonical Context," pp. 113-23.

25. Nils A. Dahl, "The Purpose of Luke-Acts," in *Jesus in the Memory of the Early Church* (Minneapolis: Augsburg, 1976), pp. 87-98.

lem to respond positively, preaching to the Gentiles began, and the significance of the apostolic mighty acts, generated by the Spirit, is narrated in the second volume as confirmation of the gospel. At this point Dahl pauses to unpack a variety of unresolved problems that lie behind these broad generalizations of purpose, such as the book's concentration on Paul, the Lukan portrait of the apostle, and the lack of attention to Paul's view of the law. Since Dahl wrote his essay, important shifts have occurred that at times support and at other times undermine his presentation.

Certainly one of the important newer emphases is the recent attempt to identify more closely the literary features of the Lukan narrative. How exactly did Luke write his history? By comparing Luke's work with that of Hellenistic historians, Daniel Marguerat has not only anchored Luke firmly in his larger historiographical milieu, but he was able also to interpret why Acts is a unified literary presentation of its one author, but with a style allowing great variety in focusing on geographical itinerary details, carefully crafted dramatic scenes, and biographical models of realistic religious intensity.[26] Quite suddenly Luke's true stature and uniqueness have emerged, which have freed him from a negative comparison with a reconstructed historical Paul of the letter corpus.

There is another aspect to this newer, far more sophisticated understanding of Luke's theological historiography. Biblical scholars have become far more sensitive to the philosophical weakness involved in the assumptions of historical rationalism. Starting with Baur's *Tendenzkritik,* major energy was expended in the search "for what really happened," as if history were an objective science constructed from "facts" apart from any interpretative mediation. Unfortunately, for much of the twentieth century a fruitless impasse developed in the study of Luke and Acts that was represented on the left by an extreme form of historical skepticism concerning Luke's work, and on the right by an equally intense and learned attempt to rehabilitate the documentary reliability of Luke-Acts. What has only recently begun to become clear is that both of these antagonistic schools of interpretation shared a common historicism used to buttress prior ideological commitments.

That said, the hermeneutical and theological difficulty of assessing the truthfulness of the Lukan presentation cannot for a moment be denied or swept under the rug. One's analysis of the Lukan presentation of Paul

---

26. Marguerat, *The First Christian Historian,* pp. 1-25.

greatly affects the evaluation of the canonical function of Acts as providing a framework for the Pauline corpus. Dibelius's solution of remaining with literary categories such as Luke's brilliant "fictional" rendering of legends and anecdotes without addressing its authenticity,[27] allowed him to purchase time for his genuine interpretive insights. However, the reader is still left in the end unsatisfied, as if the very nature of the biblical material demanded the truth question to be addressed. (I would also surmise that Hans Frei's highly influential appeal to "realistic narrative"[28] ended up with a similar theological paralysis.)

It is at this juncture that German Roman Catholic scholars, of both the past and the present generation, have made the most helpful theological and hermeneutical contributions. I begin with Heinz Schürmann's essay "Paul's Testament for the Church."[29] He argues that Paul's farewell speech to the elders assembled at Miletus (Acts 20:17-38) offers the summary of Luke's purpose in writing Acts. His farewell speech at the moment of his departure *(aphesis)* marks the end of the age of the apostolic witness and the beginning of the church's life in the postapostolic period. Luke uses this occasion to summarize for the whole church the *vita apostolica* embodied in his portrait of Paul. Paul testifies that he has been faithful to his ministry *(diakonia)* "received from the Lord Jesus" (20:24). He did not shrink from "declaring the whole counsel of God" *(boutēn tou theou)*, that is, the sacred tradition *(paradosis)* he had received. Then he admonishes the leaders from Ephesus, the elders *(presbyteroi)* and guardians *(episcopoi)*, in memory of his ministry among them and in loyalty to their appointed offices from the Holy Spirit, "to feed the church." He warns them of the coming attacks of heresies, both from within and from without, and commends them to God and his word to defend them against errors. Paul's description of his ministry as the whole counsel of God sets the parameters for the content of their proclamation and draws the battle line against the imminent threats from Jewish and Hellenistic gnostic syncretisms.

Schürmann makes it clear that this Lukan theology in Acts that summarizes Paul's witness is addressed not to an audience of the A.D. 60s, but to the church as a whole at the end of the first century that had accumu-

---

27. M. Dibelius, "Style Criticism of the Book of Acts," in *Studies in the Acts of the Apostles,* p. 25.

28. Hans Frei, *The Eclipse of Biblical Narrative* (New Haven: Yale University Press, 1974), pp. 147-50, 307-24.

29. Schürmann, "Das Testament des Paulus für die Kirche."

lated a generation of experiences. However, he insists that this Lukan presentation is not an idiosyncratic fictional construct of its author. Rather, the whole force of the speech is its stress on the continuity of Paul's ministry with an established tradition now passed on to the ecclesial leaders as guardians of the church's future. It is not surprising to see the marked similarity in content with Paul's farewell letter in 2 Timothy, which has also construed Paul's *paradosis* as the model for preserving the church's sound teaching in a post-Pauline age.

We turn next to Karl Löning's essay "Paulinismus in der Apostelgeschichte."[30] He also begins by emphasizing that the Pauline perspective of Acts reflects the time at least a generation later than the period of Paul's imprisonment (ca. A.D. 60). The problem Luke addresses turns on the development that occurred, namely, that Jews and Gentiles were now transversing their separate ways. How is it possible to continue affirming the promise that the church was the fulfillment of Israel's hopes? How can one justify the church's growth from a Jewish Christian form to one that tends increasingly to be Gentile? Löning argues that a major consideration of the portrayal of Paul's ministry focuses on this issue.

Paul is the personification of the hardening *(Verstockung)* of Judaism. His ministry began with his own radical reversal from the Jewish zealot persecuting the church as a consequence of his pharisaical piety, to becoming its most ardent apologist for the Christian faith (Acts 26:4-11, 19-23). Luke's portrayal of Paul is not primarily as a theologian, but as a figure of God's *Heilsgeschichte* who bears witness to Jesus Christ (22:15; 26:16) both in word and in deed, first by effecting the no of the synagogue (13:44-46) and then by proclaiming the gospel to all the nations (22:15). The lengthy chapters in Acts following his arrest provoked by the Jews in Jerusalem (21:27-36) offer Paul's apology for his action. He first offered his proclamation to the Jews and only then to the Gentiles as being fully consistent with what Moses and the prophets had announced (26:22-23), a manifestation of a divine plan for all peoples.

The book of Acts presents basically a defense of the accuracy (Luke 1:4) of the apostolic witness (Acts 2:36), and the credibility of Gentile

---

30. Karl Löning, "Paulinismus in der Apostelgeschichte," in *Paulus in den neutestamentlichen Spätschriften,* pp. 202-34; see his earlier article "Lukas — Theologe der von Gott geführten Heilsgeschichte," in *Gestalt und Anspruch des Neuen Testament,* ed. J. Schreiner and G. Deutzenberger (Würzburg: Echter, 1979), pp. 200-228.

Christianity in the post-Pauline era as a fulfillment of Israel's promises by God in spite of the irreversible fracture between church and synagogue. The Lukan Paul, far from being a fanciful construct of an ill-informed idealistic author who has distorted the historical Paul of the letters, is actually a historical figure now received and branded into the memory of his churches. He testifies to the faith of his Gentile churches as a consequence of God's predetermined will, executed through the ministry of Paul, the faithful missionary.

Finally, we turn to the essay of Jens Schröter recently published from the Leuven conference of 2001.[31] His contributions to the history of the canonization of Acts have already been described. Our attention now focuses on his summarizing theological observations in respect to the book of Acts. In the final section of his article, Schröter returns to Harnack's thesis of the irreconcilable contradiction between a critical historical and a canonical reading of Acts. He notes the logical connection between Harnack's larger perspective based on his history of Christian dogma and his assessment of Acts as part of the church's political effort at the end of the second century to shape its traditions toward the goal of early Catholicism. Harnack's evaluation of the tension between history and canon arises from the assumption that critical reflection consists in comparing the difference between the reconstructed events of early Christian history and their presentation in the book of Acts. Schröter suggests that an equally rigorous approach would compare the various stages between the witness of Acts and the subsequent history of its canonical shaping. In other words, a critical evaluation would also take into consideration the *Wirkungsgeschichte* of Acts, which is to say, the text's historical afterlife in the church.

When one approaches the historical tensions evoked by Acts from this perspective, some observations arise that offer serious modifications to Harnack's thesis. First, the Gospels and the Pauline letter corpus present two simultaneous stages of the development of the New Testament canon independently of each other, and each acknowledged early as authoritative. Harnack's reconstruction of the canonical history is one-sided when he relates the entrance of Acts into the canon as a response to Marcion, a threat occurring in the middle of the second century. Second, none of the early Church Fathers assigned Acts the role of buttressing the authority of

31. Schröter, "Die Apostelgeschichte," pp. 395-429.

Paul that had long since been accepted. Rather, the expansion of Pauline tradition to all the apostles allows a combination of the Lukan Pauline traditions with the substantive contents of Acts to occur without a sense of undue friction. Third, Acts contains numerous literary indications that it was intended to be read as a historical account of the early church, and not as a collection of fanciful tales. Finally, regarding the portrait of Paul in Acts: it has been increasingly recognized since Harnack that the apostle is portrayed as a representation of a specific epoch of the spread of Christianity that has resulted in a shift of emphasis and perspective from that of the Pauline letters.

In terms of a canonical reading of Acts, Harnack correctly described the three determinative corpora of the New Testament canon consisting of the Gospels, the Pauline Letters, and the Catholic Letters. From this perspective the canonical function of Acts emerges with clarity. It consists primarily of presenting the apostles as the legitimate guardians of the Jesus traditions, strengthened by the connection with the catholic letters of Peter, James, and John, and the portrait of Paul in Acts as in agreement with that of the letters. This orientation toward legitimating the apostolic proclamation is thus constitutive for an understanding of the New Testament canon, not least that it establishes the boundaries of its witness over against that of the heretics. There are therefore good reasons for maintaining that the reception of Acts by the early church is far closer to the book's own intention than that projected by Harnack. This canonical intention he described as a political strategy of the late second century can actually be roughly related to the reasons evoking Acts as a "consensus document" of A.D. 100 that was written to ensure the unified witness of the apostles and Paul. A historical critical analysis of the church's early history will undoubtedly not result in a simplistic unity, but the meaning of the past, particularly when the *wirkungsgeschichtliche* dimension of canonization is included, can increase our understanding of its multifaceted coherence.

4. The Hermeneutical Effect of the Canonization of Acts

The canonization of Acts has provided hermeneutical legitimation for a variety of different contexts from which to read the book.

a. The book of Acts can be read as a unified two-volume narrative consisting of the Gospel of Luke and the Acts of the Apostles. This exegetical enterprise may at first appear strange since in an earlier section I criticized the widespread assumption that the narrative unity of Luke-Acts as a diptych was the only proper critical stance for its interpretation. My criticisms against the reading of Luke-Acts as a narrative unity reflect those of Parsons and Pervo:[32] there are two different literary genres represented; differing handling of sources; a shift from the theme of the kingdom of God to the kerygma of the resurrected Christ; etc. I am also aware of Marguerat's recently developed thesis that the unity of Luke-Acts is not announced in the biblical text itself, but is a task of the reader, who must construct this unity in the course of reading.[33]

The thesis I am prepared to defend disagrees in part with both proposals regarding a unified reading of the Luke-Acts narrative. I disagree on historical grounds with the widespread assumption that Luke-Acts functioned as a unified narrative from the time of its composition until it was unfortunately separated at the moment of its canonization. The critical analysis of Schröter has persuasively established that the dating of the two volumes is separated by at least a generation. Again, the Gospel of Luke as a separate volume was canonized as authoritative apart from Acts. Finally, the entrance of Acts into the larger process of the canonization of the New Testament occurred in a far later period and was not of primary historical significance until the early decades of the second century, first seriously mentioned by Irenaeus.

Then again, I disagree hermeneutically with the thesis of Marguerat because he assigns a major task to the modern reader according to a postmodern hermeneutic, and so disregards the effect that the canonical shaping of Acts has had on the church's rendering of its Scripture, namely, its two traditions of canonical positioning constitutive to its final form. In a word, the narrative reading of Luke-Acts is not carried on as an early precanonical historical stage of a narrative diptych, but only on a postcanonical level when Christian interpretation of its Scripture pursued intertextual connections between the two volumes. Although such connections are not explicitly stated in the text, the legitimacy of such an intertextual interpretation can be tested, case by case, by its ability to illuminate the theological substance of its construal.

---

32. Parsons and Pervo, *Rethinking the Unity of Luke and Acts.*

33. Marguerat, *The First Christian Historian,* pp. 43-64. See also Schröter, "Die Apostelgeschichte," pp. 419-20.

b. The book of Acts can be read as a commentary on all the Gospels and vice versa. Wall argued that Acts must be read as Luke's intentional commentary on the Gospel.[34] However, apart from the intentional recapitulations in the prologue of Acts, nowhere is there an explicit reference to the "first book" or allusions to a specific word or event. Instead, the recourse to the history of Jesus is of a general nature: John's baptism, spirit-filled actions of Jesus, crucifixion and resurrection. As Schröter concludes: "These, however, assume no knowledge of the Jesus story related in the Gospel of Luke."[35] The unity of the Lukan history arises from a content orientation and does not derive from the literary character of either of the books.

Still, because Wall is aware of the canonical effects of the shaping of Luke and Acts, his frequent appeal to an intercanonical dialogue within the New Testament, especially between Acts and the Gospels, is not academically irresponsible, but offers a useful homiletical application fully appropriate for a Christian sermon. The only caveat is that one remembers that the Jesus of the Gospels did not "share his story" (L. E. Keck).

c. A variety of commentators correctly insists that the explicit relation between the witness of Acts and that of the Pauline letters remains a necessary and ongoing part of a canonical interpretation of the New Testament. However, two prevalent interpretive dangers have already been mentioned, and are to be avoided. The first is to apply a form of historical rationalism that gives historical credence solely to the Pauline letters and a priori denigrates Acts as historically valueless. The second is motivated by an exactly opposite intention of providing external evidences to support the historicity of Acts by various harmonistic ploys. In my judgment, this approach is equally a form of rationalism, hermeneutically a mirror image of the first option. The main purpose of reviewing the essays of Schürmann, Löning, and Schröter was to raise other theological options commensurate with the genre of canonical literature. Such an appeal does not assume a coherence apart from tension, but allows for freedom in anticipating a multifaceted variety of truthful witnesses that bear testimony to the theological substance of the apostolic voices, the quest for whose harmony remains an essential part of the imperative "to search the Scriptures."

d. There is a good illustration of the newer approach to addressing historical tensions between Acts and Paul's letters. One of the classic passages

---

34. Wall, "Canonical Context," pp. 115-17; Wall, *Acts of the Apostles*, vol. 10, passim.
35. Schröter, "Die Apostelgeschichte," p. 421.

used throughout the nineteenth and early twentieth centuries highlights the contrast between the historical Paul of the letters (Gal 2) and the "fictional" Lukan account in Acts 15 of the apostolic decree. Whereas in Galatians 2:6 Paul announces that the church leaders "laid nothing in addition on him," in Acts 15 the council added four cultic restrictions on Gentile Christians that ran directly in the face of Paul's understanding of a law-freed gospel. Thus, it was widely held that these rules were added much later, apart from Paul's knowledge, and were moralistic "concessions" asked by Hellenistic Jewish Christians from Gentile Christians.

More recently it has become clear that such an interpretation basically misunderstood Acts 15. The four restrictions are not concessions alien to Paul's missionary message. Indeed, just the opposite. These restrictions are the imperatives from Leviticus 17 and 18 that are listed in the same sequence as in Acts:

Lev 17:8	no foreign sacrifices
Lev 17:10-12	no eating of blood
Lev 17:13	no eating of strangled meat
Lev 18:1-23	prohibition of sexual immorality

What is most significant is that these regulations are not limited to Israel, but include explicitly the non-Israelites (Gentiles) living within the Hebrew community. The apostolic decree in Acts 15 (whether a literary expansion or not) serves to confirm from Israel's own Scriptures that Paul's mission to the Gentiles is in accordance with the will of God and is a support, not a repudiation, of Paul's gospel.

5. The Singularity of Paul's Letters and Their Corporate Form

A different issue has recently been raised by A. Lindemann,[36] who moves away from treating purely historical questions respecting the Pauline corpus to a larger hermeneutical problem. Are these letters to be read today as individual single texts or within their canonical context as a corpus? Lindemann offers several reasons for choosing the first option:

36. Lindemann, "Die Sammlung der Paulusbriefe," pp. 321-35.

a. Only by pursuing the letters individually can one recover the sharp profile of a letter's historical milieu and avoid the dangers of introducing themes from outside the text that blur its original meaning.

b. The Pauline corpus has collected the individual letters by retaining all the elements of specificity derived from the letter's original situation, and its formation did not offer an abstraction or condensation of its contents.

c. There is no sign that the Pauline letters were given a later theological redaction or harmonization in order to serve together as unified religious literature.

I fully agree with Lindemann in his insistence that the letters be studied as individual letters with careful attention paid to each letter's uniqueness and historical specificity. Where I differ is in his failure to reckon with biblical interpretation being an exegetical activity that moves, as if in a circle, between the poles of a text's singular specificity and its role within a larger literary context. No interpretation of a Pauline letter can be adequate that does not interpret the individual specificity of a letter also in its larger context within the Pauline corpus.

Several reasons support the need for employing both exegetical approaches together as a necessary component for understanding:

a. Although the Pauline letters were collected within a corpus in which the individual particularity was retained, they were not received by the church as just occasional letters but were circulated shortly among Paul's churches as authoritative.

b. The letters within the corpus were not redacted according to one uniform pattern, but they were nevertheless clearly shaped in different canonical ways. As shown above, Romans was expanded and positioned to form an introduction. The Pastorals served as a concluding valorization of Paul as the church's doctrinal model, and the corpus was framed by the canonization of the Acts of the Apostles.

c. The effect of the formation of a Pauline corpus was that intertextual interpretation was encouraged by the overlapping of events, themes, and persons among the letters until Paul's corpus was in time included with the Old Testament and the Gospels as part of the church's sacred Scriptures.

Unfortunately, the hermeneutical problems indigenous to the critical methodology outlined by Lindemann were painfully illustrated by the Pauline Seminar conducted by the Society of Biblical Literature for some ten years in the late 1980s and early 1990s, and subsequently published in four volumes.[37] Accordingly, after the scope of the canon was established as consisting only of the "undisputed letters," each individual "genuine" letter was isolated and critically analyzed in its historical particularity. Only at the end of this enterprise did it become evident to the participants that no hermeneutical glue was available to put together the pieces and fragments left from the enterprise. Perhaps the lesson to be learned from this exercise is that the "historical Paul" and the "canonical Paul" of the church have been indissolubly joined, and that any interpretation that omits either dimension is sorely deficient.

6. Kähler's Hermeneutic and the So-called Historical Paul

In conclusion, it is necessary to return to a basic hermeneutical point first developed in the introductory chapters of this monograph (see chapter 1). The struggle to do full justice to the integrity of each of the witnesses within the canonical corpora does not rule out a "quest for the historical Paul." Although I have obviously sought to relativize its dominance within the New Testament discipline, it retains nevertheless a theological significance. Again I return to the relevance of Kähler's distinction between the biblical historical Christ *(Geschichte)* and the historical Jesus reconstructed according to the conventions provided by common human experience apart from faith *(Historie)*. In my review of Kähler, I have sought to add a crucial modification that would not simply contrast the two models, but would also seek to establish a hermeneutical area of commonality in which both shared language, rationality, and conventions of their culture.

I would apply the same hermeneutical principle to the relation between the canonical portraits of Paul, with all their multifaceted contours, and those common features shared by the New Testament writers, such as Luke's application of Hellenistic historiography or Paul's apologetic speech on the Areopagus as he sought initially to gain attention from his audience before bearing witness to Christ's resurrection. The hermeneutical issues remain highly complex, and there is no simplistic resolution. However, even to recognize that the canonical Paul and the reconstructed

37. See the reference to the Pauline Seminar of the Society of Biblical Literature in chapter 1, note 1.

Paul can neither be identified nor rendered inexorably alien is to establish an important hermeneutical benchmark.

II. Hebrews

The difficulty of interpreting the letter to the Hebrews is well-known, and thought by some to be the New Testament's greatest enigma.[38] The reasons for this assessment are many: its anonymous authorship, its uncertain addressee, the date of its composition, the vagueness of its historical milieu, its literary genre, and even its structure. I do not intend to review in detail the countless essays that posit various external forces that are judged to offer the interpretive key (Philo, Gnosticism, Qumran) or to pursue Grässer's thesis for seeing the book as an early Catholic response to the delay of the parousia.[39]

My questions are much more narrowly construed, and focus in accordance with the present project on the subject of canon and the function of the book within the New Testament. First, can one discern reasons why this book was canonized as Scripture, especially why it was joined to the Pauline corpus? Second, how is the understanding of the Pauline letters affected by the inclusion of Hebrews within the corpus?

1. Critical Issues

After making an initial disclaimer of reviewing the whole range of critical problems, I am also aware that the issues with which I am concerned are inextricably entwined with many of the exegetical problems that have traditionally evoked such heated debates. Thus, a brief and highly selective review seems required to do justice to the complex problems relating to the book's canonical role.

a. The letter is anonymous, but by the end of the first century it was cited already as Scripture by *1 Clement.* The history of the book's canoniza-

38. These issues are well summarized by Harry W. Attridge, *The Epistle to the Hebrews* (Philadelphia: Fortress, 1989), and by Hans-Friedrich Weiss, *Der Brief an die Hebräer* (Göttingen: Vandenhoeck & Ruprecht, 1991).

39. Erich Grässer, "Der Hebräerbrief 1938-63," *Theologische Rundschau* 30 (1964): 130-236; Grässer, *Der Glaube im Hebräerbrief* (Marburg: Elwert, 1965).

tion differed greatly in the Eastern and Western churches. Even though its role as authoritative apostolic Scripture was accepted early in the East, doubts were expressed over its authorial ascription to Paul (e.g., by Origen). Early theories to relate the book to Paul were clearly post-canonical attempts to justify its traditional attribution to Paul. The Western church, largely under the influence of Jerome and Augustine, accepted Hebrews as canonical by the fifth century. Its sequential position within the Pauline corpus has varied considerably, showing its unstable assessment, but increasingly it has entered at the end of the corpus following the personal letters of Paul and preceding the Catholic Epistles.

b. The addressee of the letter seems unclear. References such as those in 2:3 and 10:32-34 appear to reflect a particular community, but lacking the particularity characteristic of Paul's letters. The context of the letter with its consistent appeals to the Greek Bible does seem to be addressing Jewish-Hellenistic Christians of a second generation, but the writer is not focusing on contemporary Judaism, but rather on a crisis arising from disillusionment with the faith, decreasing loyalty, and backsliding from a once-held Christian confession. Various theories regarding this spiritual crisis have been proposed, but no exact evidence has been presented by which to identify the destructive forces at work in the community. There is reference in 10:32-35 to "hard struggle with suffering," exposure to abuse, and public humiliation, but it is difficult to correlate these complaints with a specific persecution.

c. The letter is often assigned to the end of the first century, but largely from indirect evidence such as a sophisticated usage of figuration and typological interpretation by the author, his elegant Greek prose, and evidences of a second generation of Christians who have already experienced some suffering.

d. Many of the major themes of the gospel are reflected in the Christian teachings of the book: the divine sonship of Jesus, salvation offered by faith, and the role of the law. However, what is surprising and unexpected is the independence of the formulations that seem alien not only to Paul, but also to the major themes of the deutero-Pauline letters and the development of the offices of early Christianity emerging in the Pastorals.

In a word, the problem of understanding Hebrews is that the problem of the particularity of the Pauline letters is exactly the opposite in Hebrews. There is a lack of a specific historical milieu, or of a concrete congregation, or of a controversy with Judaism or Gnosticism. Rather, the focus lies in the contrast between the old and the new covenants of Scripture. The writer's interest is not in contemporary Judaism, but in the Levitical priesthood of the old economy and its replacement by the heavenly dispensation of the new.

2. Major Theological Themes of Continuity

a. An initial difficulty in sketching the book's themes is that there is no full consensus as to its exact structure.[40] Still there is agreement that following an exordium (1:1-4) there are largely doctrinal sections (1:5–2:18; 5:1–10:18), closely followed by parenetic ones (3:1–4:16; 10:19–12:29), with concluding exhortations to hold fast, and greetings. Then within the doctrinal sections a common application of an a fortiori argument seeks to demonstrate the superiority of Christ over the angels and Moses (1:5–4:13), and Christ's priesthood over the priesthood of Aaron (7:1–9:28). Another medium by which the subject matter is carried is the constant citations of key Old Testament passages as warrants for the writer's theological discourse: Psalm 2 (Heb 1:5a; 5:5) for Christ's sonship; Psalm 40 (Heb 5:9) for his willing sacrifice; Psalm 45 (Heb 1:8-9) for his enthronement; Psalm 95 (Heb 4:7) for Israel's disobedience; Psalm 110 (Heb 5:5) for the new order of Melchizedek and Christ; and Jeremiah 31:31-34 (Heb 8:8-12) for the new covenant.

b. One of the central themes of the book is given immediately in the exordium of 1:1-4:[41] "In many times and in various ways God spoke to our forefathers through the prophets, but in these last days he has spoken to us in the Son." The passage bears witness to the one and same voice of God testifying in the Scriptures of the Old Testament prophets and then in these last days speaking in his Son. The verses announce a past divine revelation by the prophets in Israel's history that culminates in a climactic finality of his speaking "to us." The writer then describes the Son in the most exalted language of praise possible: "he is the heir of all things," "through whom God created the world," "who bears the very impress of his divine nature," and "who, seated on the right hand of God, continues to uphold the universe by his word of power."

---

40. See Attridge's latest attempt, *Epistle to the Hebrews,* p. 19.

41. Otfried Hofius, "Biblische Theologie im Lichte des Hebräerbriefes," in *New Directions in Biblical Theology,* ed. S. Pedersen (Leiden: Brill, 1994), pp. 108-25.

What is so striking in this formulation is that it addresses the larger theological issue of the relationship between God's revelation in the Old Testament and that of the New. Of course, such language is anachronistic since the two testaments had not yet been formed, but this is the way the material would soon have been read within the church as a developing sense of the Christian canon slowly emerged. The initial stress falls on the continuity of God's revelation within a horizontal, historical trajectory stretching from Israel to the church. However, as the Christology of the book of Hebrews is expanded, it also becomes clear that the writer conceives of this "history" in a far more sophisticated and nuanced form that is not encompassed by a linear concept of *Heilsgeschichte*. Indeed, God reveals himself in Israel's history, and the revelation of his Son occurs in the events of the incarnation within concrete time and space of this world. However, the radical discontinuity of God's word between the Old and the New, while they are continually intertwined, is never lost. In fact, the rest of the letter largely focuses on the contrast between the Old and the New that transcends not only the time line of past history, but extends as well from the earthly sphere into the heavenly priesthood of the Son.

c. The christological themes of the letter are first developed by a series of a fortiori comparisons, and Christ emerges in his godlikeness with parallels found only in John's Gospel (1:1-2). His preexistence is everywhere assumed and his qualitative uniqueness is manifested in his now divine title as Son. Then by a direct application of a series of citations from the Psalter, Christ is seen as the "begotten of God" (Ps 2:7), joined indivisibly as Father and Son. Using Psalms 45, 110, and 104, the writer portrays Christ's enthronement as he is seated on God's right hand, and as creator of the world is ascribed worship by God's angels (Heb 2:6-8).

d. It is when one examines the soteriological activity of Christ that the full extent of the radical nature of the Son's role appears. The book of Hebrews initially stands in complete continuity with the Old Testament in an understanding of what salvation consists of. It is the full, unbroken communion of God's creatures with their creator. However, Israel's history presents one of constant fracture between God and his people, causing the whole cultic tradition of Israel to focus on the means by which the broken could be mended and the unclean purified. God's holy presence was represented by an earthly tabernacle where his glory could be truly worshiped and salvation received in the presence of God.

The whole thrust of the Old Testament fell on removing the barrier of sin that separated Israel from the holy and the just. Within the covenant, cultic law was established by the sacrificial rituals by which the Levitical priesthood interceded for the people. However, it is a fundamental mistake to suggest that the Jewish people had created their own rituals to cleanse themselves. God (YHWH) himself was the source of the Torah of Moses. It was the divine will that resounded from Mount Sinai and instructed Moses. Indeed, chapters 25–40 of Exodus provide the exact instructions to Moses for building the tabernacle and ordaining Aaron and his sons into the Levitical priesthood. Exodus 40 concludes with Moses' completion of "all that God commanded him." Then a cloud covered the tent of meeting, and the presence of God (his *kabod*) filled the tabernacle. The mechanisms for Israel's continuous restoration were in place.

3. Themes of Radical Discontinuity

a. It is in the light of this Old Testament portrayal that the extreme discontinuity of the book of Hebrews emerges as the writer pronounces the whole Levitical system hopelessly inadequate, faulty, and obsolete (8:7, 13).[42] The discontinuity begins with the contrast between the office of the Levitical priest and that of Christ. The Levitical priest is first obliged to offer sacrifice for his own sins (5:3). There must be many priests in number because death prevents a continuation of the office (7:23). The Levitical priest must continually repeat his ritual as he yearly enters the Holy Place with blood not his own (9:25). In contrast, Christ did not exalt himself as high priest, but was appointed by God as his Son (5:5). Then being made perfect through suffering, he became the source of eternal salvation (5:9). His priesthood is permanent because it continues forever. Christ is a high priest, "holy, blameless, unstained . . . exalted above the heavens" (7:26). He therefore had no need to offer sacrifices daily, first for his own sins, then for the people. Rather, "once and for all he offered up himself." By a single offering he has perfected for all time those who are sanctified (10:14).

b. Second, the Levitical priesthood receives its authority according to a legal requirement concerning bodily descent. But Christ's priesthood is of

---

42. See the impressive study of Jesus' death according to Hebrews by Roy A. Harrisville, *Fracture: The Cross as Irreconcilable in the Language and Thought of the Biblical Writers* (Grand Rapids: Eerdmans, 2006), pp. 135-49.

a different nature entirely, "after the order of Melchizedek." Melchizedek is without a human lineage, and has neither beginning of days nor end of life, but resembles the Son of God (7:1-3). Therefore, Christ's power derives from its indestructible life. Because of the "weakness and uselessness" of the old order, a new hope is now introduced by Christ's office through which we draw near to God (7:18-19).

c. The old Levitical priest sought to secure atonement by a sacrifice of the blood of bulls and goats to remove sins (10:4), but Christ as the eternal Son offered his own blood, thus securing an eternal redemption. He offered his own body prepared by God (10:5, 10). At the "end of the age" (9:26) he put away sin by the sacrifice of himself.

d. According to Exodus 19, repeated in Deuteronomy 5, following a theophany at Sinai, God made a covenant with the people of Israel, assuring them that if they would obey his commandments and keep his covenant, Israel would be God's own possession, a holy nation. However, according to the writer of Hebrews, if the old covenant had worked, if it had not been deeply flawed, there would have been no need for a new covenant (Heb 8:7). Therefore, God had promised a new covenant (Jer 31:31-34) to replace the first, which had grown obsolete (Heb 8:13). It would be written on their hearts, and Christ is the mediator of a new dispensation (9:15).

e. The old tabernacle served only as a copy and shadow of the truly heavenly sanctuary (8:5). However, Christ has entered, not into an earthly sanctuary built by human hands, but into a heavenly sanctuary (9:24). There, seated at the right hand of God (10:12), he secured access into the heavenly sanctuary through his blood, where he intercedes on our behalf (9:24; 7:25).

4. Exhortation and Parenesis

Up to this point we have not dealt with a major theme of the book that most probably evoked the chief reason for the letter at the outset, namely, its focus on exhortation. Already the description of the letter's structure shows the detailed attention paid to parenesis, which is integrally joined to the doctrinal sections.

The phraseology is dominated by the imperatives: "hold fast," "open your hearts," "exhort one another every day." Behind this rhetoric lies obviously a crisis of faith that has emerged within the community. The exact nature of the problems, as we have seen, remains vague, but this lack of precise details does not diminish its importance. Frequently there is the mention of holding firm "if only we keep our confidence strong to the end" (3:14). The appeal to the failure of the wilderness generation (3:7-19) serves as a warning not to backslide into disobedience. The admonition is then repeated in 6:1-8 concerning those who "once having tasted of the goodness of the word of God," committed apostasy from the faith. Several passages speak of holding to "the confession of our hope without wavering" (10:23), and recall former days when "you endured hard struggles with sufferings" (10:32). Again there comes the exhortation: "Do not throw away your confidence."

It is crucial in understanding the central role assigned to exhortation to see how closely it is linked to the doctrinal sections. Above all, Jesus is highlighted: the captain of our salvation (2:10), who was faithful and a model for the endurance of sufferings. The great emphasis on the humanity of the Son who partook of our common human frailty and learned obedience through what he had suffered serves as a moving challenge to imitate the Savior (13:7).

An equally powerful reminder of the great cloud of witnesses (12:1) is provided by the lengthy recitation of faithful responses by the saints of the past (11:1-40).[43] These examples serve to urge those who are waning in their faith to return to the disciplined life of faith. "Therefore lift up your drooping hands and strengthen your weak knees" (12:12). Chapter 12 ends with a stern reminder that no one can escape from the just judgment of God. Thus, be grateful and offer God acceptable worship.

There is one final feature that forms the climax of the book's parenesis. Examples of faithful living are not just artifacts from the distant past. Rather, the Christian is assured a living faith because the exalted Son has entered the heavenly sanctuary and today, seated on God's right hand, continuously offers intercession for his flock. Therefore, let brotherly love continue; remember those who are ill treated. Christ has said: "I will never fail nor forsake you" (13:5). So confess in confidence: "The Lord is my helper; I will not fear what evil men can do to me."

---

43. See the helpful interpretation of chapter 11 by Robert P. Gordon, *Hebrews* (Sheffield: Sheffield Academic, 2000), pp. 127-47.

5. The Humanity of Jesus

There is another feature of the Christology of Hebrews that first comes as a surprise to the reader. Within none of the letters of the Pauline corpus is the humanity of Jesus so emphasized as in Hebrews. "The pioneer (captain)[44] of their salvation was made perfect through suffering" (2:10). Since the children he was seeking to save shared in flesh and blood, Jesus himself "also partook of the same nature that through death he might destroy the devil who has the power of death" (2:14). "He had to be made like his brothers in every respect" (2:17). Hebrews 5:7-10 describes the earthly Jesus praying with loud cries and tears to God who was able to save from death. "Although he was a Son, he learned obedience through what he suffered." He not only suffered physically but also was "tempted like every human being, but without sinning" (2:18; 4:15). He endured the cross and its shame (12:2), and the writer even notes that he suffered and died "outside the camp" (13:12) where carcasses were disposed of and criminals executed.[45] Christ's obedient intention was expressed in his first-person adaptation of Psalm 40: "Lo, I have come to do thy will, O God" (10:7).

6. The Major Hermeneutical Issues at Stake

The issue is succinctly formulated by Graham Hughes.[46] How can the Scriptures of the Old Testament function in one context so immediately and continually as a vehicle for the living Word of God, while in another context the same Scriptures, enshrining the old covenant, are dismissed as outmoded and obsolete? Perhaps one way to begin this hermeneutical reflection on this problem is to make the complexity of the issue even more precise. A warrant for this move is given in the cautious formulation of Hebrews 1:1: "many times and various ways." Our approach is therefore to question certain interpretive options that have been advanced as solutions of the problem.

44. Rowan A. Greer, *The Captain of Our Salvation: A Study in Patristic Exegesis of Hebrews* (Tübingen: Mohr Siebeck, 1973).

45. Attridge, *Epistle to the Hebrews*, p. 399.

46. Graham Hughes, *Hebrews and Hermeneutics: The Epistle to the Hebrews as a New Testament Example of Biblical Interpretation* (Cambridge: Cambridge University Press, 1979), p. 35.

a. Several Inadequate Interpretations The relationship between the Old and the New in the book of Hebrews is not primarily one of prophecy (promise) and fulfillment. Regardless of whether one chooses from one of the varying patterns such as found in Matthew, Luke, or John, none of these schemata is primary in Hebrews. To be sure, there are elements from this pattern occasionally present (10:15-18), but even here the exact pattern is not dominant.

The relationship is not primarily formulated in literary terms such as between a literal and a figurative reading of Scripture, as if the Old Testament provided a literal story and the New its figurative reinterpretation. Actually this literary distinction is largely blurred in Hebrews, and virtually every historical event is rendered figuratively (many already from a Jewish midrashic tradition) while seldom is the literality of the Old Testament's reference totally dissolved.

The relationship is not primarily typological, although a pattern of type and antitype can be seen in 3:7–4:13, when the resting place of Israel in the land becomes an antitype for the rest of an eschatological salvation through Christ. Still, this pattern is not pursued consistently because of the dominant features of discontinuity that restrain the typology.

The relationship is not exclusively ontological, such as in copy versus reality, or shadow versus substance. Clearly this relationship is present in Hebrews (8:5), but it is not universal. The retention of a historical dimension continues to compromise consistently ontological reading.

Finally, the relationship is not that of an evolving traditio-historical trajectory, akin, say, to that of von Rad's construal that extended in interpretive stages of charismatic leaps from the Old Testament to the New. Whatever linear lines are present, the continuing vertical dimension, resounding a living divine voice, remains crucial (12:25).

In sum, the complexity of the problem arises in that elements from very different hermeneutical strategies all are present.

b. The Dialectical Relationship between Old and New Hughes's solution, that the relationship between the continuity and discontinuity of the Old and the New is dialectical,[47] is in my judgment certainly correct. However, the difficult problem still remains in defining with greater precision how the term "dialectical" functions within Hebrews. Hughes has made an important start

---

47. Hughes, *Hebrews and Hermeneutics*, pp. 101-10.

by focusing on the very different understanding of history involved in this tension.

When treating the dimension of continuity between the Old and the New in previous paragraphs, it was pointed out that the illustrations from the Old Testament of Israel's history are often construed as part of ordinary human behavior. Within a linear trajectory, historical events are portrayed that are shaped by contingent forces, even though a larger telic direction is always assumed. Similarly in the emphasis on the full humanity of Jesus in Hebrews, stress is laid on Jesus' sharing of a common body of flesh and blood with the children of Israel. He partook of the same nature of a common humanity in every respect, including temptation, suffering, and death, like every other mortal.

Yet the elements of discontinuity between the Old and the New, which actually dominate the book, are not gently developed, as if on the edges of his argument, to be subtly introduced. Quite the opposite! The elements of discontinuity are radically announced without any attempt at providing a bridge — at least, so it first appears. The New is qualitatively distinct from the Old. The New is not a flowering into the New from a common seed. The Son is related only to the Father and is thus unique in every way.

Although there are places where the radicality of the New is described in extreme apocalyptical language (12:18-29), more frequently the entrance of the New has retained a historical, even linear, dimension. Jesus learned obedience through a life of suffering (5:8), and from the initial verses in chapter 1, God's revelation of his will, encompassing different means and extending over different epochs within time, was not expressed apocalyptically, but historically. Of course, later on the reader learns that Christ's sacrifice marked "the end of the age" (9:26), which is a classic apocalyptical formulation of the dissolving of historical continuity.

An initial key in trying to understand how both the Old and the New have a historical dimension is to recognize that the concept of history in Hebrews is integrally connected with the Word of God. "The Word of God is living and active, sharper than any two-edged sword, probing to the division of soul and spirit, joints and marrow, and discerning the thoughts and intentions of the heart" (4:12). It is the voice, identified with the Holy Spirit (3:7), that speaks judgment to the disobedient wilderness generation (3:7-10) but returns long afterward to speak through David and renew his promise of rest "today" (4:7). Moreover, it is clear that the Word of God has spoken and continues to speak in the words of the Old Testament to the church, both in judgment on the old and promise from the new, as it once did to ancient Israel.

A major point to be made is that there are two historical trajectories, both in the history of Israel and in the history of the church, serving as bearers of the Old and the New, that emerge as the Word of God. The two trajectories are radically different, both in their continuity and in their discontinuity, yet are indissolubly intertwined in the understanding of the writer of Hebrews. However, in being the living Word of God, the term "history" is fully inadequate, if at times necessary, to encompass the multidimensional quality of the divine speech. It is vibrant and active; it enters ordinary human history, even in linear trajectories, but it can just as easily transcend the ordinary and explode into the sheer verticality of apocalyptical speech. It can also speak of the relationship of the Old and New ontologically as a shadow relates to its reality, but then describe the theophany that once terrified Moses as gentle compared to the coming apocalyptic shaking of the earth and the heavens of our God who is a consuming fire (12:18-29).

There is one final but crucial point with which to conclude in addressing the tension between the Old and the New. Only Jesus Christ as the humanly incarnated Son of God is able to bridge these two dimensions. He alone is able to unite the human and the divine that stand in such tension within the theology of the writer. Seated at the right hand of God as the divine equal, he intercedes for the sake of his people because he alone has overcome the barrier of separation and opened for us access to the Father through his sacrifice (10:19-25).

We return to our initial hermeneutical question. How can the Scriptures of the Old Testament function together in their continuity as the abiding Word of God, and in their discontinuity as a sign of the old order that has been replaced by the new? The writer of Hebrews does not give a set of hermeneutical rules, but uses Scripture as both the vehicle of the Old and of the New along with its tension. Yet ultimately the criterion for distinguishing is established entirely in the content of the person and work of Jesus Christ. He becomes the means by which the history of revelation is understood and by which its truth is measured. His is the voice of the same God who revealed himself in many and manifold ways, and continues to speak on behalf of his people seated at God's right hand.

7. Reasons for the Inclusion of Hebrews in the Pauline Corpus

From the historical evidence available, there is no unequivocal answer to this question. We can assess with some certainty that in the Eastern Church the book of Hebrews was received as an authoritative writing by the end of the first century. One can only speculate regarding the influence of certain other features of Hebrews for its inclusion within the larger corpus. Although the letter lacked the normal Pauline prescript, there are references to a particular congregational addressee, even though vague, as we have seen. The interaction between doctrine and parenesis, although structured in Hebrews in a manner different from Paul's style, provides an element of continuity, and shows that the structure is not that of a tractate or sermon. This point is, of course, strengthened by the conclusion with its doxology and greetings. Certainly the reference to "our brother Timothy" (13:23) must also have exerted a strong force in drawing the letter within the Pauline circle.

From the very beginning of the debate respecting its canonicity, it was pointed out by the Greek-speaking Church Fathers that the language and style of Hebrews were far different from that of Paul. It was also noticed, of course, not with the intensity and precision of the Enlightenment scholars, that many of those issues central to Paul's letters were either missing or treated in a way quite alien to Paul: justification by faith, law versus gospel, centrality of the cross and the resurrection.

Nevertheless, if read as a whole, Hebrews was undoubtedly heard as a genuine "Christian" writing. There was not a hint of Judaizing or gnostic distortions, but the letter bore testimony in the most robust and exalted form to the Lordship of Christ the Son, who was the equal with the Father. Although the letter remained strikingly independent in its formulations, when taken as a whole there is a large degree of theological overlap with the major topics of the faith.

The Word of God proclaimed in the old covenant had culminated in the incarnation of Jesus Christ, whose preexistence was everywhere assumed. The book of Hebrews represents the highest possible form of Christology that is constantly related to the salvific activity of Christ and formulated largely in priestly terms. The cross is still central, but its significance expanded in terms of Christ's suffering and priestly sacrifice. Moreover, the role of the cross is now clearly joined to its role as providing access to the heavenly sanctuary. Christ's resurrection is assumed, but now interpreted largely in terms of Christ's heavenly ascension and his present intercessory activity on behalf of his people. Ironically, it has often been observed that the theology of Hebrews is at times most closely akin to that of the Catholic Epistles, especially to 1 Peter. Finally, a review of the faithful obedience of the Old Testament saints (Heb 11) serves to bind the letter to the entire history of Israel and to lay stress on the unity of the faithful of both covenants who are joined in eager anticipation of the awaited fulfillment of God's promises.

8. *The Effect of Hebrews within the Pauline Corpus*

In an illuminating and probing essay regarding the hermeneutical contribution of Hebrews to biblical theology, Andrew Lincoln has mounted a powerful case for its interpretive role that runs directly in the face of the canonical approach I have been positing.[48]

Lincoln first summarizes his lengthy section on the various forms of christological reading by concluding that there is no one master method to be derived from a study of Hebrews (p. 330). The contribution of Hebrews does not provide an objective norm that can be simply applied by later Christian readers. He dismisses out of hand any idea that the canonization of Hebrews serves to transcend the limitations of the writer's time-conditionality (p. 332).

Lincoln argues that two key elements are lacking in an academic descriptive analysis: the role of the writer who is trying to relate the old and the new, and the audience for whom biblical interpretation is being done. In the case of Hebrews, the writer brings his contemporary worldview to shape his theological understanding. Lincoln identifies him as a Hellenistic Jew influenced by the middle Platonism of his times. The ancient writer asks himself how he can hear the word of God for the new situation in the life of God's people. What makes the writer's reflections effective is the combination of qualities and characteristics that the writer brings to the task. Imagination and creativity are crucial in combining his

---

48. Andrew T. Lincoln, "Hebrew and Biblical Theology," in *Out of Egypt: Biblical Theology and Biblical Interpretation,* ed. Craig Bartholomew et al. (Grand Rapids: Zondervan, 2004), pp. 313-38. The parenthetical page references in the following text refer to this article.

own critical reflections with the needs of the audience. He claims that the model is that of a good pastor.

In sum, according to Lincoln, no theological questions have been settled by Hebrews "for all time" (p. 332). Instead Hebrews becomes an example of how one ancient author sought to address a set of problems in his community, largely with parenetic concerns. At this juncture Lincoln adopts the insights of postmodernism in criticizing any allegedly textual objectivity. Thus, the modern interpreter has the same freedom in the use made of his insights to his audience. He can relativize and critique parts of his inherited Scriptures, and the present-day Christian might well see it as necessary to take up quite different ethical stances from those represented by Hebrews. New ways of interpreting Scripture become inevitable in order to be relevant to the new cultural settings and according to his own developing understanding of Christ.

My objections to Lincoln's interpretation of the role of Hebrews for theological reflection are many, but I shall focus on one crucial point of disagreement. Lincoln has no sympathy for the theological and hermeneutical role of canon. As we have attempted to show, the early church struggled to interpret, maintain, and preserve its apostolic tradition, as is reflected in the history of New Testament canonization. In my present project I have focused only on the shaping of the Pauline corpus, and sought to show its role as a guide of the church and for the church in understanding this crucial theological legacy. By neglecting the whole subject of the Christian canon, and replacing it with a form of philosophical postmodernism (p. 333), the modern interpreter continues to flounder rudderless in a world torn apart with countless competing agenda.

In contrast to Lincoln's proposal, I shall offer an analysis of how the inclusion of Hebrews affected the subsequent reading of the Pauline corpus. The book of Hebrews, positioned on the edge of the Pauline corpus, functioned to provide a hermeneutical warrant for addressing the larger interpretive issue of the relation between the old and the new covenants. However, very shortly, through the development of the entire Christian canon, this relationship was understood as between the Old Testament and the New.

As we observed earlier, an interpretation of the title of the book "To the Hebrews" remains undecided, and countless theories have been mounted in an effort to regain an original particularity for a specific addressee. I would suggest that the church's understanding moved in the opposite direction. The title correctly construed the epistle as addressing the theological problem of the two dispensations. The epistle to the Hebrews offers a programmatic statement of the theological relationship that received its content from Scripture and not from its historical setting in the first century. The epistle to the Hebrews was directed to those who were being attracted by a life "in the old covenant." The threat to the faith was not from contemporary Judaism, but from the old Levitical covenant that was derived from reading Scripture apart from the new order of Jesus Christ.

Hebrews offered a way of understanding the Old Testament as a revelatory *Heilsgeschichte* in which the voice of the one and only God who spoke in the history of Israel, now has spoken definitively in the Son at the "end of the age."[49] This relationship had a crucial dimension of continuity, yet was equally characterized by a radical discontinuity through the entrance of a qualitatively new covenant. Hebrews thus allows an interpretive strategy for relating a historically oriented *Heilsgeschichte* with a Pauline apocalyptical vision.

This dialectical concept of Hebrews also provided a classic formulation by which the church could understand itself to be freed from the cultic and ceremonial laws of the Old Testament because of the sacrificial death of Christ, yet still remain under the obligation of the moral laws of the Old Testament. Accordingly, Hebrews provided a strong warrant for the ethical responsibilities of the Christian toward a wide range of biblically based imperatives (Heb 13:1-3) without being accused of replacing Pauline ethics with moralism. Hebrews also offered the strongest support for continuing to receive the vertical imperatives of the Old Testament as authoritative, especially in the Psalms, as a central part of the Christian Scriptures, and thus was added further weight to the emphasis of the Pastorals on the use of the sacred writings in providing teaching and training in righteousness (2 Tim 3:16-17).

The reading of the Pauline corpus through the lens provided by Hebrews did much in unifying the so-called deutero-Pauline letters (Colossians, Ephesians) with the undisputed letters of Paul. Both Colossians and Ephesians speak of Christ the creator, seated on the right

---

49. See the recent study of Tomasz Lewicki, "Weist nicht ab den Sprechenden!" in *Wort Gottes und Paraklese im Hebräerbrief* (Padeborn: Schöningh, 2004), whose entire research focuses on the centrality within Hebrews of "the speaking God."

and of God. Ephesians pictures the church raised up and made to sit with Christ "in the heavenly places" (2:6), and the Christian life as a sacramental union within a holy temple (2:21). Moreover, both Colossians and Ephesians assume the preexistence of Christ who created all things (Col 1:16; Eph 1:9-10). Hebrews also greatly strengthens Paul's message for the Christian to expect and to embrace continual suffering as constitutive for living in a hostile world. To suffer abuse for the sake of Christ is the greatest reward possible (Heb 11:26).

Finally, the eschatological vision of Hebrews, while often expressed differently from that of Paul, has a clear family resemblance with that of the other letters. He speaks of the eschatological day dawning (10:25), of a heavenly city yet to come (13:14), and even cites Habakkuk 2:2-3 (10:37) affirming that "the coming one will not long tarry." There is also the sober note of the final judgment, described in vivid apocalyptical imagery (12:25-29), in which each person will give account (13:17). The issue continues to be debated as to the effect of the delay of the parousia on Hebrews, but it is quite impossible to argue that Hebrews has lost the connection with the church's eschatological hope (6:19).

6. Theological Implications of the Pauline Corpus for Interpretation

The purpose of this final chapter is to summarize in a more succinct, systematic fashion some of the theological implications of a canonical reading of the Pauline corpus that have emerged in the preceding chapters. My intention is not to duplicate arguments that have been made throughout the various chapters, but to integrate preeminent themes that have been addressed from different vantage points, and to establish links between chapters that were only implicit.

I. The Theological Integrity of a Canonical Reading

Throughout the preceding chapters I have used the term "canon" in its broadest sense. Canon is not just a listing of received books, but involves the process by which the letters of Paul were received, collected, transmitted, and shaped by the early apostolic church. In other words, it includes philological, historical, literary, and theological dimensions.[1] A major concern of this study has been to contest the widespread assumption of the New Testament guild that the issue of canon lies in the field of subsequent church history and is irrelevant to the study of the historical Paul and his letters.[2] As a result

---

1. This point has unfortunately been misunderstood by Bruce M. Metzger (*The Canon of the New Testament* [Oxford: Clarendon, 1987]), who insists on using the terminology of canon only in its narrow sense of list when criticizing its broader theological usages (p. 36 n. 84).

2. I find it both surprising and disheartening that a leading German New Testament scholar from Halle (the home of Tholuck, Kähler, and Schniewind!) could confidently assert

of a lengthy historical process, the letters of Paul received a particular canonical context. The recognition of this context greatly affects the interpretation
of the individual letters, and at the same time provides a hermeneutical
guide toward an understanding of whole corpus as Scripture.

II. The Canonical Context as an Interpretive Guide

The Pauline corpus was shaped by the apostolic tradents for the use of
Paul's letters by the church. Its shaping offered a theological and hermeneutical guide for the future generations of the Christian community.[3] It
offered a confessional stance confirming its truth and binding the church
to its authoritative Scriptures.

The shaping process took many different forms. Several of the letters
were shortly circulated to other Pauline churches, much like a round letter
(e.g., Eph 1:1; Col 4:10). Or again, the letter to the Romans as the introductory letter of the corpus returned to many of the topics Paul had earlier addressed, but functioned both to universalize and to draw out the theological substance of the issues with an even more profound exploration of its
content. This concern for a larger, unified coherence did not remove the
letters' original contingencies, but provided additional aid to their later application. The shaping of the Pastorals lay in assigning the letters of Paul a
normative role as a truthful model by which to measure the church's
sound doctrine in the coming postapostolic age. Paul's writings along with
the Old Testament and the evangelical traditions of the Gospels established a rule of faith, later articulated in further detail by Irenaeus against
the gnostic threats to the faith.

A major instance of the canonical shaping of the Pauline corpus was
the role assigned to the other books as an interpretive framework for the
letters. Acts served to legitimate the Pauline and Catholic Epistles as a
truthful apostolic witness of the gospel to the living Lord of the church.
For its part, Hebrews, positioned on the edge of the corpus, provided a

---

that the emphasis on the exegetical function of the final form of the canonical New Testament text has been fully overcome by 250 years of historical critical research (Udo Schnelle,
Einleitung in das Neue Testament, 4th ed. [Göttingen: Vandenhoeck & Ruprecht, 2002],
p. 26).

3. Paul C. McGlasson, *Invitation to Dogmatic Theology: A Canonical Approach* (Grand
Rapids: Brazos, 2006).

broad hermeneutical guide in addressing the larger question of the relationship between the Old and New covenants, an issue raised briefly in the
Pauline letters but not fully explored.

III. Canonical Shaping and Reader Interpretation

Another major concern of this study was in responding to Frances Young's
position that texts are mute regardless of their shaping until a fresh meaning is rendered by each new act of interpretation. I argue that the focus on
canonical shaping of the Pauline corpus does not eliminate the role of the
interpreter who continuously renders the text from his or her new cultural
context.

However, the function of canon is to privilege a particular reading of
the biblical text, which the tradents of the evangelical tradition designated
as the apostolic witness. This move thereby distinguished the form of the
apostolic testimony from all later church tradition. The process of canonization did not remove the need for continuing interpretation, but it established a canonical context within which the ongoing exegetical activity
functioned. The truth of this interpretive activity was then measured by its
coherence with the larger canonical shaping of the Christian Bible. This
process was not a static one, but was evoked by the divine promise that the
Spirit of Christ, the living Lord of the church, would continually make
alive the apostolic witness shaped by the New Testament canon by which
the church received its imperative mandates and support for daily life as a
faithful Christian community with a mission to the world.

IV. The Hermeneutical Dialectic in Reading the Corpus

The unique hermeneutical problems of assigning a canonical authority to
the Pauline corpus lay in its highly particularized quality of contingency.
We noted how different strategies were employed to overcome this apparent problem by the introductory function of Romans and the concluding
modeling of the Pauline theology by the Pastorals. A relationship was established by which contingency and coherence were held in tension. Yet an
equally important aspect is reflected in 2 Timothy's describing the stance
of the community as one struggling to find the proper analogy from these

to poles to address its own changing historical experiences. This triangular hermeneutical activity provided the warrant for the genre of preaching, catechesis, and liturgy, as a fresh Word of God was perceived in the faithful anticipation of divine instruction.

The inclusion of the deutero-Pauline letters within the corpus (Colossians and Ephesians) not only illustrated how Paul's message was extended into the area of ecclesiology with a deeper plunge into the mystery of the body of Christ within the divine purpose; these letters were also included as part of the apostolic witness to a faithful extension of the Pauline kerygma within a developing institution in need of new offices and officers.

V. The Historical and Canonical Paul

Our study of the Pauline corpus began by observing the repeated frustration of serious biblical scholars to reconstruct the theology of the historical Paul. Yet we have also affirmed that the endeavor to pursue this historical search could not be dismissed out of hand. The study of Paul's Jewish roots, the milieu of syncretistic Hellenistic sects, the fresh insights into Gnosticism from newly discovered texts, and the cultural pressures from Greco-Roman hegemony all brought new perspectives, particularly in revealing the complexity of Paul's historical setting.

Nevertheless, we have continued to defend the position that the search for the historical Paul will remain elusive because of the very theological nature of the New Testament itself. The historical Paul of the first century has been transmitted by Christian tradents who have received and shaped their testimony into the form of a canonical Paul. This canonical image is not a fictional caricature, but a historical vehicle of the Christian gospel (*geschichtlich*) and was seen and preserved by a community of faith, the impact from which continued to shape their lives long after Paul's death. This fusion of the historical Paul and the canonical (Lukan) Paul is most clearly reflected in the book of Acts. Much like the search for the historical Jesus, the historical Paul and the canonical Paul have been intertwined inextricably together. To denigrate the latter and retain only the former removes the key for understanding their subtle relationship.

Increasingly one's evaluation of the biblical texts has been determined by one's understanding of the nature of history. Postmodernism has grown increasingly critical of many of the assumptions of nineteenth-century historical criticism.[4] Yet what is now offered as a new hermeneutical sophistication "come of age" seems painfully nebulous and unsatisfactory, indeed an approach that renders the profile of Paul sterile, mute, and theologically uninteresting. The nature of the New Testament literature is such that to evaluate it as a good example of literary fiction tries in vain to suppress the truth question that was uppermost in the intention of its authors and readers.

VI. The Christological Content of the Pauline Witness

Modern Pauline research has increasingly focused on external factors that are alleged to have been constitutive to understanding Paul. One speaks of the influence of the philosophical remnants of the Cynics and Epicureans. Or again, literary conventions of the diatribe and parenesis have taken center stage in interest. Still more recent has been the emphasis placed on the sociological forces that have provided the imagery by which Paul and early Christianity have articulated their identity. Much of this research has been serious and is not to be disparaged. One only has to compare modern studies with the nineteenth-century harmonizations of William Conybeare and John S. Howson[5] or the historical rationalism of William M. Ramsay[6] to discern the different world into which scholarship has now entered.

Yet there has been a less positive side. Many New Testament scholars have developed an allergy against even speaking of Paul's theological, doctrinal witness, and read the biblical texts only obliquely, as if by reflex. However, Paul's Christology undergirds every aspect of his letters. Moreover, Paul's consistently passionate focus on the death and resurrection of Christ marked the transition of apostolic preaching from the imminent coming of the kingdom of God to his proclamation of the apocalyptic effect of the humiliation of the cross and the exaltation of the resurrection and parousia. From these mighty acts of God in Christ, Paul announced the good news of the gospel: the revelation of the righteousness of God

4. See Jocken Teuffel, *Von der Theologie. Die Kunst der guten Gottesrede in Entsprechung zur gelesenen Schrift* (Frankfurt: Peter Lang, 2000).

5. Willian J. Conybeare and John S. Howson, *The Life and Epistles of St. Paul* (London: Macmillan, 1854)

6. William M. Ramsay, *St. Paul the Traveller and the Roman Citizen,* 7th ed. (London: Hodder and Stoughton, 1903).

Rom 1:17) and the reconciliation of the world to himself (2 Cor 5:18), to be received by a response of faith.

VII. The Faithfulness of God to His Promises

One of the most promising features of recent Pauline studies has been the rediscovery of the centrality of the Jewish Scriptures for understanding Paul's theology. The importance of Romans 9–11 has emerged with new persuasiveness as Paul wrestles with the continuing faithfulness of God to his promises to Israel. Yet the importance of recognizing the role of canon in this regard has been far broader than in discerning the conceptual features of Septuagintal Greek, or the conventions of midrashic, targumic interpretation, significant though these may be. The inclusion of the book of Hebrews within the Pauline corpus pursues themes implicit in Paul's letters, but expresses the theological case in legitimating the enduring continuity between God's unfolding purpose for Israel and the church. Similarly, the Pastorals continue to assign a central role to the reading of "all of Scripture" for the future training of the church in a life of righteousness (2 Tim 3:16).

VIII. The Eschatological-Apocalyptic Witness of Paul

One of the great contributions of the modern study of Paul has been the rediscovery of Paul's apocalyptic theology.[7] Our study has affirmed its centrality in his vision of God's cosmic reign. Nevertheless, I have argued that only by seeing Paul's apocalyptic emphasis within the larger context of the whole Pauline corpus can this dimension of the message not be construed in such a way as to set it in opposition to other important features of the New Testament such as Lukan theology or that of the Pastorals. Attention to the whole New Testament canon resists portraying Paul's apocalyptic theology as a rejection of "primitive Jewish vestiges" allegedly within the Synoptics, Thessalonians, and Revelation. It also resists employing a strategy that describes Paul's apocalyptic according to an exaggerated sectarian

---

7. Ulrich H. J. Körtner, *Weltangst und Weltende. Eine theologische Interpretation der Apokalyptik* (Göttingen: Vandenhoeck & Ruprecht, 1988), pp. 326-41.

interpretation that measures the subsequent history of the early Christia. church negatively as a betrayal of Paul's true eschatological vision.

To conclude: the role of the canon sets parameters for interpretation that the church has affirmed in locating the arena in which the Word of God is heard. It is this insistence on the authoritative role of the "ruled reading" by the canon that sets my approach to canon apart from those who stress that the establishment of a fixed canon is only one moment in a continuous canonical process. Accordingly, each succeeding generation of Christians is alleged to represent a new "apostolic community" with the challenges to reenact the apostolic task in search of a new, often hitherto unknown response, measured only by its relevance to a changing modern culture. Thus, even the term "canon" has been reinterpreted to support an interpretive stance that in effect serves to undercut the essence of the church's confession of a written sacred Scripture whose witness to a living Lord continues to shape and enrich its life in the Christian faith.[8]

---

8. The attempt of H. J. Körtner, *Der inspirierte Leser* (Göttingen: Vandenhoeck & Ruprecht, 1994), pp. 108-13, to use Martin Kähler's hermeneutic to support a postmodern, reception theory of canon results in shifting the interpretive focus away from the witness of the biblical text to the inspired imagination of the reader. In my judgment, this move, shared largely by Bultmann and Tillich, strikes at the heart of Kähler's main theological concern, which was to defend the unique integrity of the church's apostolic witness.

Index of Names and Subjects

Aaron, 239, 241
Abasciano, Brian J., 185n.169
Abraham, 55, 58, 67, 76, 97-112, 119-21,
  129, 183, 185
Acts, 22, 62, 109, 158, 219-36, 254, 256.
  See also Luke-Acts
Adam, 67
Aland, Kurt, 5n.6
allegory, 14
Amtprinzip, 159. *See also* church: ecclesi-
  astical offices of
Antiochus IV Epiphanes, 196-97
apocalypticism, 194-218, 246-47
apostles: as authoritative witnesses, 16,
  21, 156; and the canon, 9, 21-22, 44;
  definition of, 82-96
Aramaic, translation into, 18, 100, 150
Aristides, 62
Art of Performance, The (Young), 40
Augustine, 36, 193, 238
authorities, Christians' relationship to,
  144, 147

Baeck, Leo, 194n.181
Barnett, Albert E., 71
Barr, James, 211
Barrett, C. K., 90, 132, 223, 225
Barth, Karl, 126
Barthes, R., 40

Bauer, Walter, 8-9, 100
Baur, Ferdinand Christian, 8, 13, 70,
  180n.159, 219, 227
Beker, J. Christiaan, 2, 34n.6, 68, 97-102,
  104, 106, 165, 180-81, 183
Biblical Canons, The, 223
*Biblical Exegesis and the Formation of
  Christian Culture* (Young), 40
Bloom, Harold, 58, 191
Boer, Martinus de, 215
Bornkamm, Günther, 66-67, 125, 145,
  179, 217
Bright, John, 13
Brox, Norbert, 70, 158n.129, 159-60, 165
Bultmann, Rudolf, 12, 72, 134, 153n.121,
  220-21, 259n.8; and apocalyptic, 194,
  200-201, 204-5, 214-15; associates of,
  83, 88, 90, 125

Cadbury, Henry, 221
Campenhausen, Hans von, 61, 82, 94
canon: and Acts, 7, 22, 26, 76, 109, 219-
  37, 254, 256; authority of, 9, 15-16,
  22n.35, 23, 60-62, 220, 225, 230, 237-
  38, 259; and the Catholic (General)
  Epistles, 7, 22, 225, 231, 238, 249, 254;
  criteria used in forming the, 19-24,
  80; definition of, 4n.4, 15; and the
  early church, 4n.6, 5, 7-11, 20-21, 43,

Index of Scripture References

274